International Acclaim for John Keegan's

The Iraq War

"A must-read. . . . Illuminating. . . . He provides exceptional detail
. . . that will enthrall military buffs."   —*Fort Worth Star-Telegram*

"Highly readable. . . . One of the best brief guides to the history
of this whole confusing field."   —*Financial Times*

"A superb strategic overview. . . . Concise and well-written. . . .
Keegan provides a basis for understanding the embers of the
insurgent conflagration."   —*The Washington Times*

"A remarkable achievement."   —*The Spectator*

"Comprehensive. . . . It is in his examination of the military
campaign itself that the insight really surfaces. He cuts directly
to the heart of the mystery and questions surrounding this
operation. . . . His analysis . . . is sound and enlightening – from
the political to the tactical level."   —*New York Post*

John Keegan

THE IRAQ WAR

John Keegan's books include *Intelligence in War*, *The First World War*, *The Battle for History*, *The Face of Battle*, *War and Our World*, *The Mask of Command*, *Fields of Battle*, and *A History of Warfare*. He is the defense editor of *The Daily Telegraph* (London). He lives in Wiltshire, England.

Also by John Keegan

Intelligence in War

The First World War

The Face of Battle

The Nature of War
(with Joseph Darracott)

World Armies

Who's Who in Military History
(with Andrew Wheatcroft)

Six Armies in Normandy

Soldiers
(with Richard Holmes)

The Mask of Command

The Price of Admirality

The Second World War

A History of Warfare

Fields of Battle

The Battle for History

War and Our World: The Reith Lectures 1998

An Illustrated History of the First World War

Churchill: A Life

THE IRAQ WAR

John Keegan

VINTAGE BOOKS

A DIVISION OF RANDOM HOUSE, INC.

NEW YORK

FIRST VINTAGE BOOKS EDITION, JUNE 2005

Copyright © 2004, 2005 by John Keegan

All rights reserved under International and Pan-American Copyright
Conventions. Published in the United States by Vintage Books, a
division of Random House, Inc., New York. Originally published in
Great Britain by Hutchinson, the Random House Group Limited,
London, and simultaneously in hardcover in the United States in
slightly different form by Alfred A. Knopf, a division of
Random House, Inc., New York, in 2003.

Vintage and colophon are registered trademarks of
Random House, Inc.

The Library of Congress has cataloged the Knopf edition as follows:
Keegan, John, [date]
The Iraq war / by John Keegan. – 1st American ed.
p. cm.
1. Iraq war, 2003. I. Title.
DS79.76.K44 2004
956.7044'3 – dc2
2004006895

Vintage ISBN: 1–4000–7920–9

Author photograph © Jerry Bauer
Maps by Reginald Piggott

www.vintagebooks.com

Printed in the United States of America
10 9 8 7 6 5 4 3 2 1

Contents

Illustrations

Colin Powell with Jack Straw (*Reuters/Kevin Lamarque*)
General Tommy Franks (*Reuters/Tim Aubry*)
Iraqi Information Minister Muhammad Saeed al-Sahhaf (*Reuters/ Faleh Kheiber*)
Central Command personnel in the Joint Operations Centre, Qatar (*AP Photo/Wally Santana*)
Lieutenant-General John McKiernan (*Defence Picture Library*)
USAF B-1 bomber (*Defence Picture Library*)
Captain Tom Bryant of V Corps walks ahead of his Humvee during a fierce sandstorm (*Defence Picture Library*)
Cobra helicopter (US Marines) (*Defence Picture Library*)
US Army medics of the 2nd Brigade (*Defence Picture Library*)
US special forces in northern Iraq with Kurdish fighters (*Defence Picture Library*)
Chinook helicopter crewmen in northern Iraq (*Defence Picture Library*)
A US Airborne soldier drops into northern Iraq (*Defence Picture Library*)
River crossing in northern Iraq (*Defence Picture Library*)
US Army M1-A1 Abrams tank (*Defence Picture Library*)
Australian special forces (*Defence Picture Library*)
US Army tanks and Bradley fighting vehicles (*AP Photo/John Moore*)
A-10 ground support aircraft (*Defence Picture Library*)
An Apache helicopter which crashed during preparation at Assembly Area SHELL (*Defence Picture Library*)

US Naval special operations units south of Basra (*Defence Picture Library*)

US Marine Sergeant Dan Lockward leads his fire team (*Defence Picture Library*)

Saddam's sons Uday and Qusay in a mortuary (*Defence Picture Library*)

A British Royal Marine fires a Milan wire-guided missile (*AP Photo/Jon Mills*)

British gunners from 7 Parachute Regiment Royal Horse Artillery (*Defence Picture Library*)

British soldiers of the 1st Battalion the Parachute Regiment (*Defence Picture Library*)

Lead elements of the 3rd Battalion the Parachute Regiment advance into the northern part of Basra (*Defence Picture Library*)

A British Army Warrior vehicle passes a destroyed Iraqi T-55 tank (*Reuters/Chris Helgren*)

A convoy of Humvees of the 5th Marines pictured during a sand-storm (*Defence Picture Library*)

A US Army 3rd Division tank rolls across the tarmac of Baghdad International Airport (*Getty Images*)

US Marines fight their way through the streets of Baghdad (*Defence Picture Library*)

A statue of Saddam Hussein falls at his palatial grounds in Tikrit (*Reuters/US Army photo by Staff Sgt. Craig Pickett*)

Saddam Hussein being dragged out of an underground hole by US troops near his home town of Tikrit (*AFP/Getty Images*)

The former President minutes after capture (*Defence Picture Library*)

Maps

Acknowledgments

I should like to thank my colleagues at *The Daily Telegraph* with whom I covered the Iraq War on a daily basis during March and April 2003, particularly Charles Moore, then the Editor, Michael Smith, the Defence Correspondent, Alec Russell, the Foreign Editor, Con Coughlin and Kate Baden, my secretary. I was encouraged to undertake this book by my editor at Hutchinson, Anthony Whittome. I was at first unwilling to do so because of the difficulties I foresaw but he predicted that they would dissolve. He was right and I am glad that he persuaded me to take up what has proved to be an unusually interesting commission.

I am also grateful to Donald Rumsfeld, US Secretary of Defense, whom I twice interviewed in his office at the Pentagon. He also made it possible for me to interview General Tommy Franks, CENTCOM Commander, immediately after the war was over. I am extremely grateful to General Franks for his openness. I also received valuable help from Colonel Christopher Vernon, Colonel Michael Dewar and Lt-Colonel Richard Hoare, all of the British army.

I should also like to thank my American editor, Ashbel Green at Knopf, my literary agent, Anthony Sheil and my irreplaceable assistant, Lindsey Wood. Without her ability to meet very tight deadlines the book could not have been produced.

Finally, my love and thanks to my children, Lucy, Tom, Rose and Matthew, and to my darling wife, Susanne.

Kilmington Manor,
Wiltshire,
15 March 2004

THE IRAQ WAR

1

A Mysterious War

Some wars begin badly. Some end badly. The Iraq War of 2003 was exceptional in both beginning well for the Anglo-American force that waged it and ending victoriously. The credit properly belonged in both cases to the American part of the coalition. It was the Americans who provided the majority of strength on the ground and overwhelmingly the majority in the air and at sea. The British contribution was important and warmly welcomed by the Americans but it was that of an esteemed junior partner.

The war was not only successful but peremptorily short, lasting only twenty-one days, from 20 March to 9 April. Campaigns so brief are rare, a lightning campaign so complete in its results almost unprecedented. For comparisons one has to reach back to the 'cabinet wars' of the nineteenth century, Prussia's victory over Austria in six weeks in 1866 or over the French field army in less than a month in 1870. Walkovers, as by the Germans in the Balkans in 1941, do not count. The Iraqis had fielded a size-able army and had fought, after a fashion. Their resistance had simply been without discernible effect. The Americans came, saw, conquered. How?

While reporting the war in *The Daily Telegraph* I frequently found myself writing that its events were 'mysterious'. It was a strange word for a military analyst to use in what should have been objective comment. Even in retrospect, however, I see no reason to look for another. The war was mysterious in almost every aspect. Mystery shrouded the *casus belli*, the justification for going to war. The war was launched because Saddam Hussein, President of Iraq, refused to co-operate with United Nations inspectors in their search for his forbidden weapons of mass destruction. Yet even after his defeat laid the whole territory of Iraq open to search, such weapons eluded discovery. Mystery surrounded the progress of operations. Iraq fielded an army of nearly 400,000 soldiers, equipped with thousands of tanks, armoured vehicles and artillery pieces. Against the advance of an invading force only half its size, the Iraqi army faded away. It did not fight at the frontier, it did not fight at the obvious geographical obstacles, it scarcely fought in the cities, it did not mount a last-ditch defence of the capital, where much of the world media predicted that Saddam would stage his Stalingrad.

The régime, so bombastic in speech before and during the conflict, mysteriously failed to take elementary defensive precautions. In a country of great rivers, the Euphrates and Tigris pre-eminently but also their tributaries, it failed to destroy the bridges, or even in many cases to prepare them for demolition. While the regular army and the vaunted Republican Guard apparently demobilized themselves, the soldiers disappearing to their homes at the appearance of the invaders, their place was taken by mysterious 'fighters' of the skimpiest military training, devotees of the ruling Ba'athist party or foreign Islamicists with an urge to die. Perhaps most mysteriously of all, much of the population of Iraq, the ordinary town dwellers and country people, exhibited a complete indifference to the war going on around them, carrying on their everyday lives apparently oblivious of its dangers. To the bewilderment and fury of the coalition soldiers, traffic often travelled as normal, civilian cars and trucks proceeding headlong into the middle of firefights and stopping only if shot at, by young soldiers terrified that the driver might be a suicide bomber.

Mystery ultimately enfolded the fall of the régime. Following the capture and occupation of Baghdad on 9–10 April, no trace of the government could be found. Not only was there no large number of prisoners of war, the usual index of victory, there were equally no captured generals or staff officers nor, most puzzlingly of all, politicians treating for peace. The Ba'ath leaders and their party officials had disappeared, just as the army and the Republican Guard had disappeared. The disappearance of the soldiers was easily explained. They had taken off their uniforms and become civilians again. The disappearance of the leaders was baffling. It was understandable that, fearing retribution for the crimes of the régime, summarily at the hands of the population, judicially by process of the conquerors, the principal perpetrators and their associates should seek to make their escape; but where had they gone? The American high command distributed packs of cards, each bearing the photographic image of a wanted man. The distribution yielded results. The owlish Tariq Aziz, Deputy Prime Minister, was arrested. So were a number of other important if less prominent Saddam apparatchiks. On 22 July 2003 Saddam Hussein's sons Qusay and Uday, both steeped in the brutality against political opponents which was their father's trademark, were betrayed, by the inducement of a $15 million reward, and killed during a gun battle in the northern city of Mosul. Kurdistan might have been thought an ill-chosen hiding place for the dictator's sons. One of the most extreme Islamicist terror organizations, Ansar al-Islam, had however set up what amounted to a 'liberated zone' in Kurdistan, so perhaps encouraging the two thugs – whom Saddam had hardened to their inheritance by sending them to witness torture and executions – to seek refuge there.

The final mystery of the whereabouts of the dictator himself persisted. In the immediate aftermath of the defeat rumours circulated that he had made his escape to a friendly Muslim country. The rumours were cumulatively discounted. Such stable régimes, Libya or Syria, as might have been willing to welcome him were also prudently cautious of the danger of offending the United States. Countries where anti-Americanism flourished, such as Yemen or Somalia, were judged too unstable for Saddam to risk his survival in their turbulent politics. The occupation authority in Iraq eventually concluded that he remained within the country, probably hidden by family or tribal supporters in his home area around Tikrit. Frequent searches were mounted without result. A more methodical procedure proved productive. An intelligence team, by working through his family tree, identified the whereabouts in the Tikrit neighbourhood of residents who might be sheltering him. On 13 December 2003 a party of American troops from the 4th Infantry Division, revisiting a farm already searched but now with better information, uncovered the entrance to an underground hiding place. When the trapdoor was lifted, a bedraggled and heavily bearded Saddam was found cowering inside. He held up his hands and announced, 'I am the President of Iraq and I am ready to negotiate.' He was swiftly transferred to American military custody.

Saddam's arrest put an end to the last contingent mystery of the war. A greater mystery remained, attaching not to the war's events but to its fundamental character. How had it been possible to fight a war which was not, by any conventional measure, really a war at all? All the components of a war had been in place, two large armies, huge quantities of military equipment and, that most essential element of modern hostilities, an enormous press corps, equipped and alert to report, film or broadcast its slightest incident. Beyond the battleground, moreover, the world had been transfixed by a war mood. Governments had been thrown at loggerheads over the war's rights and wrongs, the workings of the great international organizations had been monopolized by debate over the war, populations had marched against the war, the world's religious leaders had uttered the direst warnings about the war's outcome, the international media had written and spoken about little else but war for weeks before, during and afterwards. Yet, when war engulfed their country, the people who ought to have been most affected by it, the population of Iraq itself, seemed scarcely to give it their attention. American cheerleaders had predicted that the invading army would be overwhelmed by the gratitude of the liberated once it appeared on Iraqi territory. Opponents of the war, particularly in the media, puzzled at first by the lack of opposition the invaders encountered, consoled themselves with a prediction of their own: that when the American army reached Baghdad, it would be resisted block by block, street by street. There would be a Stalingrad-on-Tigris and the West would regret that it had ever flouted high-minded opinion by mounting such an expedition.

In the event, the invaders found the population largely absent from the scene of action. There were no crowds, either welcoming or hostile. There were scarcely any people to be seen at all. In the countryside the mud hut dwellings of the cultivators displayed at best a scrap of white flag, flapping from a stick, as a sign the occupants recognized that a war was in progress. Often they gave no sign at all. Herders and ploughmen wended their heedless way about the landscape. Mothers shooed their children to shelter at the sight of military vehicles. Camel drivers stood to gaze. Otherwise the dusty countryside lay empty under a pall of apparent indifference at the world crisis that had come to visit Iraq.

Civilian unwillingness to engage with the war was matched, and more than matched, by that of the rank and file of the Iraqi army. Saddam commanded some 400,000 men in uniform, 60,000 of them in his loyalist Republican Guard. Few were well trained and most of their military equipment, once of the Soviet first-line, was now antiquated. The coalition high command nevertheless expected them to fight. Its soldiers, particularly the younger men who had never been in battles, were spoiling to meet the challenge. They were to be largely disappointed. Here and there they found spots of resistance, Iraqi infantrymen who manned their positions, tank crews who exchanged fire. In most cases as the invaders advanced to places where defences had been prepared, however, they found them abandoned, often clearly in the last minutes before action threatened. Pathetic scraps of evidence of occupation lay about, pots of rice, packets of tea, newspapers, discarded clothing and even abandoned boots and weapons. The owners had fled, not to better positions or to regroup, but to go home. Western military intelligence officers identified two waves of desertion: the first following coalition air attack preceding the advance, a second as the sound of approaching coalition armour was heard. By the time the coalition forces actually appeared, the Iraqi soldiers were gone, to disappear into the civilian population and not to be seen again.

The phenomenon was disconcerting, particularly to military theorists committed to the view that war is animated by politics. Such theorists expect the defenders of a country under attack to resist, because the attack threatens the essentials of their society. They accept the reality of collapse, such as that which overwhelmed France in 1940, but associate collapse with objective military events, such as encirclement or deep penetration of a flank. Failure to fight altogether defies their theories, particularly their central theory that military structures are an amalgam of army, government and people. The circumstances of Iraq in 2003 demonstrate that classical military theory applies only to the countries in which it was made, those of the advanced Western world. Elsewhere, and particularly in the artificial, ex-colonial territories of the developing world, usually governed as tyrannies, it does not. Iraq is a particularly artificial construction; three former provinces of the Ottoman Empire, each inhabited by disparate populations, ethnically and religiously separate from one another. The central and southern regions are respectively Sunni and Shi'a Muslim Arab, the north, though Muslim, not Arab at all but Kurdish. The Ottoman Turks had not treated the three regions as a unit but ruled them separately. It was the British, exercising a League of Nations mandate, who had attempted to unify the country and bequeathed their shaky creation to the successor governments. It had worked erratically at best and only by according dominance to the Sunni of the centre. Monarchy had been supplanted by dictatorship, eventually, in its most ruthless form, that of Saddam Hussein.

Saddam had tested his dictatorship to its limits. Had he been content merely to modernize, spending his country's vast oil revenues for the benefit of all, he might have made Iraq a successful country. Modernize he did, but out of megalomaniac ambition he also attempted to establish Iraq as the dominant Middle Eastern state, a regional military superpower. He waged internal war against the Kurds. He dragooned his population into a costly invasion of neighbouring Iran over a trivial border dispute. He finally provoked a war with the world by an aggression against Kuwait designed to pay his debts.

Defeated and humiliated, he persisted in playing the big man, refusing to demonstrate to the United Nations that he had desisted from developing the weapons of mass destruction with which he had buttressed his ambition. For twelve years, between 1991 and 2003, he fenced with the United Nations and its supporters, the United States foremost, over inspection and disclosure. Eventually, having exhausted American patience, he was confronted by the challenge of war again. He declined to offer the facilities and guarantees that would have staved off the consequences of his intransigence. He thus brought war on himself.

It was not a war into which the peoples of Iraq would follow him. In one sense Western military theorists were right. Ordinary Iraqis ought to have been willing to fight to defend their homeland, as theory dictated, had Iraq been an ordinary country. Iraq, however, was not an ordinary country. It was not merely an artificial creation; it was also a monstrosity. Artificial states, of which there are many in the world, can survive for long periods through the medium of carefully calculated concessions by the dominant centre to the minorities. Saddam did not concede. He brutalized. Not only were individual opponents of his régime tortured and murdered; whole sections of the population were murdered also, while those not currently chosen for Saddam's cruelties were held in check by fear of his disfavour.

Ultimately there is no mystery about the collapse of Saddam's régime and the failure of his people to fight his last war. Saddam had waged war against Iraq itself, repeatedly, relentlessly, revengefully. He had exhausted the will of the population to do anything for him and it was entirely appropriate that he should have been driven as a last resort to seek refuge underground in the soil of his tortured country.

2

Iraq Before Saddam

'Iraq' in Arabic means the shore of the great river and the fertile land surrounding it. The word has been used since at least the eighth century AD to describe the alluvial plain of the Tigris and Euphrates valley, known in Europe since Antiquity by the Greek term 'Mesopotamia', the land between the rivers.

Long before the Greeks, the land between the rivers was of local, and far wider than local, importance. Mesopotamia has genuine claims to be the cradle of civilization. There are other river valleys to dispute the title. The Indus is one, the Nile another, and in both power rested with rulers who controlled or appeared to control the life-bringing flood. Geography made Mesopotamia different. The central valley is so flat, descending only 34 metres in 338 kilometres (112 feet in 210 miles), that the annual snow-melt from the surrounding highlands spreads across the whole face of the land and can be utilized only by constantly renewed irrigation work. The 'irrigation societies' which consequently grew up were eventually unified under a succession of dynasties, Akkadian, Sumerian and Assyrian. Assyria became a great power and it was under the Assyrian kings that the magnificent works of temple and palace architecture, some still surviving, were created. Assyria was eventually overthrown in the seventh century BC by barbarian invaders from the Central Asian interior but Mesopotamia was restored to civilization by incorporation in the Persian Empire. Briefly Hellenized under Alexander and his successors,

Mesopotamia became a borderland between the later Persian Empire and Rome and thus remained until conquered by the Arabs in the early expansion of Islam in the eighth century AD. After the transfer of the seat of the Islamic Caliphate from Damascus to Baghdad in the tenth century, Iraq became the centre of the most powerful state west of China and Baghdad a city of wealth and splendour under its Abbasid rulers, particularly under the famous vizier Nizam al-Mulk. This was the era of the Arabian Nights and the Thousand and One Tales, when Abbasid life was a byword for luxury and extravagance wholly at variance with the austerity of the early Muslim régime. Baghdad's time of glory was brought abruptly to an end in 1258 when the Mongols, the latest wave of interlopers from the Steppe, terrorized the last Abbasid Caliph into surrender and had him strangled within his own city.

Mongol power did not last and Iraq, having temporarily fallen under the power of Tamerlane, last of the great Steppe conquerors, reverted to Persia. Persian rule was ended at the beginning of the sixteenth century by the arrival of the Ottoman Turks, under whom Iraq was to be governed until the beginning of the twentieth century. The Ottomans, though originally a horse people of the Steppe, had absorbed from the Byzantines, after their capture of Constantinople in 1453, a sophisticated understanding of statecraft and ran their enormous empire, stretching from the Red Sea to the Balkans, on lines that owed much to those descendants of Rome. They understood the mechanisms of taxation, they were masters of the principle of divide and rule and they made the maintenance of an efficient imperial army the basis of their authority.

The Ottomans divided Iraq into three *vilayets*, or governorships, centred on Mosul, in the Kurdish north; Baghdad, a largely Sunni city in the centre; and Basra, in the Shi'ite south. Iraq was ready-made for the exercise of their skills in manipulating minorities. In both the Mosul and Basra *vilayets* a traditional tribal society predominated and the Ottomans ruled indirectly through chieftains and heads of leading families. The situation was further

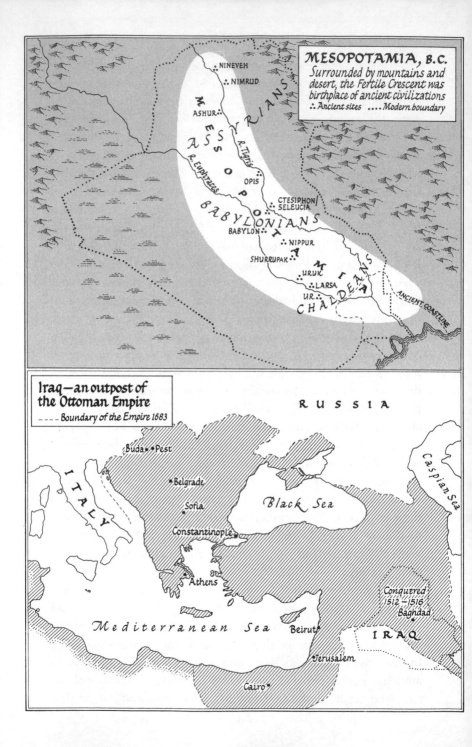

MESOPOTAMIA, B.C.
Surrounded by mountains and
desert, the Fertile Crescent was
birthplace of ancient civilizations
∴ Ancient sites .... Modern boundary

NINEVEH
NIMRUD
ASHUR

M
E
S
S
O
P
O
T
A
M
I
A

ASSYRIANS

R. Tigris
R. Euphrates

OPIS

CTESIPHON
SELEUCIA

BABYLONIANS

BABYLON
NIPPUR
SHURRUPAK
URUK
LARSA
UR
CHALDEANS

ANCIENT COASTLINE

Iraq—an outpost of
the Ottoman Empire
----- Boundary of the Empire 1683

RUSSIA

Buda Pest

Belgrade

Sofia

Black Sea

Caspian Sea

ITALY

Constantinople

Athens

Mediterranean Sea

Beirut

Conquered
1512–1516
Baghdad

IRAQ

Jerusalem

Cairo

complicated in the Baghdad *vilayet* because of the city's proximity to the Shi'a holy places of Najaf and Karbala. The Shi'a religious leaders, though disfavoured by the Sunni Ottomans, had to be respected because of the readiness of the Shah of Persia, the most important Shi'a ruler in Islam, to intervene on their behalf. In the Basra *vilayet*, from the seventeenth century onwards, the most significant locals were the merchants trading with the British East India Company. Throughout the country there was a scattering of religious and ethnic minorities, including Eastern Rite Christians, heretical Muslims, such former Steppe people as the Turkomans and an ancient and large Jewish community, present since the Babylonian captivity.

A final complexity of the Ottoman system in Iraq was that rule was exercised, until the nineteenth century, through a slave, or *mameluke*, class. The *mameluke* principle had been devised in early Islam to evade the Koranic prohibition on Muslim fighting Muslim; since conflict is an irrepressible feature of human life, pious Muslims sought to get round the ban by buying slaves to fight for them. Boys were purchased from the Steppe horse people, trained as soldiers and inducted into the Caliph's army; after the conquest of the Balkans boys were forcibly recruited there from Christian families and taken to Constantinople, where they formed the formidable Janissary corps. Inevitably slave soldiers soon came to exercise power. In Constantinople the Janissaries dominated the court; in Egypt and Iraq, farther from the centre, the *mamelukes* achieved autonomous power. Outwardly obedient to the Caliph, effectively they governed in their own right. It was a peculiarity of the *mameluke* régime in Iraq that its members were brought from the mountain region of Georgia, to which the recruiters constantly returned to refresh their numbers. The position of *mameluke* was not hereditary.

Even though not hereditary power-holders, Ottoman government slaves, Janissaries and *mamelukes* alike, were deeply reactionary in outlook. Their position depended upon resisting change of any sort and theirs was the principal influence which kept Ottoman society static and increasingly backward. By the beginning of the nineteenth century, after several hundred years of military success, the Ottoman Empire – Turkey as it was now often called – faced defeat by the Christian world. The Caliphs bestirred themselves. In 1826 the Janissary corps was bloodily disbanded and Western institutions introduced. The reforms spread progressively to the empire's outer provinces. In Iraq, in 1831, the *mameluke* governor of Baghdad was turned out of office for disobedience and by 1834 all three provinces, Baghdad, Mosul and Basra, had been brought under the direct rule of Constantinople. The new Ottoman officials brought with them procedures designed to recruit soldiers to the imperial army by conscription, to super-impose secular courts over those of the religious and tribal author-ities and to organize land-holding, the basis of the economy, through a government-controlled land register. All these reforms met local resistance, often local revolt, but the *tanzimat* (reforms) proceeded inexorably and by the last decades of the nineteenth century the Nizam-i Celid (New Order) was established.

What impeded its complete realization was reaction at the centre, as so often the response of traditional power to a reform movement. Abdul Hamid II, who became Sultan-Caliph in 1876, was temperamentally absolutist and resented the rate at which central power was slipping from the absolute ruler's hands. He attempted a confrontation with the reforming Young Ottomans, as the reformists were known, and suspended the constitution his predecessor had been obliged to grant. Too late; in 1908 a new group of reformists, the Young Turks, members of the under-cover Committee of Union and Progress (CUP), formed largely of Ottoman subjects from the European provinces, staged a revo-lution and seized power. They accelerated the pace of reform but without conceding power to the empire's non-Turkish subjects. That was to prove a mistake. The Young Turks looked to Europe for example, to Germany for alliance and sought to heighten the Westernization of the empire. They were secularists, not prac-tising Muslims, were ethnic Turkish nationalists devoted to the idea of a greater Turkey pushed into Central Asia (Turanianism) and they adopted an imperialist policy towards the empire's Arab subjects. As Ottoman Arabs equalled or even outnumbered the empire's Turks, the policy was unpopular and was particularly resented by the educated Arabs who, though few in number, were influential, particularly in Syria and Lebanon. There lay the heartland of what was to become known as 'the Arab Awakening', a movement mounted by idealists who looked forward to the reunification of the Arab lands as a single political unit, to the liberation of the Arabs from imperialist rule, Ottoman, British, French and Italian, and to their intellectual emancipation through the pursuit of Western education but within Muslim belief. Many of the nationalists were Ottoman officers who by 1914 had formed a secret society within the army's ranks, al-'Ahd (the Covenant). To it belonged several men destined to become prominent in post-Ottoman Iraq, notably Nuri al-Sa'id.

The first stage in the detachment of Iraq from Turkish rule came in November 1914 when, following the Ottoman entry into the First World War on the side of Germany and Austria-Hungary, Britain despatched an expeditionary force from India to seize Basra. The move had two aims: to open a front against the Turks to assist the Russians, but also to protect British oil interests at the head of the Gulf. The expeditionary force was well received in Basra, where many of the merchant houses had a long association with their British and Indian equivalents, going back to the Honourable East India Company. The ease of occupation tempted the British to push farther and by November 1915 the Mesopotamian Expeditionary Force (MEF) had advanced to within fifty miles of Baghdad. There it was counter-attacked and pushed back to Kut on the Tigris and besieged. Kut proved a humiliating disaster. After four months the garrison was starved into surrender. Not until 1917 did the advance resume. Progress then accelerated and by October 1918, when the Ottomans agreed to an armistice, the whole of Iraq came under British occupation, including the oil-rich north around Kirkuk and Mosul, ethnically Kurdish territory.

In the immediate aftermath of the Ottoman collapse the British imposed a military and semi-colonial administration, proclaiming regulations based on those operating in the Indian empire. It was clear that the arrangement would be only temporary, though there was a nascent acceptance among many Arab Iraqis of the idea of Iraq becoming a unitary state. It was not shared by the Kurds who quickly began to demand separate political status. The most prominent Kurdish leader, Shaikh Mahmud Barzani, was appointed governor of part of Kurdistan but proclaimed independence in May 1919. After his removal by military force, the British resumed control.

In Baghdad and the surrounding central provinces, the al-'Ahd society, of which the Iraqi branch was now localized in the city, attracted considerable support from the urban notables, who were anti-British and opposed also to the aspirations of both the Kurds and the southern Shi'a; another Sunni faction, however, of which Nuri al-Sa'id was a leader, while better disposed to the British, advocated unification under Faisal, one of the sons of the Sharif of Mecca who had led the Arab Revolt against the Ottomans. Nuri and many of his associates had served under the Sharif and looked to his Hashemite family to head the future Arab kingdoms. Nuri enjoyed the advantage of intimacy with the officials of the British administration, from whom he had detected that they too were divided over the future of Iraq. While some favoured maintaining direct rule, others hoped to elevate the Hashemites to kingship, chiefly as a means of curbing the Islamicism of the southern Shi'a.

Ironically what precipitated the decisive postwar crisis was not division between the Sunni and Shi'a but a sudden recognition by some of them of shared interests. During 1919 the victorious Allies, meeting at the Versailles conference, had begun to formalize plans for imposing European rule on the former possessions of the German and Ottoman empires, under authority devolved by mandate from the new League of Nations. The mandate for Iraq was to be allotted to the British. Foreseeing a return to imperial subject status in a new guise, the southern Shi'a, under their religious leaders, and then the Baghdad Sunni, showed their opposition. There were large-scale demonstrations which led to armed resistance. British garrisons were brought under attack. By June 1920 the revolt affected most of the Sunni centre and the Shi'a south, while there was a recurrence of rebellion in the Kurdish north.

Support for the revolt, however, proved patchy; many notables and tribal leaders were chiefly concerned to safeguard their traditional position. By July the revolt had largely subsided, though at the cost of 6,000 Iraqi deaths and 500 in the British and Indian Army garrison. The Shi'a had suffered the brunt of the repression, an experience that heightened their disaffection from the Sunni minority in and around Baghdad.

The British, now empowered by the League of Nations to administer the Iraq mandate, chose to react to the revolt by establishing a form of indirect rule, which it was hoped the population would find more acceptable than the military administration. A council of Iraqi ministers was appointed, with Iraqis also replacing British political officers in the old Ottoman districts. Perhaps inevitably, however, a majority of the appointees at all levels were chosen from the Sunni minority, since they were identified by the British as more dependable and experienced than Shi'a or Kurds. Sunni domination was particularly evident in the new Iraqi army, which was officered almost exclusively by men who had held rank in the Ottoman army; the Chief of Staff was none other than Nuri al-Sa'id, the most prominent Sunni in the old al-'Ahd society.

In a typical exercise of imperial divide-and-rule practice, moreover, the British decided to create a parallel army to the new national force, which would be under their direct control. The Iraq Levies, which during the first decades of the mandate would be the real instrument of central power, were raised not from the major but the marginal Iraq communities. Those chosen were Kurds, Marsh Arabs and Assyrians, a Nestorian Christian people who had fled Turkey during the First World War and were not Iraqi at all. The Assyrians nevertheless made excellent soldiers and proved fiercely loyal to the British. Eventually history caught up with them and almost all left post-mandate Iraq, where they had acquired a reputation as colonial lackeys, to make a new communal life in the United States.

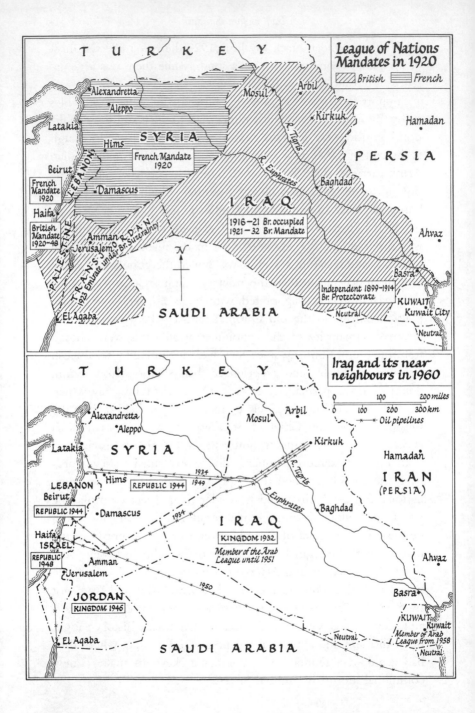

League of Nations
Mandates in 1920
///// British   ═══ French

TURKEY

Alexandretta
• Aleppo
Latakia
SYRIA
Hims
French Mandate
1920
Beirut
French
Mandate
1920
• Damascus
Haifa
British
Mandate
1920-48
Amman
Jerusalem
El Aqaba
PALESTINE
LEBANON
T-R-A-N-S-J-O-R-D-A-N
1923 Emirate under Br. Suzerainty)
N
SAUDI ARABIA

Mosul •
Arbil
Kirkuk
Hamadan
R. Tigris
R. Euphrates
PERSIA
Baghdad
IRAQ
1916–21 Br. occupied
1921–32 Br. Mandate
Ahvaz
Basra
Independent 1899–1914
Br. Protectorate
KUWAIT
Kuwait City
Neutral
Neutral

Iraq and its near
neighbours in 1960

TURKEY

0   100   200 miles
0   100   200 300 km
—×—×— Oil pipelines

Alexandretta
• Aleppo
Latakia
SYRIA
LEBANON
Beirut
REPUBLIC 1944
Hims
REPUBLIC 1944
1934
1949
• Damascus
1934
Haifa
ISRAEL
REPUBLIC
1948
Amman
Jerusalem
JORDAN
KINGDOM 1946
El Aqaba
SAUDI ARABIA

Mosul •
Arbil
Kirkuk
R. Tigris
Hamadan
IRAN
(PERSIA)
R. Euphrates
Baghdad
IRAQ
KINGDOM 1932
Member of the Arab
League until 1951
1950
Ahvaz
Basra
KUWAIT
Kuwait
Member of Arab
League from 1958
Neutral
Neutral

The creation of the council of ministers and the national army did not solve the principal problem in postwar Iraq: sovereignty. The mandate system was posited on the principle that the countries adopted by the League of Nations for mandate rule were already sovereign and, as soon as sufficiently developed, should emerge into independence. The most evolved were to be furnished with appropriate heads of state from the outset. In the case of Iraq, by reason of the sophistication of its urban population and its potential wealth clearly a candidate for early release from mandate rule, the choice fell upon the Amir Faisal, a Hashemite prince and son of the Sharif of Mecca, who had taken part in the Arab Revolt and had originally been appointed to the throne of Syria (until the French, who administered the Syrian mandate, fell out with him). There was much to favour him as a future king of a sovereign Iraq. He descended from the family of the Prophet and so, though a Sunni, enjoyed respect among the Shi'a; he had authentic nationalist credentials, as a leader of the Arab Revolt; and he was well-known to the British, among whom he had friends. He was, moreover, personable, charming and politically astute. Nevertheless he was not by birth or affiliation Iraqi; by origin he was an Arab of the distant deserts, by upbringing a child of Ottoman society in Istanbul.

Little wonder, therefore, that he was to find it difficult to establish the legitimacy of Hashemite authority over the old land between the two rivers. In the eyes of Iraqi nationalists he was too closely associated with the British; to Kurds and Shi'a he depended too heavily for domestic support on his comrades of the Arab Revolt, who were overwhelmingly Sunni and often former officers of the Ottoman army. Under the mandate constitution Iraq became notionally a democracy, with an elected parliament; but the franchise was indirect and the vote consistently manipulated both by the British and the royal government to assure a compliant majority. Manipulation ensured that the constituent assembly, forerunner of the national parliament, voted in 1922 to ratify an Anglo-Iraqi treaty giving Britain executive authority over the foreign and security policies of a nominally co-equal Iraqi kingdom.

Britain's desire to secure the passage of the treaty was greatly assisted by two extraneous factors, one of which was to persist in importance – apparently in perpetuity. The first was Turkish intervention in Iraqi affairs. The new Turkey, since the collapse of Ottomanism, was an ethnically exclusive Turkish state, but it retained territorial ambitions. They included that of incorporating northern Iraq's oil-bearing regions, with their Kurdish population, into Turkish national territory. Britain was unwilling to see Iraqi territory ceded to a foreign power, even though its holdings in the Turkish Petroleum Company (soon to be the Iraq Petroleum Company) would ensure its access to the oil reserves. Iraqis of most communities recognized that acquiesence in the passage of the treaty offered the best means of blocking Turkish predation. The second factor was Kurdish rebellion. Seeing in Turkey's intervention an opportunity to further their ambition for independence, some Kurds rose against the mandate administration, forcing the British first to stage a costly campaign of repression and then to install the chief Kurdish strongman as regional governor. The expedient did not endure. Shaikh Mahmud, the new governor, rapidly demonstrated that he intended to make himself Kurdish King, forcing the British to take military action in Kurdistan again, which resulted in Mahmud's flight to Iran.

Turkish aggression and Kurdish rebellion had the combined effect, paradoxically, of bringing about the settlement Britain sought. Because the southern Shi'a themselves were simultaneously refusing co-operation in the passage of the treaty, their religious chiefs judging that it threatened their privileges, both the King and the Sunni leaders were brought to conclude that acceptance of the treaty, repugnant as they found it, was a lesser evil. Without it they could not count on British support and without that support they risked losing the north and the south becoming a chronically dissident region. The King meanwhile announced important electoral concessions which granted the Shi'a notables a commanding position in the projected parliament. The result was that a constituent assembly was successfully convened in March 1924 which ratified the treaty and led swiftly to the election – by indirect and carefully controlled means – of a sovereign parliament later that year.

The independent Iraqi government, nominal as its independence was, swiftly declared its position on two key points of policy. It sought to raise a conscripted national army and it pressed repeatedly for a declaration by the British of a date at which the mandate would be surrendered, allowing Iraq to become a full – and so fully independent – member of the League of Nations. In the first policy it was only partially successful. Conscription, which recalled the bad old days of Ottoman imperialism, was deeply unpopular with the Iraqi people; moreover, the British did not believe that the Iraqi treasury could afford the cost of a large army. The new Iraqi army which emerged was therefore neither to be a conscript force nor as large as the court, dominated as it was by ex-Ottoman officers, wished. Over the termination of the treaty the government was more successful. In 1929 a new British administration, formed by the Labour Party, more sympathetic to nationalist aspirations in the territories for which it held responsibility overseas than the Conservatives, promised independence by 1932. Its implementation was dependent on the Iraqis agreeing provisions acceptable to Britain. That condition was achieved thanks to the political skills of the new Iraqi prime minister, appointed in March 1930, Nuri al-Sa'id. Nuri, who was to dominate Iraq until the fall of the monarchy in 1958, was an archetype of the Arab leader in the late colonial era. A traditionalist, he was pro-Western for strictly realistic reasons, but sincerely patriotic. As an ex-Ottoman officer, but a member of the al-'Ahd association of Arab nationalists, he had excellent credentials as a military leader but was also quickly able to demonstrate governmental capacity. His wider vision was of an Arab world dominated by states under Hashemite leadership; his domestic policy was for Iraq to be ruled by a military administration which held popular loyalties by wise distribution of its oil wealth.

The British liked Nuri and he appeared to like them. Under his premiership it was therefore not difficult to negotiate a new Anglo-Iraqi treaty that would form the basis for emergence from mandate status. Its key provisions were that, while full responsibility for external defence and the maintenance of internal order should be vested in the Iraqi government, the British should be given rights of military transit through Iraq if necessary, while two bases, including the great air base at Habbaniyah, should remain in British hands. That presumed Britain's right to maintain the Iraq Levies as a base protection force. The treaty was ratified, after Nuri had called a general election to endorse his policy, in November 1930. Predictably the Kurds objected, protesting that it did not meet the obligations allegedly undertaken by the British to protect their special status, but the rebellion was put down, with British help. In October 1932 Iraq was admitted to the League of Nations as a sovereign and independently governed state.

Independent Iraq was destined, during the first twenty-six years of its existence, to be neither a democratic polity nor a truly autonomous state; the achievement of democracy, indeed, was to elude its people long beyond 1958. Domestically, Iraqi politics during the years of the Hashemite monarchy were to be the arena of élites, of which the urban Sunni grandees and landowners were to be the most active, grouped into parties which frequently re-formed and changed their names. The more successful parties, such as al-Ikha, also, however, included representatives of the better-educated and more prosperous Shi'a. The role of the parties was to preserve the élites' privileges, particularly by the denial of all but the most modest land reform and by monopolizing access to paid government appointments. Behind the parties, at all times, stood the army, whose officers were cultivated by the court and who could assert their power at any time when regional or minority disorder threatened, as it frequently did in Kurdistan, the authority of the centre. Many of the officers were originally Sharifian, having risen to prominence under the Hashemites during the Arab Revolt. The most important group formed the Circle of Seven, an inner grouping of four the Golden Square. Nuri al-Sa'id did not belong but remained nonetheless a permanent and dominant political figure, frequently in power as Prime Minister and, even when not, the rock on which royal rule rested.

Externally, Iraqi politics were constrained by the continuing fact of British power in the Middle East, which persisted even after the grant of independence to India in 1947 and the withdrawal from Palestine in 1948. The Royal Navy controlled the Gulf and Indian Ocean, while the British army maintained garrisons, directly or indirectly, in Egypt, Jordan, Saudi Arabia, Sudan and Libya until the mid-fifties. During the Second World War the Middle East was base area for the largest of Britain's overseas garrisons. As Nuri al-Sa'id recognized, British power had therefore to be accommodated at all times. He was content that it should be, since he regarded the British as most dependable guarantors of the power of the Hashemites, to which he was committed. Nuri was conscious of the growing power of Arab nationalism, particularly in Egypt and Syria, and he was himself a supporter of the idea of pan-Arabism; but he hoped that a unified Arab polity would emerge in a monarchical form under Hashemite leadership. He was also disturbed by the rise of Jewish power in Palestine and, after 1948, became an active opponent of Zionism, while fearing the effects that militant anti-Zionism would have on stable Arab societies. At heart he was an Iraqi patriot, of a moderate and pro-Western cast of mind. For all his undeniable political skills, his essentially traditionalist attitude would eventually doom him to defeat by younger Arabs possessing fiercely anti-Western, anti-Zionist, anti-capitalist beliefs.

Economically Nuri was a modernizer who would seek, through the investment of Iraq's growing oil revenues, to better the lot of the people and to improve the resources and efficiency of the state. He was not helped by the characters of the monarchs he had to serve, or by the monarchy's erratic fortunes. Faisal, a charming and intelligent man, died in 1933. He was succeeded by Ghazi, whose vaguely pan-Arab and anti-British feelings attracted support from nationalists; he associated himself too closely with Sunni favourites, however, to foster national unity. His reign, like his father's, was brief (1933–39), ended by a car crash. He was succeeded by his son, also Faisal, but, as he was only three years old at his accession, the monarchy became a regency, exercised by Prince Abd al-Ilah, brother of the infant King's mother. Abd al-Ilah, who was to be Regent until 1953, shared Nuri's pro-British outlook but unfortunately did not possess his political subtlety. His main interest lay in securing the future of the Hashemite dynasty, of which he saw the British as the best guarantors. That priority separated him from the Arab nationalist officers of the army – a force of increasing size, 41,000 by 1941 – whom he farther alienated by failing to disguise the social disdain he felt for them.

That was bad politics. The officer corps, which had staged a minor *coup d'état* in 1936 to bring about a change of cabinet, was now the effective force in the country; no government could be formed without its approval and any government was obliged to promote the policies it favoured, pan-Arabism and, increasingly, friendship for the totalitarian régimes of Western Europe foremost. Matters came to a head in 1941. The Regent had attempted to reassert the principle of civilian control, with the object of strengthening the connection with Britain, by appointing his chief courtier, Rashid Ali al-Kailani, as Prime Minister, with Nuri as his Foreign Minister. The move was less well-judged than it appeared. Rashid Ali, like many Arab politicians of the period, admired Hitler and Mussolini and expected their victory. He also resented Britain's preponderant role in Iraqi affairs, which the outbreak of the Second World War had emphasized. Britain demanded strict adherence to the Anglo-Iraqi treaty and, in particular, confirmation of its right to move troops through the country. By the end of 1940 Britain was also demanding Rashid Ali's removal. He was determined not to resign and, during early 1941, set in train a series of events which led to the flight of the Regent and Nuri to Transjordan and to a military *coup d'état*. A new Regent was installed, Rashid Ali reappointed as Prime

Minister and, when the British insisted on extracting permission to send troops into the country, a military confrontation staged outside the British base at Habbaniyah.

A curious little campaign then ensued. While Britain organized an intervention, to be launched from India and Transjordan, the Habbaniyah garrison attacked the Iraqi forces deployed outside the base on 2 May. The attackers consisted largely of RAF aircraft, which bombed and strafed the Iraqi ground troops to great effect; they were supported by a battalion of the Iraq Levies and two companies of the King's Own Royal Regiment. Startled by the strength of the British resistance, the Iraqis fell back on Baghdad. Meanwhile Rashid Ali had indicated to Germany that he would welcome assistance and some thirty German aircraft, staging through Vichy French Syria, arrived at Mosul. The appearance of Habforce, the column that had driven across the desert from Transjordan, consisting of mechanized units of British Cavalry and the Arab Legion, settled the issue. Rashid Ali and his supporters fled, the Germans withdrew. By June the Regent and Nuri had returned and a pro-British government was restored; in the interregnum, however, disgruntled nationalists had vented their anger at the British intervention on the Baghdad Jewish community, killing over 200. This *farhud* was the precursor of events which, in 1950, would cause almost all Iraq's 100,000 Jews to leave for the new state of Israel, thus ending a presence of over two thousand years and one of the richest minority cultures to be found anywhere in the Middle East.

The restoration of 1941 was a restoration not merely of the legitimate regency, but also of the primacy of Nuri al-Sa'id. With intermissions, he was to hold the premiership thenceforth until 1958, making Iraq, in outward appearance, one of the most stable states in the Middle East. Internal problems persisted, particularly those of Kurdish separatism and of Shi'a discontent, caused by the persistent denial to the Shi'ite majority of the political power their numbers demanded. Nuri had also to deal with the problem of a growingly important Communist movement, strongly supported by the Soviet Union, and with nationalist hostility to the establishment and consolidation of the Israeli state. He found means, however, to placate or diffuse internal dissent, to contain the Communists and to persuade the nationalists of his anti-Israeli credentials.

His most substantive anti-Israeli gesture was the despatch of Iraqi troops to fight Israel during its war of independence (1948–49). In 1948 a contingent of 18,000 was sent to Transjordan (soon to be Jordan) to defend the annexed Palestinian West Bank. Its intervention was successful but Iraq was later accused by Egypt of operating too passively, acting merely as a defender of Jordanian territorial acquisitions and failing to mount an offensive which might have diverted Israel from its conquests of Galilee and the Negev. Nevertheless the Iraqi contingent was for a time the largest Arab force in Palestine, a commitment which invested Nuri with influence in the attempts to negotiate a postwar settlement. His solution was to recognize the existence of Israel in return for its surrender of much of the territory conquered during the war. It was rejected by all parties and the great powers as well, a reaction which provided him with the opportunity to bring the Iraqi troops home.

Nuri's principal initiative to limit the Communist political threat, and the influence of the Soviet Union, was his creation of the Baghdad Pact in February 1955. It came at the end of a disturbed period in domestic politics which had seen him often out of office, manipulating power from the sidelines rather than as head of government. In 1948 he had renegotiated the Anglo-Iraq Treaty of 1930 in what ought to have been a popular move; the Portsmouth Treaty was judged by many, however, still to concede too much to the old mandate power. During 1954, when premier once again, he was attracted by the example of Turkey and Pakistan, who had entered into a mutual assistance treaty. Nuri first succeeded in bringing Turkey to sign a similar agreement with Iraq, later extended to include Pakistan, Iran and Britain. The signing of the Baghdad Pact, besides creating a formidable anti-Soviet bloc in the region, also had the effect of cancelling out the domestic harm done by the Portsmouth

Treaty, since by it Britain agreed at last to surrender its rights at Habbaniyah and other bases in Iraq without securing other concessions from Iraq.

The signing of the Baghdad Pact was greeted with enthusiasm in the West; though the United States was not a signatory, it associated itself with Britain's commitment to equip and train the Iraqi armed forces. Nuri, however, either failed to see or chose to ignore its negative effects at home. The Soviet Union, as a self-proclaimed anti-imperialist force in the world, was regarded as a friend and ally by most Arab nationalists, particularly the younger officers in most Arab armies and above all by the Free Officers who had overthrown the Egyptian monarchy in 1952. Because Nuri believed that his relationship with Iraq's generals ensured his control of the army, he seemed indifferent to the growth of an undercover Free Officer movement in its junior ranks. Communist subversion was what worried him; and, from his resumption of the premiership in 1954 onwards, he conducted a campaign of repression against the Iraqi Communist Party, but also against all dissidents, wherever disorder or its threat was evident. He was also, meanwhile, attempting to invest Iraq's growing oil revenues, so as to raise the level of general prosperity, create work and increase material wealth.

The trend of events, however, was against him. Nuri was now increasingly seen as a figure of the past. The Arab Revolt and the overthrow of Ottomanism no longer seemed the central events of modern Arab history, as they had done to the ageing generation of Sharifian officers who had ridden with Lawrence of Arabia. The younger generation looked to leaders untainted by association with the British and French, who had won their spurs in the war against Israel, even at the cost of defeat in the field, and who saw the Soviet Union as a better source of support for a united Arab nation than the old régimes of the West. Egypt's Colonel Nasser was their *beau idéal*. He was outspokenly anti-Western, pragmatically pro-Soviet and a champion of Arab independence in every form. His nationalization of the Suez Canal won him adulation throughout the Arab world. When it provoked

France and Britain to conspire with Israel in an attack on Egypt in November 1956, even Nuri aligned himself with Arab protest, breaking off relations with France and excluding Britain from meetings of the Baghdad Pact. However, he also took action against anti-Western street protesters in the major cities and displayed in other ways his continuing pro-Western stance.

His opponents responded by forming a National Front in February 1957, combining the older domestic parties and the Communists with the new Ba'ath (Renaissance) Party, a secular and modernizing organization founded in Syria in the previous decade by the Arab Christian Michel Aflaq. The Front quickly established close connections with the Iraqi Free Officers movement, an undercover organization which modelled itself on the Egyptian Nasserists. Nuri again failed to detect or else ignored these developments, apparently believing that his management of Iraqi foreign policy during the Suez crisis had secured his domestic position. In June 1957 he retired from the premiership once more, though continuing to control the government from behind the scenes. He remained ostensibly outside politics until March 1958 when, following the union of Egypt and Syria in a United Arab Republic (UAR), he resumed the premiership, on this occasion as head of an Arab Union of Iraq and Jordan, hastily formed as a riposte to the creation of the UAR in the last days of the previous administration.

The logic of the Arab Union was that both of its component states were Hashemite monarchies. Monarchy, however, outside Jordan, was almost as discredited in the eyes of nationalists as the pro-Western régimes that underpinned it. It attracted no support from the Free Officers who were instigating their own measures to secure Iraq's future. Under the leadership of Brigadier Abd al-Karem Kassem and Colonel Abd al-Salim Arif, they had decided to overthrow the Hashemite dynasty, declare a republic and form a government drawn from the ranks of the army. They had also decided to act quickly since they foresaw that the growing discontent within the officer corps could not much longer be disguised. The opportunity to act was given them by Nuri himself who, alarmed by an American intervention in Lebanon, to avert a civil war, and by the evident hostility of Nasser's United Arab Republic to the Arab Union, decided to send elements of the Iraqi army to the Jordanian border as a measure of support to Jordan's King. The deployment was seen by Kassem and his military allies as providing the opportunity to mount a coup and on 14 July 1958 army units moving towards Jordan entered Baghdad and attacked the royal palace. The young King, Faisal II, and the Regent, Abd al-Ilah, and other members of the royal family were shot in the courtyard. Nuri, allegedly attempting to escape the city disguised in woman's clothing, was shot in the street the following day.

Immediately after this bloody end to Iraq's royal government, the country was proclaimed a republic and Kassem Prime Minister, Minister of Defence and Commander-in-Chief. Supreme power was vested symbolically in a three-man sovereignty council. Arif was appointed Deputy Prime Minister. Tension between the two soldiers revealed itself at once. Arif belonged to the Nasserist school of nationalists whose overriding aim was to create a single Arab nation within which the states descending from the old imperial system would lose their identity. Kassem was an Iraqi nationalist, committed to Iraq's economic development and its evolution as a rich and powerful independent state. Half Sunni, half Kurdish Shi'a by birth, he was presumably well positioned to foster national unity. Temperamentally, however, he was an authoritarian, whose inclination, when he encountered opposition, was to use force to resolve his difficulties. He genuinely sought to build a homogenous Iraqi society and tried to integrate both Kurds and Shi'a with Sunni, promising prosperity and permitting the public organization of political and interest groups – women, youth, nationalists, the Muslim Brotherhood – hitherto suppressed. He recognized Kurdish separateness, though not the right to separatism, revoked the Iraq Petroleum Company's oil exploration rights and announced a scheme of radical land reform, designed to end the days of absentee landlordism over wide areas of agricultural holdings.

Kassem's policies, combined with his undoubted personal magnetism, brought him widespread popularity. It was a shallow popularity, however, dependent on his ability to mobilize crowds in the street; his role as 'Sole Leader' was ultimately supported, as the previous régime had been, by the intelligence and security forces and the army. Shallow popularity was opposed, moreover, by the hostility of displaced rivals and well-organized covert groups, Nasserist Free Officers who rejected his policy of 'Iraq First', the Ba'ath, which was growing in strength, and the Communists.

He was obliged early on to remove Arif, his co-conspirator, whom he imprisoned but did not execute; Rashid Ali, who had led the military revolt of 1941 and who returned from exile expecting to enter into his inheritance, he did execute. He was also driven to fall out with the Communists; after a preliminary attempt to draw them into his scheme for broadening his political support, he found their determination to work for their own ends a threat to his position and he progressively withdrew the privileges he had begun by granting them, without actually coming to an open breach. His management of the Communist problem was the most successful strand in his dictatorship.

He also began well in his attempt to palliate the Kurdish problem. In 1960, as part of his liberalization programme, he allowed the Kurdish Democratic Party (KDP) to organize openly. Its co-operation with the Communists and its efforts to draw the Soviet Union into Iraqi domestic politics understandably alarmed Kassem, however, and he rejected its over-bold demand for the grant of regional autonomy. That move provoked armed protest in Kurdistan and by the autumn of 1961 serious fighting had broken out in the north, engaging the army in a campaign of repression. The leader of the most important Kurdish group, Mulla Mustafa Barzani, a long-time opponent of the Baghdad government, returned to the field with his *peshmerga* guerrillas, who were to become a permanent cause of internal disorder during Kassem's period in power and under Saddam.

Kassem's most dedicated opponents, however, came from the

groups apparently closest to him, the Arab nationalists and the army. His foreign policy pleased both, for he reasserted Iraq's rights over Iran's in the Shatt el-Arab and he revived the claim to Kuwait, so menacingly in June 1961 that Britain, Kuwait's traditional protector, was prompted to send an expeditionary force to the emirate, from which it had only just been withdrawn. Because so much of the Iraqi army was committed to Kurdistan, Kassem was unable, however, to respond with a corresponding military deployment to the Kuwait border. At British representation, the Arab League, to which all Arab states belonged, recognized Kuwait as an independent country and on the withdrawal of the British troops replaced them with others of their own, largely drawn from the army of the United Arab Republic (Egypt and Syria).

Kassem's response was to remove Iraq's representation from the Arab League and to break off relations with several Arab states that had recognized Kuwait's independence. These were empty gestures. Within Iraq the Free Officers and other nationalists, and the Ba'ath, took the view that he had humiliated Iraq, left it isolated in the Arab world and, most critically of all, caved in to British imperialism.

The Kuwait affair left Kassem in a precarious position. Outwardly he retained his popularity; his use of oil revenues for the general good, particularly by the improvement and expansion of the electrical and health care system, was widely welcomed and his reduction of the rights enjoyed by the Iraq Petroleum Company was seen as proper and patriotic; but his hold on power was maintained only by a balancing act. Believing he was accepted as 'Sole Leader' by the masses, he had failed to protect himself by creating a real network of power groups loyal to himself. Other power groups, covert and conspiratorial, resented his refusal to position Iraq at the centre of the Arab nationalist movement and his determination to pursue a policy of 'Iraq First'. He had already survived several attempts to unseat him: a crude conspiracy led by the returned Rashid Ali in 1958, a rising in the north in 1959 and an assassination attempt in October of that year, in which the young Saddam Hussein had fired on his car. The decisive stroke, however, was to be launched by the Ba'ath, now a well-established and efficient force in Iraq's unofficial politics. Its leaders, particularly Kassem's former confederate Arif and Brigadier Hasan al-Bakr, were dissatisfied by Kassem's isolation of Iraq within the Arab world and by his dependence on the Communists for support. They also hated his insouciant belief in his own popularity as a safeguard of his personal security. That was perceptive. Kassem, though apparently aware that trouble was brewing, merely arrested some of the leading Ba'athists. He did not deploy dependable units of the army to protect himself. On 9 February 1963 others in the Ba'ath struck against the air force, which was loyal to Kassem and also had Communist connections. Meanwhile they brought their supporters into the streets in Baghdad and sent army units they controlled to the Ministry of Defence. Had Kassem armed the Communists he might have survived but he disdained to do so. In the prolonged street battle that followed he and his supporters were eventually overcome, captured and shot.

Power now seemed to belong to the Ba'ath but the leaders of the coup appointed the non-Ba'athist Abd al-Salim Arif as President, with the Ba'athist Hasan al-Bakr as Vice-President. There ensued a troubled period of disputed authority. The Ba'ath had become the most important political force in Iraq but its factions could not agree, the points of difference, as usual, being over the relative weight to be given to the pursuit of Iraqi and wider Arab nationalism. Arif, who enjoyed wide support in the army, eventually used his military position to quash the Ba'ath, ruling thereafter as a military dictator. He created the Republican Guard as an inner army, recruited from dependable tribal allies, and he trod a narrow path between Nasserism and straightforward Iraqi nationalism. He proved a skilful politician and might have enjoyed a long period of power had he not been killed in a helicopter crash in 1966, apparently a genuine accident. Power then passed to his brother Abd al-Rahman Arif, another soldier, who attempted to perpetuate his system of personal rule. The second Arif, however, lacked the former's skills and encountered more difficult problems, including the aftermath of the Arab disaster of 1967 in the war with Israel, a deteriorating situation in Kurdistan and the outbreak of a Communist-led revolt in the south. Under his uncertain hold on power, the Ba'ath was able to reorganize and to extend its tentacles, notably into units of the army and the Republican Guard. In July 1968 the Ba'ath staged a semi-coup, which disposed of President Arif by putting him on an aircraft out of the country. It was subsequently unable, however, to agree on the division of power with the non-Ba'athists in the army who had joined in Arif's removal and a fortnight later, on 30 July, it staged a second coup, which appointed the veteran Ahmed Hasan al-Bakr President, with his young kinsman Saddam Hussein as his deputy. Bakr's base of power, though he held the post of secretary-general of the Iraqi Ba'ath party, was in the army. Saddam's power, which he was already and secretly dedicated to making absolute, derived from his role as a Ba'athist, an experienced conspirator and a member of an extended family, clan and tribal network centred on the provincial centre of Tikrit. Hasan al-Bakr has been described by Charles Tripp, a leading historian of modern Iraq, as 'a typical regimental officer, solicitous of the welfare of his subordinates and able to use the language of military collegiality to create a certain bond with fellow officers. Despite the radical Ba'athist rhetoric that he used when occasion demanded, his views were conservative and rather typical of his provincial background: pan-Arab to some degree, but also imbued with a keen awareness of status distinctions between different lineages and clans among the Sunni Arabs . . . of Iraq.' Saddam, by contrast, was a completely uncollegial figure, solicitous of no one's welfare but his own and animated by a Stalinist ruthlessness to acquire and maximize personal power.

3

Saddam Hussein

Saddam Hussein, a poor and uneducated provincial youth, came to exercise absolute power in Iraq by a mixture of violence and political intrigue. His rise followed a novel and unusual path. Leadership in the Muslim world is traditionally associated with birth or religious status, often both together. Indeed, traditional Muslim society offered the ambitious none of the ways upward customary in the West. Worldly ambition was anyhow not a quality thought proper by pious Muslims. At the heart of the Muslim system lies the idea of the *Umma*, the community of fellow believers, commanded by the Koran to live in harmony under the authority of the Imam or Caliph, the successor of the Prophet. The succession divided Muslims almost from the beginning, soon after the death of Muhammad, into the Sunni majority, which believed that the Caliph, though he should preferably descend from Muhammad's tribe, the Quraysh, was to be elected and accepted by the faithful as long as he showed himself 'rightly guided' by the law of God; and a number of minorities, of which the Shi'a was the largest. The Shi'a hold that the succession was flawed from the start, believing that the Caliphate should have passed to the Prophet's cousin and son-in-law, Ali. This dispute gave rise to murder and civil war and divides Islam to this day. Nevertheless, neither faction diverged from the central idea, that Muslims live under the law of God, revealed in the Koran and to be upheld by Muhammad's successor.

Practical difficulties made the idea difficult to sustain; the history of Islam for many centuries is a record of dissent and dispute, often violent, of succession by victory in war, not election, and, at times, of competing caliphates. Internecine violence always, however, affronted pious Muslims, so much so that Islam invented a unique institution, that of slave soldiery, to absolve those in dispute of the sin of fighting fellow believers. A unified Caliphate was only reestablished in comparatively recent times when the Ottoman Turks, a non-Arab people from Central Asia who had been recruited to serve as slave soldiers, imposed their authority over the Arabs by military force and assumed the Caliphate by diktat. From the sixteenth century onwards the history of Islam became largely that of the Ottoman empire, with its seat at Constantinople (Istanbul). Areas of the Islamic world, notably in India and South-east Asia, never formed part of the Ottoman Empire; many of its subjects, in south-eastern Europe and the Near East, remained Christian. The empire, however, embraced the historic heartland of Islam and almost all Arabs were, from the sixteenth to the early twentieth century, directly or indirectly subjects of the Ottoman Sultan-Caliph.

Power in the Ottoman world, both secular and religious, was dynastic; sons succeeded fathers, though favoured wives were often able to evade the principle of primogeniture and new sultans commonly consolidated their accession by murdering brothers en masse. The traditional principle persisted nevertheless; birth and religious status were the bases of worldly authority. Religious status could be quite widely drawn; the servants of the Sultan-Caliph, his ministers and military commanders, derived their authority from association with him. Thus, for example, the Muhammad Ali dynasty of Egypt, whose leaders ruled the country during the nineteenth and early twentieth century, were legitimized as the Sultan-Caliph's viceroys (Khedive). Unnervingly, alternative legitimate power could also arise spontaneously, through the appearance of a Mahdi, a man directly guided by God. The most famous Mahdi of modern times was Muhammad Ahmed, who became ruler of Sudan in the 1880s.

Mahdism, dynastic usurpation, fragmentation of the Caliphate or patronage by it were the only means, until the twentieth century, by which power could be transferred in the Muslim world. The historic ideas of the *Umma*, the community of believers, of the Caliphate and of the overriding authority of the Supreme Being and his law as revealed in the Koran, impeded the emergency of secular politics. Much was changed in the Islamic and particularly the Arab world, however, by its penetration by European imperial powers in the nineteenth century. The conquest of Algeria by the French after 1830 and the subordination of Egypt to British rule after 1882 subjected large numbers of Muslim Arabs to the processes of European government, based not on the ideas of religious fraternity or divine authority but on those of administrative efficiency and economic development; with them the Europeans brought also secular education and law, both quite alien to the Muslim mind, which for centuries had used schools as a means of Koranic instruction and the courts as a forum for judgement by *Sharia*, Koranic law.

European imperialism did not extinguish the power of Muslim ideas; in the long run, indeed, by a process of reaction, it was to reenergize Islam and in a highly aggressive form. In the early twentieth century, however, the worldly behaviour of some young Muslims was decisively altered by exposure to European thought and practice. In the Ottoman empire, dissatisfaction at the failure of the Sultan-Caliph's government to stem the encroachment of European powers prompted a group of army officers, the 'Young Turks', to set up a modernizing régime; its leaders were irreligious Turkish nationalists; their tendency to treat the Arabs of the empire as subjects rather than fellow-Muslims led to the beginnings of what has been called 'the Arab awakening'. The awakening was accelerated by Turkey's defeat in the First World War which led to the fall of the Sultanate, the abolition of the Caliphate and the attachment of the Ottomans' Arab provinces to the French and British empires as League of Nations mandated territories. Cast adrift in a world where a supreme Muslim authority no longer existed, the Arabs within the mandates and in the British protectorate of Egypt began to respond to direct rule by

Europeans by emulating European political forms. One manifestation, the Muslim Brotherhood, which appeared in Egypt in
1928, was specifically Islamic in character but sought to preserve
religious values by adopting such European practices as recruiting
young people into a Scout movement, founding schools, hospitals and clinics and building factories, all run on Islamic principles. The Muslim Brotherhood, eventually to be persecuted by
Arab régimes of specifically secular character, has survived into
modern times; one of its adherents, Sayyid Qutb, conceived the
theory of Islamic renewal which inspired the terrorists of 11
September.

Another direction taken by the Arab awakening was the creation
in Syria after the Second World War of a political party dedicated by title to 'resurrection'. The Ba'ath Party, founded in 1944
by a Syrian Christian, Michel Aflaq, proclaimed the unity of all
Arabic-speaking people and their right to live in a unitary state.
It specifically denounced the boundaries imposed on the Arab
lands by the empires – including the Ottoman. Aflaq went farther;
Christian though he was, he invoked the idea of Islam, propounded
by Muhammad, as the common inheritance of all Arabs, Muslim
or not, and its rise as an historical experience which gave the
Arabs a particular mission in the world. The Arabs were to transform themselves first by spiritual renewal and then their political and social systems. Paradoxically, Aflaq was politically a secularist
and the Ba'ath was to become the first secular party in the Arab
world. It gave no place as leaders to traditional religious figures
and emphasized Western rather than Islamic social values: the
importance of scientific and technical education and the equality
of the sexes. Nevertheless the roots of Ba'athism were meta-
physical, which perhaps explains its appeal to the Arab mind.
Aflaq was also rigidly anti-Communist, regarding Communism
as another form of foreign imperialism.

Ba'athism's influence was geographically limited. It did not
flourish in Egypt where during the 1950s another movement,
loosely known as Arab socialism, achieved dominance through a
revolution led by young army officers, notably Abdul Nasser.

Nasser adopted several of Aflaq's ideas; he was an egalitarian and a secularist, fervently anti-imperialist and a champion of Arab unity, which he did much to advance by creating a United Arab Republic which briefly joined Egypt to Syria and established a presence in Yemen. Ba'athism's most notable success was achieved elsewhere. During the 1950s it found followers in Iraq, several of whom were advanced to ministerial positions after the overthrow of the monarchy in 1958.

A junior Iraqi Ba'athist was Saddam Hussein, twenty-one in 1958. His prospect of advancement then looked slim. He was uneducated, uncouth and without connections; crucially he lacked any military position, a serious deficiency in view of the domination of the Ba'ath both in Iraq and Syria by young army officers, who were also the leaders of the revolutionary movement in Egypt. Saddam had sought admission to the Iraqi military academy but did not take the entrance examination. Frustrated in that ambition, he had become little more than a semi-criminal drifter, with a reputation for troublemaking and a talent for violence. Possessed of exceptional self-confidence and a ruthless will to succeed, qualities contained in a large and strong physical frame, he was nevertheless determined to become a man of power. In doing so, during the decades of the 1960s and '70s, he single-handedly defined an entirely new form of Arab leadership, dependent neither on birth nor position nor assumption of religious authority but on the use of force and his personal skills in political manipulation. Saddam's Arabism was irrelevant; had he been born German or Russian in the age of the dictatorships – and he greatly admired Stalin – he would have understood how to exploit disorder and instability to his advantage and could well have risen to dominance in the Nazi or Marxist-Leninist systems.

Saddam was born in the village of al-Ouja, a small and poor village on the Tigris near the provincial centre of Tikrit, sometime between 1935 and 1939; his birth date was not officially recorded and he is believed, in any case, to have altered it on marriage to make himself appear older than his wife. His father may not have been married to his mother, Subha Tulfah, who was the dominant influence on his life. A strong-willed and outspoken peasant woman, who made a living as a clairvoyant, Subha was certainly married after Saddam's birth to a fellow villager whom Saddam came to hate; he was scorned and mistreated. Subha, however, had a brother, Khairallah Tulfah, who assumed the role of surrogate father to Saddam and guided his early development. Khairallah, despite his humble origins, had been commissioned as an officer in the prewar Iraqi army, a status that greatly impressed Saddam. Khairallah also fixed Saddam's political outlook. He hated foreigners, particularly the British, declared his admiration for Hitler and the Nazis and was a supporter of Iraq's wartime ruler, Rashid Ali, who in 1941 had tried to arrange an alliance with Nazi Germany and for a German expeditionary force to enter Iraq. For his complicity in the plot Khairallah had been cashiered from the army and jailed for five years.

During Khairallah's imprisonment Saddam, still a child and apparently often driven from the hut which was the family home by his stepfather, kept himself alive by thievery and odd jobs. He had, however, conceived the idea of getting an education and when Khairallah was released, joined him in Tikrit, where his uncle got him into school and supported him. Khairallah was a survivor. He found teaching jobs himself, joined the fledgling Ba'ath party and became sufficiently well-regarded as an educationist to be appointed director of education in Baghdad after the overthrow of the monarchy in 1958. By then he had moved to the Karkh district of the capital, taking Saddam with him. Saddam enrolled at Karkh high school and appears to have applied himself. He was still, however, the local provincial rough who ran a street gang and who fought with anyone who opposed him, mocked his peasant ways or supported the pro-British, monarchical government which represented the established order before the revolution of 1958.

The revolution of July 1958 led to Saddam's initiation into the culture of political violence and opened his eyes to the possibilities of personal advancement to power by killing. He had joined the Ba'ath party in 1957, apparently for idealistic reasons; since it then had only 300 members in Iraq the move was certainly not opportunistic. It was no doubt, however, influenced by his uncle Khairallah's espousal of Ba'athism and by the advantage membership of the Ba'ath provided, as shown by his uncle's appointment as Baghdad's director of education. But Khairallah did not last long in the job. An Iraqi Communist, Saddoun al-Tikriti, denounced him as a man of unsavoury reputation and he was removed. Shortly afterwards Saddam, apparently at his uncle's prompting or to avenge family honour, arranged to lie in wait for Saddoun outside his house and murder him by a shot to the head. It was too blatant a crime to be overlooked. Both Saddam and his uncle were arrested and taken into custody, where they remained for six months. In the absence of incriminating evidence, however, they were eventually released.

In another sense, the killing of Saddoun did Saddam no harm, rather the contrary. It conferred on him among fellow Ba'athists a reputation for ruthlessness, at a time when the party was looking for ruthless party loyalists. The Iraqi Ba'athists had been disappointed by the outcome of the 1958 revolution. Its leader, Abd al-Karem Kassem, was a regular officer of conventional views, anti-British and anti-monarchist but equally neither Nasserist nor Ba'athist in outlook. As an Iraqi nationalist, he was unwilling to see Iraq become subordinate to Egypt in an Arab socialist union and was equally resistant to the Ba'athist message of merging Iraq with its neighbouring states in a pan-Arab renaissance.

Had Kassem merely held aloof both from the Nasserists and the Ba'athists, his régime might have survived. Alarmed by the activism of the Nasserists and Ba'athists among the group of so-called Free Officers who had brought him to power, he turned to the Iraqi Communists, who in their enthusiasm for a Soviet alliance necessarily opposed both movements. In March 1959 some of the Free Officers therefore decided to stage a coup. It was an unwise move. The coup was badly organized, lacked popular support and quickly failed. Kassem took a savage revenge. Using the Iraqi Communist Party as his agency of repression, he encouraged it to hunt down and murder all the complicit Free Officers. The avengers went farther; they also killed many of the officers' nationalist supporters and in Mosul organised a mob reprisal which lasted a week and culminated in mass executions. The surviving Ba'athists were outraged. Not only had Kassem set back their dream of creating a pan-Arab state, by severing Iraq's ties with the Egyptian Nasserists. He had also killed many of the men who had risked their lives in rising against the monarchy. The Ba'athists decided on revenge in their turn. Their difficulty was that, as a still tiny party of professional people and students, they lacked members who had any familiarity with violence. A general who had survived Kassem's purge, Ahmad al-Bakr, was a Ba'athist sympathizer, however, and he had appropriate contacts. As a Tikriti, he knew Khairallah and through the uncle he met the nephew. Recognizing that Saddam could be useful to the party as a thug and enforcer, he introduced him to Ba'athist party members. Saddam was not to be admitted to the party at once but he was selected to take part in the attempted assassination of Kassem which was being prepared in the autumn of 1959.

The attempt was botched, perhaps by Saddam's hastiness in opening fire on Kassem's motorcade on 7 October 1959. Kassem was only wounded and recovered. Saddam may have been wounded by return fire; he certainly always claimed to have been so. In the confusion which followed the shooting he made his escape, got home to his native village and then succeeded in crossing the frontier into Syria. Once arrived in Damascus, he was sheltered by local Ba'athists and introduced to the founder of the movement, Michel Aflaq. Aflaq, impressed by what were now Saddam's credentials as a serious revolutionary, apparently admitted him to full party membership and arranged for him to find safer refuge with other Ba'athists in Egypt.

Saddam was in exile four years, which he spent completing his high school education and mingling with other political revolutionaries. He also enrolled as a law student at Cairo University, though he did not complete his degree, and married his cousin,

Sajida, Khairallah's daughter. Marriages within the family are common practice in the Arab world and it is possible that the two young people had been betrothed since childhood. Saddam also joined the Egyptian Ba'ath party and collected friends. One of his closest comrades in Cairo was a fellow survivor of the plot to assassinate Kassem, Abdul al-Shaikly, who was studying medicine and would later become Iraqi Foreign Minister before the two fell out. It is alleged that Saddam, during his Egyptian exile, became associated both with Egyptian intelligence and with the CIA. Of that there is no proof though he was apparently financially supported by the Egyptian government, which was concerned to foster its political contacts with foreign Ba'athists after Syria withdrew from political union with Egypt in 1961.

Saddam's chance to return from exile came in 1963 when Kassem was overthrown in a coup, apparently engineered by the CIA and led by Ahmad al-Bakr, Khairallah's friend and Saddam's early sponsor. The 1963 coup was particularly bloody. Kassem was removed from power only after prolonged street battles in which hundreds died; he was shot after a peremptory trial and his bullet-riddled body was then exhibited on Iraqi television. Bakr became Prime Minister in the change of régime, which effectively established the Ba'ath as the ruling party, and shortly after the transfer of power Saddam, with Abdul al-Shaikly, flew from Cairo to Baghdad, to be welcomed home by a crowd of exultant Ba'athists at the airport. Saddam the pan-Arab revolutionary seemed to be about to enter into his political inheritance.

The reality of his return proved different. Despite his undeniable record as an early enemy of Kassem and as an anti-Communist Arab nationalist, Saddam's humble origins still told against him in his homeland. To the better-educated, middle-class Ba'athists he looked and sounded like a peasant. He was aware of their contempt and resented it. He also knew, however, that he could compensate for his lowly personal standing by winning respect by force; and in the immediate aftermath of Kassem's overthrow the political situation in Iraq offered plentiful opportunities for violence. Kassem's successor, President Arif, filled his government with Ba'athists but failed to quell dissent between its two factions, a civilian group of pan-Arabists and a military group loyal to the army's traditional 'Iraq first' policy. Eventually he expelled all the Ba'athists from their ministerial posts but left the party in being. Bakr, Saddam's party mentor, exploited the situation to achieve dominance, using Saddam, now head of internal party security, to bully and browbeat his opponents.

Saddam remained committed to seeking personal power. That required the removal of Arif, a risky undertaking as the President had the full support of the army. There were several plots, all premature; nevertheless, Saddam proceeded and, in one of the most mysterious episodes of his career, was identified as a conspirator, arrested and imprisoned in October 1964. How he escaped execution has never been explained; nor was his escape in July 1966, after a period in gaol when he was not harshly treated. How he occupied his time between his escape and the successful removal of Arif's brother Abd al-Rahman from the Presidency in July 1968 is also unclear, as are his whereabouts. On 17 July 1968, however, he arrived outside the presidential palace, riding on a tank and dressed as a lieutenant. By telephone Bakr ordered Arif to go to the airport; a bloodless change of power was completed by a broadcast announcing that the Ba'ath party had assumed control.

Bakr had engineered the coup by persuading the leading Ba'athists in the army, notably Generals Daud and Nayif, to lend him their support. He had given them his assurance that, once Arif was removed, the army would be accorded ultimate authority within the country. Not only had he no intention of keeping his word; in the aftermath of the coup he had Daud exiled to Morocco and Nayif to London (where, in 1978, Saddam, then President of Iraq, arranged for him to be murdered). The new government was filled with ministers from the civilian wing of the Ba'ath party, relegating the army to a subordinate position. Saddam was not given a ministry; instead he became head of state security, a position of decisive importance which he would use to advance himself to supreme power eleven years later.

He was also appointed deputy chairman of the Revolutionary Command Council (RCC) of the Iraqi Ba'ath, the supreme party organ in the country; although the Ba'ath had not so far achieved its programme of creating a unitary Arab state, it was organized into Command Councils in each of the countries, notably Syria and Egypt, where it had sizeable numbers of followers, a system devised by Aflaq himself. The success of the 1968 revolution diminished rather than increased, however, Aflaq's influence in Iraq. Instead it was the Tikrit connection which would now come to dominate. Bakr brought many Tikritis beside Saddam into positions of power after 1968. One was his friend and Saddam's uncle Khairallah, who became mayor of Baghdad. Khairallah, according to Con Coughlin, Saddam's biographer, constantly reminded Bakr to depend on Saddam. 'You need family to protect you, not an army or a party. Armies and parties change direction in this country.'

The relationship between Bakr and Saddam was not one of blood ties. They were unrelated. Bakr nevertheless had from an early stage fostered Saddam, got him into the Ba'ath and sponsored his career. In the years after the 1968 coup, they would work intimately together, Bakr consolidating the Ba'ath's hold on power, Saddam providing force whenever needed to protect Bakr's position and intimidate or dispose of his enemies. Saddam was already an accomplished thug and murderer. During the seventies he would become a master of state-directed repression; he ran a pervasive domestic security and intelligence system, supported by an apparatus that incarcerated, interrogated, tortured and killed the régime's opponents as necessary.

Saddam was also pursuing the parallel policies of extending the Ba'ath's power into every institution and organ of public life, on the Stalinist model he favoured (though it equally equated to the Nazi programme of *Gleichschaltung*), meanwhile ensuring that his own personal power was enlarged in unison. Some of his acts of repression were deliberately ostentatious, such as the condemnation to death of fourteen Iraqi Jews in January 1969 and their public hanging in Baghdad's central space, Liberation Square. The

Iraqi Jewish community had once been one of the largest and most emancipated in the Middle East. Saddam had early, however, detected that anti–Semitism, which he represented as anti–Zionism, was popular with the masses, who shared the common Arab hatred of Israel and resented the consistent failure of the Iraqi army's participation in the Arab–Israeli wars.

Saddam also pursued the régime's domestic enemies, as he privately characterized them, the non-Arab Kurds of Iraq's northern provinces and the Shi'a southerners. Historically the Arab Muslim population of Iraq has been dominated by Sunni. Statistically, however, they are a minority within the country, making up only a fifth of the population. Better educated and more successful in every branch of public life, they formed the main body of the Ba'ath party. It was to the disadvantage of both Kurds and Shi'a that they were associated with Iran, Iraq's neighbour but traditional enemy. Iran is the only Middle Eastern country in which Shi'a predominate; Saddam suspected Iraq's Shi'a of complicity with the Shah of Iran in his effort to expand his territory by encroachment. He also suspected the Kurds of disloyalty, with some justification. The Kurds, a stateless people whose homeland is divided by the national frontiers of Iran, Syria and Turkey as well as Iraq, have a long history of seeking liberation and unification by playing their host countries off against one another. They had sustained a state of rebellion in the north ever since the creation of Iraq by the British in 1920. This blew sometimes hot, sometimes cool. In the early seventies the Kurds grew troublesome again and were supported both by the Shah and the Soviet Union, which saw in lending them support an opportunity to punish the Ba'ath for its persecution of Iraq's Communists. The Ba'ath regime could not afford to ignore the problem. The Shah's support for the Kurds was not wholly opportunistic, since Iranians and Kurds are ethnically linked; more important, some of Iraq's largest oil resources are centred around Mosul, effectively the capital of Kurdistan.

In an uncharacteristic display of moderation, Saddam decided to deal with the Kurdish rebellion by diplomacy rather than force;

he may also have been brought to that decision by the notable failure of the Iraqi army to make headway against the rebels on their own ground. What followed demonstrated that Saddam could be a realist as well as a violent revolutionary. He first approached the Soviet Union, from which Iraq was beginning to buy arms to re-equip its forces. As a valuable commercial client, he got a hearing; Kosygin, then Soviet premier, promised in 1970 to withdraw support from the Kurds, as long as Saddam agreed not to take revenge; on his return from Moscow Saddam actually consented to grant the Kurds a measure of the autonomy they had long been demanding. The catch was that the implementation of the concessions was to be postponed for four years. The Kurds saw the catch and continued to make trouble. Saddam trumped them in 1975 when he submitted to the Shah's demand that Iraq should renegotiate the 1937 treaty which aligned the Iraqi–Iranian border along the Shatt el-Arab in midstream (the *Thalweg*). This Algiers Agreement was greatly to Iraq's disadvantage but, as a short-term means of pacifying Kurdistan, Saddam judged it desirable. So it proved; within two weeks of the new treaty being signed, Iran had withdrawn its support from the Kurds, whose rebellion collapsed. That would not, however, be the end of the *Thalweg* issue; it was to underlie Saddam's ill-judged decision to attack Iran in 1980, the inception of a war of eight years that would exhaust both countries.

While Saddam was seeking to settle his military difficulties – and though only Deputy President during the seventies he increasingly exercised full executive power – he was also extending and consolidating his control over the party, armed forces and government. President Bakr proved increasingly easy to control. It was his subordinates at Saddam's nominal level whom he decided it was necessary to eliminate if he were to achieve complete supremacy, which was now his object. The three men he identified as principal obstacles between himself and the Presidency were: General Hasdam al-Tikriti, the air force officer who was armed forces Chief of Staff; Salih Mehdi Ammesh, Deputy Prime Minister; and Abdul Karim al-Shaikly, Saddam's old friend and political confederate, whom he had once called his 'twin', now Foreign Minister. Tikriti was a dedicated Ba'athist, with high standing in the party, and a tough nut; he could read Saddam's intentions, rightly feared him but exercised sufficient power to keep him in check. In 1969 he persuaded President Bakr to exile Saddam to Beirut; unwisely he allowed him to return. The following year, while away on an official visit to Spain, Saddam arranged for him to remain outside the country as ambassador to Morocco; in 1971 he was murdered by Saddam's gunmen while visiting his children at school in Kuwait. Ammesh was also shunted into ambassadorial appointments, first in Moscow, then Paris, then Helsinki. He survived to die of natural causes (unless, as is widely believed, he was poisoned). Saddam's close friend Shaikly was also sent abroad as an ambassador, to the United Nations in New York, his fault apparently having been to refuse to marry Saddam's sister. He was dismissed as Foreign Minister in 1971, spent many years abroad and was murdered on his retirement to Baghdad in 1980.

Saddam's brutal measures to assure the security of the regime, which were often also personal score-settling, made him feared and hated by many Ba'athists, particularly those who had been admitted to the party earlier than he. In compensation for what he knew was his personal unpopularity, Saddam set out in his early years as Vice-President to win a following among the masses. The opportunity was provided by Iraq's enormous oil reserves, the second largest known deposits in the world and only slightly smaller than those of Saudi Arabia. The Arab states had been slow to recognize the potential oil offered to transform their economies and to enlarge their international standing and influence. Many of the governments, dynastic, backward and deeply Islamic, actually did not want to exploit their oil wealth, fearing that money would entail modernization and so a disturbance of their traditional ways. Most in any case lacked an educated class capable of investing revenue productively. As a result, many of the rulers were content with whatever disproportionately small percentage of oil income the great foreign petroleum companies allotted them, taking it for themselves and leaving their subjects to subsist as before in poverty.

The first of the Middle Eastern oil-producing countries to rebel against the foreign petroleum companies was Iran which, under Dr Mussadeq, nationalized the British-owned Anglo-Iranian Oil Company in 1951, precipitating a crisis which almost led to war. The crisis was resolved in Britain's favour but the damage was done. The oil producers had learnt that the petroleum companies, even when acting as a consortium, were not all-powerful and so began to negotiate extraction terms more favourable to themselves. The dynastic governments, particularly in Saudi Arabia and the Gulf States, some of which remained under semi-colonial regimes long after nationalists had come to power in the Mediterranean Arab countries, were timid in their dealings with the great corporations. Post-monarchical Iraq took a more robust line. Kassem took control of the land on which the Iraq Petroleum Company (IPC) – a consortium of BP, Shell, Esso, Mobil and the French CFP – operated in 1961. President Arif set up the Iraqi National Oil Company (INOC) in 1964, to develop the fields which the foreign companies preferred to hold in reserve, intending to sell the oil extracted from the new fields on the international market. The consortium reacted by refusing to sell oil they produced, in Iraq or elsewhere, to buyers who dealt directly with INOC.

The quarrel between the consortium and their own government naturally enraged popular opinion in Iraq. It was heightened by the consortium's introduction of a policy designed to reduce production in the IPC's fields and so the oil revenues of the Iraqi government. President Bakr's administration responded by developing the fields the consortium had put into reserve, so expanding output and replacing revenue lost through the consortium's reduction of extraction by direct sales onto the international market. Iraq was able to pursue this policy because, as a secularist state with a developed educational system, it had, unlike the dynastic Arab countries, enough engineers, technologists and commercial experts to run an exploration and distribution programme of its own. Saddam, who was intimately involved in the programme, also helped to ensure its success by negotiating an agreement under which the Soviet Union guaranteed to buy any unsold Iraqi oil surplus and an agreement with France to respect its interests in return for a promise that it would not join an anti-Iraq boycott.

The pact with Moscow was signed in April 1972. Two months later Saddam took the logical step of nationalizing the Iraq Petroleum Company, after which all its revenues would accrue to the Iraqi state. Short of military intervention, there was little that the foreign governments represented in the Iraq Petroleum Company could do by way of reprisal. Saddam had taken the precaution of acquiring a guarantee of Soviet support, at a time when the Soviet Union was at the height of its postwar power; he knew that Britain was in the doldrums, its economy depressed and its government paralysed by domestic problems; the United States, attempting to extract itself from the misery of Vietnam, was in no position or state to undertake another overseas intervention. France, though its interests were hemmed by the nationalization, was bought off by the promise of a preferential price for oil purchases.

Nationalization transformed Iraq's economic situation. In 1968, the year the Ba'ath seized power, Iraqi governmental oil revenue amounted to $476 million, or 22 per cent of what was then national income. By 1980, when the benefits of nationalization (multiplied after the quadrupling of oil prices in 1973 by the Organisation of Petroleum Exporting Countries, OPEC) had come fully on stream, oil income had risen to $26 billion, representing 50 per cent of the country's greatly expanded national income. The new money was spent in a way that, as was not the case in so many of the oil-rich dynastic states, would benefit the country at large, to include many of the common people. A large proportion admittedly went on the armed forces, which doubled in size and acquired much modern equipment, including Soviet armoured vehicles and French aircraft. The larger proportion, however, went to modernize the country's infrastructure and expand its industry. The programme of investment was closely overseen by Saddam, who had had himself made chairman of all the central planning and spending committees. He knew, moreover, what he wanted and, as even his enemies admitted, was a far-sighted and efficient economic manager. Thus he was directly responsible for the electrification of the country, for building large numbers of schools and hospitals, for creating a radio and television network, for adding to the railway system, for building national highways and for setting up industrial and raw-material plants.

Brutal though he was in his persecution of political rivals and enemies of the Ba'athist party, Saddam did not look for victims among those willing to work with him in the modernization programme. The talented and patriotic were identified, encouraged and promoted. Under his leadership during the 1970s the Ba'ath became a popular movement, recognized by many Iraqis as a force for good within the country and enjoying high levels of support. When membership was thrown open to the masses, after Saddam had decided that it should cease to be merely a revolutionary élite, hundreds of thousands joined. Despite his anti-Communism, moreover, Saddam also propagated Ba'athism as a socialist movement, dedicated to distributing wealth and promoting egalitarianism. A major token of his equalizing purpose was shown by his land reform programme, under which state-owned land was distributed to 222,000 farmers, who were also provided with agricultural equipment.

Saddam was also a social progressive. He sought to abolish illiteracy, raise educational standards and improve the status of women, in sharp distinction to the policies of many of the rulers of neighbouring states. Thanks to Iraq's start as a mandate state, under European influence, its population was more evolved and better educated by mid-century than many in the region. The Iraqi élite was often educated abroad and the female members of better-off families enjoyed freedoms denied in traditional Arab societies. Saddam sought to extend the privileges of the few to the many and with success. The Ba'athist revolution created a sizeable middle class and consolidated the country's educational establishment. By the end of the 1970s Iraq belonged, with Egypt and Syria, to the group of Arab countries which were manifestly emerging into the modern world. Such had been the founding principle of Ba'athism, one which Michel Aflaq, who survived until 1989, lived to see at least half-realized. Had Saddam been content to persist simply as a modernizer, he might have become a widely respected Middle Eastern statesman, with friends throughout the region and in the Western world. Some in the West continue to think indeed that his descent into isolation and obloquy represents a failure of Western diplomacy; that had the United States and its allies pursued different policies at key stages in Iraq's relations with its neighbours during the last two decades of the twentieth century, Saddam could have been restrained from his excesses and retained as a valuable ally and even a moderating influence in a volatile strategic region.

That may have been to expect too much of his violent and self-centred character. Saddam was apparently able to subordinate his impulse to settle differences by brute force when fully in control of the circumstances in which he operated, as when he was masterminding the Ba'ath investment programme. When opposed, however, he seemed instinctively to resort to the methods by which he had ascended to power in the cruelly competitive world of Arab politics. Saddam was patently not a religious Muslim, not a believer who had imbibed the idea of fraternity and who sought to progress through life by submission to Allah and amity with his fellows. When opposed, Saddam struck out, by the underhand blow if necessary, with outright force if desirable and possible.

During the 1980s and '90s, Saddam was frequently opposed, always by the Kurds, who remained irreconcilable, from 1980 onwards by Iran, Iraq's traditional enemy, and during the 1990s and beyond by the West, for reasons for which by then only he could be held to blame.

Before the coming of his time of troubles, Saddam was to achieve one more personal triumph, advancement to the Presidency of Iraq. During the era of modernization, Saddam had displayed sedulous loyalty to President Hasan al-Bakr. Bakr's growing passivity had made it easy for Saddam to rule in his name while avoiding any confrontation; he had nonetheless taken care to consult the older man at every stage, to submit all matters to him for approval and to withdraw if his chosen solution to a problem failed to meet with Bakr's approval. By 1979, however, Saddam had decided that the sham by which Bakr remained in office and he, as Deputy President, concealed his effective authority could no longer be sustained. External problems demanded that he should emerge from behind the throne and take full power.

The principal problems concerned Israel, Syria, a fellow Ba'athist state, and Iran. The existence of the state of Israel had unsettled the Middle East since its creation in 1948, giving rise to four wars, in 1948, 1956, 1967 and 1973, in three of which Iraq had been involved. At the end of the 1970s, however, it was the successful American mediation of a peace settlement between Israel and Egypt, the Camp David Accords of September 1978, that provoked Saddam. He had long hankered to inherit the leadership of the Arab world exercised by President Nasser and resented its assumption by Anwar Sadat on Nasser's death. The Camp David Accords, deeply unpopular with all Arabs outside Egypt and many within, provided Saddam, as he saw it, with the opportunity to displace Sadat, but only if he could get full control of Iraqi foreign policy. That was desirable for another reason. President Bakr was an enthusiast for closer co-operation between Iraq and Syria. Their Ba'ath parties agreed in October 1978 to merge the countries' ministries of defence, information and foreign affairs. In January 1979 Saddam was sent to see President Assad in Damascus to formalize the arrangement. It was not one which, however, he truly supported, partly because he was an Iraqi nationalist, more importantly because he feared that the alignment – designed to lead swiftly to full union – would frustrate his personal ambitions. Finally, and at the same time, he was growingly concerned by the rise of Islamic fundamentalism in Iran. Although Iraq had given Ayatollah Khomeini asylum during his exile from Iran, it had thereby won no gratitude. Khomeini execrated Iraqi secularism and had a particular reason to dislike the Ba'athist regime in its disfavouring of the Shi'a population of the south. The Shi'ites, 200,000 of whom Saddam had expelled from Iraq to Iran as aliens, hated the Ba'athist régime and Saddam was right to fear that, with the most charismatic of the world's Islamic leaders established as a *de facto* theocrat just across the border, the situation in the south was likely to become more disturbed.

In any case, he doubted the capacity of a government led by Bakr to deal effectively with the problems. It was this consideration that prompted him to decide, in mid-July 1979, to remove his former patron from office. He correctly judged that, given Bakr's isolation and enfeeblement, it would not be necessary to stage a coup but that Bakr would go quietly. So he did. On the evening of 16 July, Saddam, his cousin Adnan, the Defence Minister, and Khairallah called on Bakr in his office and told him that his resignation was required. If given, he would be allowed to retire in dignity and comfort. Bakr's son staged a token protest but was overpowered. Next day, Bakr announced that he was retiring for reasons of ill-health. He lived for another three years and, though mysterious circumstances surrounded his death, it cannot be proved that he was a victim of Saddam's malfeasance.

Many deaths did follow Saddam's assumption of the Presidency, deaths that were deliberately publicized. Saddam had prepared the ground for the removal of Bakr by seeking support for the move at a meeting of the Ba'athist Revolutionary Command Council on 11 July. He had not expected to be opposed and was outraged when the secretary-general, Abdul Hussein Mashhidi, insisted that the decision be put to the vote. He had Mashhidi removed within the week but this display of independence may have disquieted him. Either because of it, but probably because he had scores to settle anyhow, his first public act after his accession was to announce and carry out a purge. On 22 July the thousand senior members of the Ba'ath party were summoned to an extraordinary conference in Baghdad. The proceedings were opened by the new Vice-President, Taha Yassin Ramadan, who announced the discovery of a plot. The plotters, he went on, were all present in the room. Saddam then took the podium to denounce the plotters and called on the recently dismissed Mashhidi to elaborate the details.

What followed was a grisly compression into a single act of a Stalinist show trial and of its bloody outcome. Mashhidi first explained that he had, since 1975, been a member of a Syrian conspiracy to overthrow both Saddam and Bakr, to bring about the Iraqi-Syrian union. He gave the key dates of the preparatory moves and the names of his confederates. Then Saddam took over again, announced that the enemies of the party had all personally confessed their guilt, had their names read out, sixty-six in all, and ordered those named to leave. Finally, after orchestrated expressions of loyalty from the floor, Saddam called on the audience to join the firing squads that would execute the guilty. A puppet court was immediately convened, twenty-two were condemned to death and, in a carefully filmed event, Saddam led a representative group of senior Ba'athists in carrying out the 'democratic executions'. The victims were all shot in the head.

The film of the show trial and its aftermath was widely distributed; Saddam made a triumphal speech to the nation later in the day he had taken part in the executions. It was the start of his campaign to bring all activities in national life and all elements of Iraqi society under Ba'athist but more strictly his personal control. Just as Stalin had subordinated all bodies in Soviet Russia to the Communist party, either by deeming them to be organs of state or by inserting party officials into their command structures, Saddam insisted that the Ba'ath should take control or oversee every public body in Iraq and any significant private one also. Teachers were obliged to join the party; after 1980 all journalists, writers and artists were required to join the General Confederation of Academicians and Writers. Although the court system remained intact, it was left to deal only with routine cases; those of importance were referred to the Baghdad Revolutionary Court or to special temporary courts under Presidential control, from neither of which were appeals allowed. The armed forces were kept under the closest supervision and, in a classically dictatorial practice, the Ba'ath ran its own parallel military organization, the Popular Army, which in the first year of Saddam's Presidency was doubled in size to 250,000.

For ordinary Iraqis content to lead private lives, doing their jobs dutifully and evincing no interest in politics beyond conforming with the official party programme, Saddam's rule was not burdensome. On the contrary; his régime was popular. Saddam's Ba'ath ran something like a welfare state, in which all Iraqis got free schooling up to, if they were capable, university level. Health care was free and available to all; food was cheap; the domestic economy, underpinned by the country's oil income, was buoyant. Women were truly emancipated, free to find work in the professions, educated to the same standard as males, and going unveiled and unharrassed by the sort of religious police so tiresomely intrusive in other Gulf states. In many respects Iraq was a model of what the West hoped modernizing Arab states would become.

The price paid by ordinary Iraqis for their material well-being under Saddam's régime was the restriction of their political and intellectual liberties, taken for granted in Western countries, and the awful penalties suffered by those who disobeyed or dissented. In a memorandum submitted to the United Nations by a group of exiled Iraqi intellectuals soon after Saddam's rise to power, they wrote:

> The dictatorship of Saddam Hussein is one of the harshest, most ruthless and most unscrupulous régimes in the world. It is a totalitarian, one-party system based on the personality cult of Saddam Hussein. The man and his family and relatives have control of the regular army, People's Army, police and security services. All news media are under the strict control of the régime and there is no opportunity for freedom of expression. Political organization is limited to the Ba'ath party and a number of insignificant, obsequious organizations. Trade Unions do not exist. Membership in any opposition party is punishable by death. Any criticism of the President is also

punishable by death. Torture is the norm. The security system
is all-powerful, omnipresent and enjoys unlimited powers.

Westerners who hoped for a different Iraq may have been
indulging in wishful thinking, misled by the Ba'ath's commitment to secularism and modernization. The mind of Islam is
deeply resistant to the ideas of individual freedom and political
diversity which lie at the heart of Western liberalism. Muslim
illiberalism is particularly strong in the Arab lands, Islam's heartland; no Arab country has ever been a true democracy and even
in the other secularist states, such as Syria and Egypt, the political tradition favours single parties and strongman leadership.
The tradition connects to the most salient elements of Muslim
religious belief: the idea of the Caliph, the successor of the
Prophet, as ruler of the *Umma*, the Muslim community; the
unique power of the Koran as a guide to human behaviour, not
to be challenged by secular writings; and the role of the *Sharia*,
religious law, as the code by which communities are to be regu-
lated. The primacy of these elements has been protected since
the fourteenth century because the religious leadership of the
majority Sunni sect then 'closed the gates' of *ijtihad,* the practice of independent reasoning which had hitherto permitted
Muslim scholars to adapt the *Sharia* to changing circumstances.
Thereafter the past, not the present, has determined how Muslims
should think.

Secularist though he was, Saddam was enormously assisted in
his imposition of a totalitarian system on Iraq by the Islamic
adherence to conformity of thought and behaviour. It was farther
reinforced by the Ottoman inheritance, which emphasized the
dominance of the ruler and the leading roles of the army and
state bureaucracy and had institutionalized the practices of
draconian punishment of any infringement of that order. Only
sixty years, after all, had elapsed between the withdrawal of
Ottoman rule and the elevation of Saddam to supreme power.
It is not surprising that both he and his subjects should have
resumed so easily the respective habits of unquestioned authority

and subservience to it that had been second nature to their grand-parents' generation.

Ultimately, however, neither Islamic tradition nor Ottoman inheritance wholly explains the nature of Saddam's totalitarian authority. The man, by any index of his personal behaviour, public policy and spoken pronouncements, was as President of Iraq a monster of cruelty and aggression. The nature of his régime owed more to twentieth-century ideologies of intolerance and systems of repression than to anything derived from the more distant past. Michel Aflaq, the founder of Ba'athism, had modelled the organ ization of his party on Hitler's Nazi movement, of which he was an admirer. Saddam was an acknowledged admirer of Stalin. The examples of those two mass murderers seem the most patent influence on his policies and ambitions. It is commonly said that the principal motive animating Saddam has been the instinct to survive. Saddam seems much more than a survivor. The impulse to dominate appears to have informed all his acts on his way to power and then on his exercise of it. Saddam has sought first to become leader of Iraq, then the chief warlord of the Gulf region, a nuclear warlord if he could assemble the means, with the leader-ship of the Arab world as his culminating aspiration. If he has been frustrated in his life plan, it is important to know how. The records of his military adventures supply much of the answer.

4

Saddam's Wars

Saddam was never a soldier. That omission in the story of his life may help to explain much about his behaviour as he grew to manhood and afterwards. It had been his ambition to train as an officer at the Iraq Military Academy in Baghdad but he lacked the education even to attempt the entrance exam. He resented his exclusion and conceived what was to prove a lasting jealousy of contemporaries who did secure commissions. He believed that they were unfairly privileged and probably with reason. As was not the case in many developing countries, the composition of the officer corps in Iraq was class-based. The military profession was a middle-class occupation, dominated by families which had often supplied officers to the old Ottoman army. Indeed, many of the leading figures in mandate and post-mandate Iraq, such as Nuri al-Sa'id, Prime Minister at the time of the overthrow of the monarchy, had been Ottoman officers. They were favoured by the British and often Anglophile in consequence.

There was an alternative, nationalist tradition in the army, represented by such officers as Rashid Ali, who led the attempt in 1941 to form an alliance with Nazi Germany and the brief military action against the British army and RAF garrison. Saddam's uncle, Khairallah, was a supported of Rashid Ali but, like other officers who took part in the action, suffered by doing so. He was sentenced to a lengthy term of imprisonment. The leaders were hanged. The British successfully quashed the nationalist trend in the officer corps after 1941 and it was not to revive until the appearance of the Free Officers movement in Egypt in the 1950s inspired Arab officers all over the Middle East to espouse the anti-colonialist cause.

Saddam's hostility to professional officers may, however, have bitten deeper as he rose higher in Ba'athist politics and perhaps became a dominant sentiment once he achieved power. Self-made dictators are often so affected. Hitler nurtured a deep suspicion, eventually amounting to hatred, of the German regular officer class, particularly those qualified as staff officers. His attitude may have been differently based from that of Saddam, since he had been a frontline soldier who regarded staff officers as shirkers. Stalin, Saddam's idol, probably better anticipated his attitude. Stalin, though closely involved in warfare from the beginning of the Bolshevik seizure of power, was also never a soldier; instead he served as a political commissar, imposing party control over the decisions of commanders. The generals of the First Cavalry Army, with whom he served on the southern front during the Russian civil war, retained his favour, irrespective of their military talents, after he became ruler of the Soviet Union. Others, all too often the most promising, became the victims of his suspicion and died in the great military purge of 1937. Saddam betrayed the same trait. He identified successful generals as potential rivals and had them removed and often killed once they achieved popularity.

Events presented Saddam with ample opportunity to humiliate and victimize Iraqi generals for, under his dictatorship, his country was almost continuously at war. His first war, against Iran, began almost immediately after his seizure of power in 1979 and lasted from 1980–88. His second, now known as the First Gulf War, effectively began with his annexation of Kuwait in August 1990 and culminated in total defeat in February 1991. His third war, the subject of this book, began on 20 March 2003 and resulted in the capture of Baghdad on 9 April, the collapse of the Iraqi armed forces and Saddam's disappearance (but eventual discovery in hiding on 13 December). Even the years between 1991 and 2003 had failed to bring peace to his country; immediately after the army's collapse on 28 February 1991, the UN imposed restrictions on Iraq's freedom to operate military aircraft in the Kurdish zone, north of the 36th parallel; in 1992 the United States, Britain and France announced the imposition of another 'no fly zone' in the Shi'a region south of the 32nd parallel. The bans on the operation of military aircraft were enforced by the coalition air forces and by missile forces, which attacked radar stations, air bases and anti-aircraft sites.

Saddam was entirely responsible for setting his country on the path of this twenty-year war. In the period before the seizure of power when, as deputy to President Bakr, he had had control of Iraqi foreign policy, he had correctly judged that the Shah's Iran, then supported by the United States, was too powerful a neighbour to be opposed. Its armed forces outnumbered those of Iraq, as did its population, and it had allies who were not to be crossed. It was for those reasons that Saddam had in 1975 judged it necessary to yield to the Iranian demand for a realignment, in Iran's favour, of the Iraq–Iran frontier on the Shatt el-Arab waterway, to follow the Iraqi shore instead of the *Thalweg* (centre line); the adjustment had been announced as a unilateral act by the Shah in April 1969.

Saddam's reconciliation with the Shah in 1975 was brought about entirely through his calculation that a cession of national territory in the south was necessary if the north of the country was not to escape from Ba'athist control. During the early seventies the Iraqi Kurds, who regarded the nationalization of the Iraq Petroleum Company as a usurpation of their oil-bearing regions around Mosul, and who in any case felt excluded as non-Arabs from the country's political system, completely dominated as it was by the Sunni Arab minority, initiated an insurgency which rapidly turned into a bitter internal war. It was a conflict that the Iraqi army, trained as a national defence force, was ill-equipped to fight; tanks and artillery were not the weapons needed to win a guerrilla war in the Kurdish mountains. Moreover, the Kurds were supported by the Soviet Union which saw their resistance as a means of bringing pressure on Saddam to desist from his persecution of the Iraqi Communist Party. The calculation was well-judged. In January 1970 Saddam visited Moscow and agreed to scale down operations in Kurdistan if the Russians would cease supplying weapons to the guerrillas (the Iraqi army was also a major beneficiary of Soviet army supplies).

Inevitably, given his devious nature, Saddam found ways round the agreement. The Iraqi army was not withdrawn from Kurdistan, and a serious assassination attempt was even mounted on the life of the Kurdish leader, Mustapha Barzani. Nevertheless, the security situation improved in Kurdistan until in 1974 the Shah, who had many Kurdish subjects of his own, chose to intervene on his own account. He, as leader of the largest Shi'a community in the Middle East, was affronted by Iraq's mistreatment of its Shi'a majority; he also sought means to force Iraq to accept his claim to the west bank of the Shatt el-Arab. The Iranian intervention was decisive. At a meeting in Algiers on 6 March 1975, Saddam, acting as President Bakr's deputy, conceded the territorial adjustment, though it effectively gave control of Iraq's tiny coastline on the Persian Gulf to Iran, in return for an Iranian promise to withdraw support from the Kurds. 'It was either that', Saadoun Hammadi, the Iraqi Foreign Minister, was reported to have said, 'or lose the north of the country.'

The situation remained, nevertheless, highly unstable. The Kurds were not reconciled to the régime, nor were the Shi'a. The Soviet Union remained a powerful patron of the Iraqi Ba'athists but continued to feel concern for the country's surviving Communists. The Shah was as involved as before in the welfare of Iraq's Shi'a community, which, in the province of Khuzistan, spilled over into his own country. Ultimately it was Iranian rather than Iraqi politics which determined the next twist of events. The Shah's programme of modernization had alienated the religious leadership of his own Shi'ites, who regarded it as a violation of Islamic orthodoxy. The *imams* found secular education and the emancipation of women particularly repugnant. Theirs was an attitude that was gaining strength throughout the Muslim world and emboldening traditionalist leaders in many states. The most influential of the Iranian traditionalists, Ayatollah Khomeini, who had been expelled from his homeland, was in 1977 living in Najaf, one of the holy cities of the Shi'a sect in southern Iraq. At the Shah's request he was expelled again, finding refuge in the West, but within Iran the demand that he should be allowed to return became irresistible and in February 1979 he was welcomed home to Tehran in triumph. His reappearance doomed the Shah but also created the circumstances in which Saddam, once installed as Iraq's President, should embark on a disastrous war.

Although the Ayatollah Khomeini had been given sanctuary in Iraq after his expulsion from Iran, and despite Saddam's efforts to conciliate his Islamic régime after his return from exile in Paris, he evinced no gratitude. Khomeini was an Islamic fanatic, who had devised a new interpretation of Shi'ism. Pious Shi'ites believe that the successors of Muhammad had disappeared from human view but continued to exist as 'hidden' *imams*. In their absence, and until the reappearance of the latest hidden *imam*, other religious leaders were forbidden to exercise any political role. Khomeini taught that, despite traditional Shi'a belief, a true mystic inspired by Allah and a master of religious law – implicitly himself – was entitled to teach and rule. His preaching and his dominating personality captured the imagination of millions of Iranian Shi'ites and brought him to power. He at once initiated an internal Islamic revolution, which caused the deaths of thousands of the Shah's modernizers; but his vision went farther. He saw his mission to be that of spreading the revolution throughout the region and that entailed confronting secularists everywhere. The nearest, who was also a notorious persecutor of Shi'a believers, was Saddam Hussein. While in exile in Paris Khomeini had named his enemies as 'First the Shah; then the American Satan; then Saddam Hussein and the infidel Ba'ath Party'.

Immediately after Khomeini's return home, Saddam attempted to ingratiate himself with the Islamic régime in Iran by declaring a policy of 'mutual respect and non-interference in internal affairs'. He began to pray in public, to show consideration for Shi'a religious practices and holy places and generally to demonstrate his respect for Islamic belief. Khomeini was quite unmollified, correctly judging Saddam's sudden demonstration of piety as merely expedient. He called on the Iraqis to overthrow Saddam and openly supported Shi'ite resistance to Ba'athist rule. Iranian involvement in an attempt to assassinate Tariq Aziz, Saddam's Deputy Prime Minister and, anomalously, an Eastern Rite Christian, was barely disguised.

During 1980 Saddam was progressively driven to conclude that all attempts to placate the régime of the ayatollahs were pointless; Iranian Islamicism was not only hostile but also dangerous to Ba'athism, while, as long as Khomeini ruled, there could be no hope of settling the Shatt el-Arab dispute. Force alone, Saddam decided, could rectify the situation. Objectively, moreover, the resort to force was a logical option. Khomeini's revolution had devastated the Iranian armed forces, a leading element of the modernization programme, and a disproportionate number of the victims had been senior officers. Military morale had been heavily depressed as a result, as had operational efficiency. Saddam had good reason to conclude, therefore, that Iraq's armed forces, though only half the size of those of Iran, were capable of achieving a quick and cheap victory.

Saddam began the Iran–Iraq war on 22 September 1980 by launching squadrons of his air force, equipped with French Mirage fighter-bombers, against ten Iranian air bases. His hope was to repeat the success of the Israelis on the first day of the 1967 war when, by co-ordinated surprise attacks, the air forces of Egypt, Jordan and Syria had been destroyed in a few hours on their airfields. His hope was not achieved. As Saddam was later often to complain, geography was against Iraq. Iran is a large country and its military bases were distributed all over its territory, many distant from the frontiers; Israel's targets in 1967, by contrast, had all been concentrated close behind enemy frontiers in easy reach of attack. In 1980 much of the Iranian air force survived the initial strikes and was able to mount retaliation on the same day, not only against Iraqi air bases but also against Iraqi naval units and some oil facilities, which were to prove critical targets throughout the ensuing eight-year war.

Nevertheless Saddam had been correct in his prewar judgement that the disorganization brought about by the ayatollahs' purge of the secularist, but efficient and well-trained, Iranian military leadership would make it difficult for Iran to mount an effective defence. Within a month of the start of the war the Iraqis had advanced into Iran on a front of 600 kilometres (373 miles), to a depth varying from 10 kilometres (6.2 miles) in the north to 20 kilometres (12.4 miles) in the south. They had captured several towns and got within artillery range of Dezful, a key transportation centre in the northern oilfields. In the south, after a bitter battle in the streets, the city of Khorramshahr had been taken, but at a cost of 7,000 dead and wounded. The Iraqis had, however, failed to take nearby Abadan, the old Anglo-Iranian Oil Company's refinery centre through which most of the country's oil was exported down the Gulf; without Abadan, moreover, they were ill-positioned to recapture the east bank of the Shatt el-Arab.

Having achieved his initial advance, Saddam, who was acting as supreme commander despite his complete lack of military experience, ordered the army to dig in on a defensive line. He apparently wished to avoid inflicting casualties, in the belief that the Iranians would give in if offered the chance to do so; he also calculated that the ground captured could be used in bargaining for a settlement. On both counts he was wrong. The Iranian people had been seized with patriotic fervour and, as events would demonstrate, were prepared to accept very heavy casualties to avoid defeat, while the Iranian government had no interest in negotiating a settlement on any terms favourable to Iraq.

Saddam's pause had the farther effect of allowing the Iranians to regroup, reorganize, and induct hundreds of thousands of new recruits into the army. In May 1981 they were able to launch a counteroffensive which forced the Iraqis to pull back from Abadan to Khorramshahr and in October they were driven across the Karun River, one of the first objectives. In November the tide of battle turned markedly in the Iranians' favour. They began to organize mass attacks, sending human waves of untrained juveniles to march into Iraqi minefields and barrages of automatic fire. Step by step, during the rest of the 1981 campaign and into the spring of 1982, the Iraqis were forced to give ground, losing thousands of prisoners in the process. Saddam was unable to mount an effective defence, let alone a counter-offensive, and in June 1982 declared a cease-fire, claiming that Iraq had achieved its objects.

Iraq was in fact close to defeat, less because of military losses, grievous though they were, than financial difficulties. The fighting in the south, at the head of the Gulf, had severely diminished Iraq's ability to export oil, but not so Iran's which, with outlets onto the lower Gulf and the Indian Ocean, could continue to earn oil income. Iraq, as the war became protracted, was increasingly dependent on subsidies from neighbours, particularly Kuwait and Saudi Arabia, to which Saddam successfully represented the war as a struggle against Islamic fundamentalism in which he fought to protect not only his régime but also theirs. Kuwait and Saudi Arabia both transported essential supplies to Iraq and provided oil credits to foreign suppliers, which paid, among other things, for war material. After two years of fighting, Iraq was effectively sustaining its war by borrowing and the loans, unsecured, unserviced and mounting, were putting the country into an increasingly unfavourable financial position. Its financial situation was to worsen throughout the following years and collapse to be staved off only by persuading neighbours to lengthen credit and, eventually, the United States to lend its support. During the 1980s Iran was regarded by the United States as the most dangerous of its Third World enemies, because of the violent anti-Americanism of the ayatollah régime and for its seizure of the staff of the American embassy in Tehran, in gross violation of international law. The extension of support to anti-Iranian Gulf States was a natural consequence; it eventually included the reflagging of Kuwaiti tankers as American ships, hastened after Iran began air attacks on tankers in 1984, and the strengthening of the American naval presence in the Gulf to protect them.

Yet despite foreign assistance, the war began to go badly against Iraq after 1982 and the turn of events was not to be disguised.

Internally the cost, running at a billion US dollars a month, began to reduce funds available for imports; after an initial boom, deliberately sustained by Saddam to buoy civilian support for the war, the economy began to show signs of recession. Between 1980 and 1983 Iraq's foreign currency reserves fell from $35 billion to $3 billion, with a consequent drop in imports; the reserves were farther adversely affected by Syria's action in closing the pipeline to the Mediterranean, in retaliation for Saddam's rupture of relations with the Syrian Ba'athist party. The human as well as financial costs were high, with casualties running at 1,200 a month, a figure that rose sharply during offensives. Militarily, from 1982 onwards, Iran was able to mount offensives with increasing frequency. During the summer of 1982 Iran embarked on a major offensive designed to cross the Tigris and reach Basra, Iraq's second city and capital of the Shi'a south. The methods were as before: mass attacks by waves of untrained, under-age volunteers. After the initial shock, however, the Iraqis proved equal to the strain. Their engineers constructed extensive and deep lines of fortifications, in places creating artificial lakes which funnelled the direction of the Iranian thrusts. Behind strong defences the Iraqis fought well, inflicting heavy losses on the attackers; if ground was lost, it was recaptured by ground–air counter-attacks. The Iranian air force had difficulty in operating, because of American refusal to supply spare parts for its aircraft, while the Iraqi air force, flying French and Russian aircraft, was not so penalized; it was also equipped with large numbers of helicopters which Iran lacked. Moreover the Iraqi ground forces, encouraged by their defensive successes, displayed markedly improved morale; even the Shi'a conscripts, deterred at the thought of the ayatollahs exporting their joyless regime in the wake of victory, found a sense of patriotism and battled with a will.

Between 1982 and 1984 the struggle degenerated into a war of attrition, with the Iranians maintaining the offensive but Iraq inflicting the heavier casualties. Although by 1984 the total of Iraqi war dead had reached 65,000, with up to 60,000 taken prisoner, the equivalent Iranian figure was 180,000 dead and half a million wounded. Moreover, the Iranians were not gaining ground. The exception to their consistent failure to do so came in early 1984 when, by a cunningly organized night attack, Iranian amphibious forces succeeded in surprising the garrison of the Majnun Islands, near Basra. Despite repeated attempts to recapture the islands, the Iraqis failed. Saddam therefore decided to resort to unconventional methods. He was already manufacturing chemical weapons at two plants, at Salman Pak and Samarra, and now used two products, mustard gas and Tabun, in helicopter attacks on the Iranian positions. Mustard gas is a blistering agent, developed and widely used during the First World War, Tabun a nerve agent developed by the Nazis for use in extermination camps.

Chemical agents are notoriously unsatisfactory as weapons of war. They are difficult to deliver with precision and, once launched, are wholly subject for effect on the vagaries of the local weather; low humidity robs the agents of effect quickly, high humidity causes them to persist; favourable wind direction carries them into the enemy positions, unfavourable wind direction causes 'blow back' or results in dispersion away from the battlefield. The Iraqis in the Majnun Islands encountered all those conditions; the Iranians, by contrast, soon acquired protective clothing and antidotes which rendered the use of chemical agents pointless.

In the long run, Saddam's resort to chemical weapons was to do him nothing but harm. Not only did his chemical warfare campaign fail to achieve its intended results; it also alerted the attention of the United Nations. The use of chemical weapons had been outlawed by the League of Nations during the 1920s and the ban had been sustained with remarkable consistency throughout the Second World War and afterwards. As one of the few demonstrable successes of international arms control, the United Nations was determined to support it and in March 1984 a team of UN inspectors was despatched to Iran to investigate its complaints. The team confirmed that Iraq had broken the ban, a report that prejudiced most countries previously favourable to Saddam against him. For a time Saddam was brought to desist;

in 1987–88, however, he resumed his use of chemical weapons, in that period against his own people in Kurdistan, in an attempt to terrorize them against co-operating with Iranian incursions into their area. Notoriously, at Halabjah in March 1988, his use of chemical agents killed at least 5,000 Kurdish civilians in an operation directed by his cousin, Ali Hassan al-Majid, later to be known as 'Chemical Ali'.

Between 1984 and 1988, however, Saddam's distasteful reputation as a chemical warmaker was offset in foreign opinion by what appeared to be the much more threatening behaviour of his enemies, both in Iran and in the wider Middle Eastern world. The ayatollahs made no attempt to placate either the West or the Soviet Union. They persisted in persecuting the Tudeh, Iran's Communist Party, and they made little effort to disguise their links with Islamic anti-Western terrorists. The Syrians, meanwhile, were continuing to provide refuge and training facilities to a number of violent Islamic terrorist groups and President Gaddafi so provoked the United States by his support for terrorists that it launched airstrikes against Libya in early 1986. In these circumstances it was comparatively easy for Saddam to represent himself as a force for stability in a troubled region. He was, from the middle of the Iran–Iraq War, certainly so treated. The small Gulf States, terrified that Iran might infect their populations with anti-monarchist and fundamentalist feeling, increased their donations to Iraq's war chest, eventually to the tune of $25 billion. The Soviet Union began to supply high-technology equipment, including intermediate range missiles, capable of reaching Iran's major cities from Iraqi bases. Egypt recycled some of its Soviet equipment to help Iraq with spare parts. France, if on a strictly financial basis, delivered dozens of high-performance strike aircraft, enhancing Iraqi capability to attack the Iranian tanker trade.

Most tellingly of all, the United States, which had throughout the years of Saddam's rise kept Iraq on its list of countries suspected of supporting international terrorism, now decided that a shift of policy would be advantageous. Saddam's enemies were also America's, a perception heightened by anti-American terrorist outrages in Lebanon in 1983, when, in what was to prove the first instalment of suicide bombing, a Marine barracks was truck-bombed with great loss of life, following a devastating attack on the US embassy in the city. Saddam's Foreign Minister was invited to Washington; in December 1983 his visit was returned by Donald Rumsfeld, then acting as a special Middle Eastern adviser to President Reagan. David Mack, a former State Department official who accompanied Rumsfeld to Baghdad, explained later that 'we wanted to build a Cairo–Amman–Baghdad axis'. The warmer relationship thus established did not lead to the US supplying arms to Saddam (though in 1982 it did send sixty military helicopters designated as crop-sprayers, which Saddam peremptorily had adapted to fire anti-tank missiles), but Washington used its good offices to facilitate the construction of new pipelines to port outlets in Saudi Arabia and Jordan, thus easing Iraq's financial difficulties, and it also began covertly to supply intelligence to Baghdad, derived from satellite overflights and surveillance by American AWACS aircraft operating from Saudi Arabia.

Despite Saddam's success in attracting foreign support after 1984, he was not at first able to shift the balance of the war decisively his way. He began by using the advanced weaponry with which he had been supplied to intensify his attacks on Iranian cities. The Iranian air force responded in kind but its stock of warplanes had been so reduced by losses in combat that the contest proved unequal. Iraqi missile strikes actually provoked demonstrations against the war in the affected cities. Saddam had better success by using his French-supplied strike aircraft, Super Étendards equipped with Exocet sea-skimming missiles, to intensify attacks on Iranian tanker traffic and the terminals at which the tankers loaded; there were seventy missile strikes in 1984–85. Iran responded by shifting its attacks to Kuwaiti tankers, in retaliation for Kuwait's financial support of the Iraqi war effort, a move which, as mentioned above, led to an extensive reflagging of the tankers as American ships. This strengthening of the American position against the ayatollah régime was set back in a bizarre fashion when evidence came to light that Washington was simultaneously supplying Iran with weapons – the Iran–Contra affair – in an effort to secure the release of American hostages held by Islamic terrorists in Lebanon; the repercussions severely shook the Reagan administration. It did not assist Saddam's position, in any case, when a damaging attack on the USS *Stark* in the Gulf, on 17 May 1987, was revealed to be the result of an Iraqi Exocet strike.

Nevertheless Saddam's efforts to involve Western and other navies in the protection of Gulf tanker traffic against Iranian attack had become so comprehensive that even the *Stark* affair did not dent the defence they offered. His finances, despite the punishing costs of the war, also continued to hold up. Although by 1987 Iraq's foreign debts amounted to $50.5 billion, or thrice its gross domestic product, with another $45–55 billion owed in loans from client Gulf states, sympathetic treatment by American, Saudi and even Soviet institutions allowed it to make interest payments and find purchasing power abroad. Iraq was effectively bankrupt but was able to continue fighting because no interested state, outside a small coterie of Islamic and anti-Israeli countries, wished to see it defeated.

Then in February 1988 the shift in advantage, for which Saddam had always worked, at last swung Iraq's way. The terrible suffering brought by the war to Iran, which had sustained nearly a million military casualties, out of a population of 9 million males of military age, combined with the unremitting air attacks on its cities, which had caused a widespread flight of the civilian population, had so weakened the ayatollah régime's power that it could no longer mount an effective defence. Saddam opened his decisive counter-offensive with renewed air and missile attacks on Iranian centres. In April, assisted by intelligence support, he unleashed a ground offensive on the Fao peninsula, lost to Iran in 1986; it was captured and by early July so was all Iraqi territory lost to the Iranians since 1980. The Iraqis also expelled the remaining Iranian forces from Kurdistan and even succeeded in seizing a foothold across the enemy border.

As Iran was also undergoing damaging attacks by Iraqi aircraft on its tanker traffic and coastal oil outlets, which it was unable to counter, reality forced the ayatollah régime to accept that the war could not be won and could only be prosecuted farther at increasing and pointless loss. Since 1982 Ayatollah Khomeini had insisted that only Saddam's relinquishment of power – 'régime change' as it would later be known – would induce him to enter into a settlement. He was now brought to recognize that he could not achieve that outcome. On 18 July 1988, therefore, Iran announced to the United Nations that it would accept Security Council Resolution 598, calling for a cease-fire, and it came into effect a month later. Ayatollah Khomeini died the following year, at the age of eighty-seven.

Saddam, still only in his early fifties and in vigorous health, had therefore won a sort of victory; but at terrible cost. Besides the war dead, totalling perhaps over 100,000, the conflict had also severely weakened the Iraqi economy. War debts, largely owed to the Gulf States and to Saudi Arabia, amounted to $80 billion; reconstruction costs were calculated at $230 billion. Ordinary state expenditure exceeded income from oil, about $13 billion a year; there was no other significant export except dates. The country could not service its debts, was surviving after 1988 only by begging for time to pay from its creditors and was effectively bankrupt. At the outset of Saddam's taking power, Iraq was a prosperous country with an excellent credit rating. By 1988 it was mired in borrowing which it could not manage. Moreover, Saddam's institution of an austerity prog- ramme at home, designed to reduce government spending, brought him unpopularity. Large numbers of soldiers were demo- bilized into unemployment, the number of state employees was abruptly reduced, state spending projects were curtailed, with a farther loss of jobs, and the sale of state enterprises was seen to benefit only a small group of Iraqi capitalists.

Saddam had other difficulties. Despite the departure of Iranian troops from Kurdistan, Kurdish resistance continued, provoking him, unwisely, to resort to the use of chemical weapons against the rebels. In March 1988 he had deluged the township of

Halabjah, the last place to be occupied by the Iranians, with hydrogen cyanide, killing 5,000 of the inhabitants and injuring 10,000 more. During the summer of 1988 he subjected another sixty-five Kurdish villages to chemical attack, causing heavy casualties and the flight of a quarter of a million Kurds to Iran or Turkey. He was meanwhile persisting with his efforts to develop an Iraqi nuclear weapons programme, despite the success of the Israelis in destroying the Osirak reactor centre in 1981. The West, generally so exigent in its efforts to prevent nuclear proliferation, as indeed was the Soviet Union, at first displayed a careless indifference to Saddam's lust to acquire unconventional weapons, including the missile systems necessary to deliver them. The West's unconcern, originally conditioned by its estimation that Saddam, for all his known faults, was preferable as an agent of power in the Gulf region to the incomprehensible ayatollahs, persisted into the post-Gulf War period. Then, the balance of opinion, unpredictably fickle as it so often is, swung against him. He made what proved to be the grave mistake of arresting and executing a Western journalist, after a travesty of a trial, for reporting on his unconventional weapons programme. Suddenly international opinion took against him. The United States was already suspicious of his efforts to develop nuclear weapons, a clear threat to its client state of Israel; the judicial murder of the *Observer* journalist, Farzal Bazoft, attracted the condemnation of Margaret Thatcher, who, as British Prime Minister, was the principal non-American influence on the outlook of President Ronald Reagan.

Saddam had by that stage of his career killed so many critics of his régime that he no doubt failed to comprehend why one more elimination of a troublesome individual should have serious international repercussions. Had he allowed the dust to settle it might not have done so. Almost immediately after the Bazoft affair, however, he embarked on a new foreign policy initiative which farther provoked Western disapproval. The matter was, politically if not morally, of far greater weight. Saddam made it clear that he was bent on recovering the crippling costs of the Iran war.

Though he had attacked Iran without any thought that he might be biting off more than he could chew, the first two years of the war had shown him otherwise. As difficulties developed, he turned to the other Gulf States for help, in the expectation that repayment would be neither difficult nor inconveniently demanded. As the war drew out he had found that loans and subsidies were made with increasing reluctance, and eventually arranged only out of fear of an Iranian victory. By the time the ayatollahs conceded, the cost to the Gulf States, Kuwait foremost, of sheltering behind Iraq equated, in financial if not human terms, to what might have been incurred had they fought themselves.

Saddam's 'victory' thus left a bitter aftertaste. He expected, if not gratitude, at least financial understanding from his neighbours. They, however, wanted their money back. Both parties pitched their terms too high. Saddam began to demand not only the cancellation of his debt, $40 billion by 1988, but a large farther subsidy, $30 billion, to pay for reconstruction. His creditors, increasingly doubtful of his willingness or ability to repay, began to recompense themselves by increasing oil production, in breach of OPEC agreements to stabilize quotas. As oil prices on the international market were falling at the time, the Gulf States' policy doubly disadvantaged Iraq, which found its income shrinking in consequence. The Emir of Kuwait, despite the evidence of Saddam's growing displeasure, nevertheless emphasized that he would not reduce oil output, would not grant new loans and would continue to demand repayment of Iraq's debts.

That was foolhardy on a number of counts. Whatever else was wrong with Saddam's international position, lack of military force was not one of his postwar weaknesses. He controlled the largest and most experienced army in the Gulf region and the sixth largest air force in the world. Moreover his difference with the Emir of Kuwait was not born of any recent and material dispute but went back to the early days of Iraqi independence. Under the Ottomans, who had ruled Mesopotamia since the sixteenth century, Kuwait had been administered as part of the province (*vilayet*) of Basra. Under the tutelage of the British, who had run

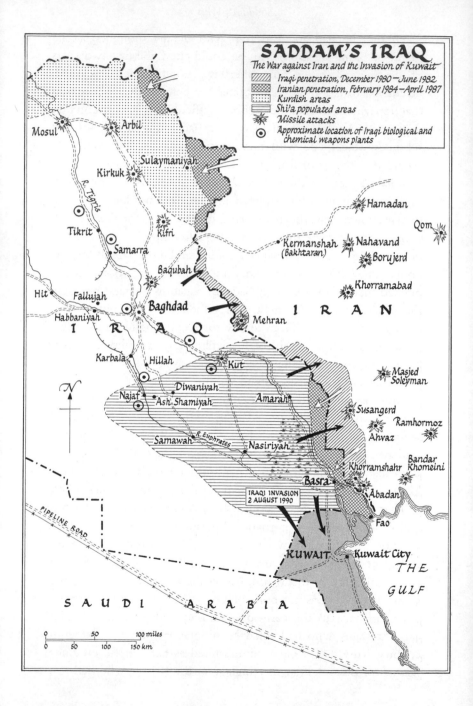

an undeclared empire over the Gulf States through the government of India and the Royal Navy throughout Victoria's reign, Kuwait had acquired a sort of independence from the Turks. This was not accepted by the Iraqi political class which, as soon as the mandate was ended in 1932, began to articulate a claim to Kuwait as part of the national territory. The claim was in part nationalist but was perhaps more strongly driven by Kuwait's oil wealth, contained in fields which straddled the common border, and by Kuwait's better access to the waters of the Gulf across its longer coastline. Whatever the merits of the Iraqi case, and they were not widely supported in the international community, it was a popular cause at home.

Saddam, moreover, was determined to persist in pressing his demands. During July 1990 Tariq Aziz, the Iraqi Foreign Minister, put his country's case forcefully to the secretary of the Arab League, arguing that both Kuwait and the United Arab Emirates (UAE) were depriving Iraq of a considerable portion of its legitimate oil income through depressing the price by overproduction; 'a drop of $1 in the price of a barrel of oil leads to a drop of $1 billion in Iraqi revenues annually'. He went on to argue that Iraq had, during the war with Iran, fought to protect the whole Arab homeland. It had spent in hard currency $102 billion on weapons and had lost $106 billion in income because of disruption of production. Yet Kuwait and the UAE were still demanding repayment of loans. 'How can these amounts be regarded as Iraqi debts to its Arab brothers when Iraq made sacrifices that are many times more than these debts in terms of Iraqi resources during the grinding war and offered rivers of blood of its youth in defence of the [Arab] nation's soil, dignity, honour and wealth?'

The threat, particularly to Kuwait, was made more explicit in a television broadcast by Saddam Hussein on 17 July. 'Raising our voices against the evil of overproduction is not the final resort if the evil continues. There should be some effective act to restore things to their correct positions.' What that act might be he indicated to the American ambassador, April Glaspie, in Baghdad on 25 July. In a letter he gave her to be sent to President Bush, he warned, 'We don't want war . . . but do not push us to consider war as the only solution to live proudly and to provide our people with a good living.'

The dialogue that followed has been minutely dissected. Supporters of April Glaspie hold that she made clear to Saddam Washington's disapproval of an attempt to settle the dispute with Kuwait by force. Critics believe that her exposition of American policy was ambiguous. The strongest point she made was that his deployment of troops (30,000 had just been concentrated on the Iraq–Kuwait border) made it 'reasonable . . . to be concerned'. Weakly, she conceded that 'we have no opinion on the Arab–Arab conflicts, like your border dispute with Kuwait . . . we hope that you can solve this problem via [the Arab League] or President Mubarak [of Egypt]'. Saddam responded by saying that he wanted a meeting with the Kuwaitis and that that might settle the matter. 'But if we are unable to find a solution, then it will be natural that Iraq will not accept death.' On that note Saddam and Glaspie parted, she apparently believing that she had merely been present at another instalment of Arab rhetoric. She would later tell *The New York Times*, 'Obviously I didn't think, and nobody else did, that the Iraqis were going to take all of Kuwait.'

Glaspie seemed to be attempting to excuse her misinterpretation of Saddam's despatch of a large army to the Kuwait border by suggesting that the troops might have occupied only the disputed Rumeila oil field and the oil-bearing islands of Warba and Bubiyan. It was an odd evasion of responsibility by a professional diplomat; even partial annexations of foreign territory are infractions of international law. Whatever her thinking, and however muddled or not, her exchange with Saddam can only be described as disastrous and rightly led to the extinction of her career.

Saddam had already made his intentions clear, in a communication to Kuwait which must have been made known to Washington. On 17 July, the twenty-second anniversary of the 'Ba'athist revolution' that had overthrown President Arif, he had demanded a stabilization of the oil price, the renunciation of the war loans and the creation of an Arab 'Marshall Plan' to rebuild

Iraq. In the event of Kuwait's failure to accept, Saddam threatened that 'we will have no choice but to resort to effective action to get things right and ensure the restitution of our rights'. King Fahd of Saudi Arabia, also one of Saddam's creditors, urged the Emir of Kuwait to capitulate and was eventually able to tell Saddam that the Emir was willing to do so. Saddam, however, chose to disbelieve him. 'At that moment', said one of Fahd's closest advisers, 'the King realised Kuwait was doomed.'

That indeed appears to have been the case. Saddam, acting as Stalin or Hitler might have done in dealing with a stiff-necked neighbour, had simply decided that he wanted to have his way. He had also concluded that he would not be opposed. It is significant that Saddam appears to have known more about Stalin than Hitler. Hitler overreached himself, in attacking Poland in 1939. Stalin never did. By one of the great injustices of history he got away with all his aggressions. Saddam probably calculated that he could do the same. It was certainly in a spirit of invulnerability that he set out on his annexation of Iraq's 'nineteenth province' on 2 August 1990.

The Iraqi army was experienced and plentifully equipped. Fully mobilized, it numbered a million men, organized into sixty divisions, including twelve armoured and mechanized. Seven of the divisions belonged to the Republican Guard, better equipped and chosen for political reliability. These, however, were paper strengths; the coalition identified only forty-three divisions on the ground. Equipment figures were better verified: over 4,000 tanks, over 4,000 infantry fighting vehicles and over 1,000 self-propelled guns. On paper the Iraqi air force had over 700 fighter and strike aircraft, at various levels of serviceability. In the event, at an early stage, it was flown to refuge in Iran and took no part in operations after the twelfth day (28 January 1991). The Iraqi navy was tiny and of no military importance, except for its minelaying before the war. The coalition eventually discovered that 1,200 mines, both of contact and influence types, had been laid, which required a heavy clearance effort; two major US warships suffered serious mine damage. The Kuwaiti army was only 16,000 strong and was swept aside by the initial onslaught, mounted by three Republican Guard divisions. They were shortly followed by 100,000 other troops which took up positions on either side of the Iraq–Kuwait border and began to construct entrenchments. In the first shock of the Iraqi invasion, however, what Saddam's enemies in the wider world feared was not his consolidating his conquests but extending them. The forward elements of the Republican Guard immediately established outposts on the Kuwait–Saudi Arabian border, thereby positioning itself to advance also towards Bahrain, Qatar and the United Arab Emirates. Nearly half the world's oil reserves had fallen under the shadow of Saddam's power.

The unprovoked and illegal occupation of Kuwait – from which 300,000 people at once fled into Saudi Arabia – was of itself enough to galvanize the powers into activity; not only the powers but lesser nations also and the international organizations. The UN Security Council passed a series of resolutions, in August, September, October and November, condemning Iraq's actions, calling for withdrawal and imposing sanctions and embargoes of various severity. On 2 August, the day of the invasion, it passed Resolution 660, not only condemning the invasion but also demanding that Iraq withdraw and begin negotiations. Resolution 661, on 6 August, embargoed all trade with Iraq. Resolution 665, on 25 August, imposed a naval blockade. Resolution 670, on 25 September, called on all member states to restrict flights to Iraq and to detain Iraqi-flagged ships that had been breaking sanctions. Finally, Resolution 678, on 29 November, the last of twelve, approved 'all necessary means' to drive Iraq from Kuwait if it had not left by 15 January 1991.

Against the background of UN diplomacy, President George Bush, strongly supported by the British Prime Minister, Margaret Thatcher, was meanwhile assembling a coalition of states that would be prepared to send troops to an international liberation force and, if necessary, to fight. Initially it was Mrs Thatcher who supplied the spark; the President did not think Saddam would attack Saudi Arabia and hoped to settle the crisis by negotiation. His outlook was influenced by a current domestic dispute with

Congress as to who controlled foreign policy. Mrs Thatcher convinced him that negotiations would entail delay without an eventual solution and that military preparations were essential. Once persuaded, the President was relentless in pursuit of supporters of his coalition, telephoning constantly around the world and extracting promises of troops, ships and aircraft. There was dissent: the USSR, China and France initially opposed the use of force but, in the event, did not oppose Resolution 678. The European Union revealed its weakness as an instrument of pan-European policy-making; the Western European Union had to be enlisted as a strategic instrument, and it co-ordinated a mine-hunting operation by six member states. Eventually, under one guise or another, sixteen states contributed naval forces, eleven air elements and eighteen ground troops, including Egypt, Syria and Pakistan; the adhesion of these Muslim countries to the coalition and the size of their contributions – Egypt sent two divisions – was of the greatest importance in depriving Saddam of title to represent himself as a champion of Arab nationalism or a Muslim religious leader. Saddam tried hard nonetheless; despite his secular past as a committed Ba'athist, he began to have himself filmed at prayer. He also concocted a spurious genealogy, falsely showing his descent from the Shi'a *imams* Hussein and Ali. Above all he worked strenuously to establish a link between his quarrel with Kuwait and his hostility to Israel. During the coming war he would attempt to widen the conflict, and detach from the coalition its Arab supporters, by bombarding Israel with Scud missiles.

His diplomacy did not avail; even his effort to mend his relationship with Iran, by offering to return the last scraps of occupied territory and the west bank of the Shatt el-Arab, failed to extract any support from the ayatollahs, despite their continuous hostility to America and the West in general. As the crisis persisted and he stubbornly refused to withdraw from Kuwait, he found himself increasingly isolated. After 13 September, when 400 Islamic leaders meeting in Mecca authorized the Kuwaitis to proclaim a holy war against him, he was entirely alone.

It was in those circumstances that on 16 January 1991 the First

Gulf War opened, at 2330 GMT. The first phase, that was to last until 24 February, was fought by the coalition exclusively as an air campaign. The coalition was completely dominant and was scarcely opposed; after 26 January, when the Iraqi air force fled to Iran, it was not opposed at all, except by anti-aircraft missile and gun defences. The lack of opposition was not surprising; at the outset, though Iraq possessed 700 aircraft, the size of the coalition air force was 2,430 aircraft and by 24 February it reached 2,790.

The air campaign fell into four phases. The first was designed to destroy Iraq's military and civil communications systems – radars, cable networks, radio and television stations – its nuclear, chemical and biological weapons research and development centres, its military industry, such as it was, and its main transportation points, bridges, railroad stations and freight yards. Targets also included civil and military headquarters, ministries and government offices. The principal weapons used in this phase were F-117A stealth bombers and Tomahawk cruise missiles, launched from submarines and surface ships. After the opening day, the British, Canadian, French and Italian air contingents joined in, flying Tornados, Mirages and Jaguars; the US Air Force and naval air force provided the main might of the attack.

In the second and third phases the attack was directed against the Iraqi army's positions in Kuwait, to destroy equipment and defences and to interdict supply. The burden of the campaign was carried by B-52 bombers delivering patterns of carpet bombing to a round-the-clock timetable.

Phase 4 accompanied the ground attack, to hit targets of opportunity, to disrupt Iraqi ground manoeuvres and to deliver firepower at the point of assault.

During the thirty-four days of preliminary air attack, the RAF flew 6,000 missions and the US Navy 18,000, while the USAF flew about 1,000 missions each day. By the end, a quarter of Iraq's electricity-generating capacity had been destroyed and another half severely damaged. Supplies to the Iraqi front line had been reduced from 20,000 tons a day to 2,000. As the coalition troops would discover, this reduced many of the invaders to near-starvation.

The most striking feature of the air campaign was the very high degree of precision attained. The war of 1991 was the first in which high-precision weapons – cruise missiles with on-board guidance systems and laser-guided bombs – were deployed. The results, by comparison with those achieved in previous air campaigns, appeared sensational. On-board television cameras showed cruise missiles, at the termination of flight, hitting targets within a margin of error of a few feet. 'Smart' bombs achieved similar accuracy. Indeed, almost anything the coalition sought to destroy, from static targets as large as bridges to mobile targets as small as individual tanks – were hit. The only failure in targeting was in the attack on Iraq's Scud missile launchers. At the outset Iraq possessed about 100 Scuds, a surface-to-surface missile mounting a one-ton conventional explosive warhead, launched from a mobile transporter-erector, to a range of 150 miles. The Scud was a development of the German V-2 rocket of the Second World War; like the V-2 it lacked accuracy and derived its military value from its elusiveness as a target. The missile could be launched from any piece of hard ground and, from arrival to departure, the system needed to be static for less than an hour. For that reason it was difficult to catch both when moving between launch positions or at the moment of launch; when not deployed, it was easily hidden under highway overpasses.

Iraq fired about ninety Scuds, half at US military targets in Saudi Arabia, the other half at civilian targets in Israel. The most successful strike was on an American barracks in Dahran, which killed twenty-eight US servicemen. The attacks on Israel were intended to provoke Israeli retaliation, in the hope that Israel's involvement would weaken or end Arab support for the coalition; diplomacy was successful in deterring Israel from responding in any way and, in the event, the casualties inflicted – four dead, 120 injured – were too low to provoke an Israeli reaction. American deployment of Patriot anti-missile missiles, which successfully intercepted about thirty-five Scuds, did much to quell alarm.

One of the few recorded failures of the ground forces during the campaign was in the destruction of Scud launchers. Though special forces ranged far and wide behind enemy lines, allegedly as far away as Baghdad itself, their success in finding and eliminating Scuds and their platforms was low. Only sixteen are known to have been destroyed and numbers remained hidden after the conclusion of hostilities.

The conventional ground campaign, however, from its opening on Sunday, 24 February to its termination on Thursday, 28 February, was an unequivocal success. Iraq's efforts to disrupt the preparation of the offensive before it was launched were ineffective. During 20 January – 1 February 1991 the Iraqis launched a spoiling attack on the town of Khafji, just inside Saudi Arabia, but failed to secure the place and were driven out, largely by forces of the Saudi Arabian National Guard, chosen by the coalition high command to emphasize the multinational character of the alliance. Other border incursions staged by the Iraqis also proved costly and ineffectual. Most of the Iraqi ground forces' activity in the weeks before 24 February were devoted to fortifying their positions. Saddam's strategy was determined by his experience in the war with Iran, which he believed had taught that air power was of secondary importance, that fixed positions were the critical element of a successful defence and that the infliction of heavy casualties would halt any offensive. What had been true against the Iranians proved not the case against the coalition. Its air resources vastly exceeded those his troops had encountered in the war of 1980–88, his fortifications were easily penetrated or outflanked by the American and British mobile formations, which deployed mine-clearing and obstacle-breaching equipment of a sophistication not matched by the Iranians, while their ability to inflict casualties exceeded that of the enemy many times. Saddam had simply failed to appreciate the disparity in strength and capability between his own troops and those of the enemy.

The situation at the outset of the coalition attack found the Iraqis concentrated in a narrow sector between the head of the Gulf and a dry desert watercourse, the Wadi al-Batin. Their forward positions were manned by about thirty divisions of the regular army, with six divisions of the Republican Guard holding the ground behind them, both to stiffen their resistance and to act as a counter-attack force if necessary. The coalition forces, by contrast, were deployed on a much wider front. While the heavy formations, largely American armour and Marines, faced the Iraqis between the Gulf and the Wadi al-Batin, more mobile formations – airborne and airmobile divisions, mechanized divisions and the French and British armoured divisions – had been thrown out into the desert to outflank the Iraqi defences and strike at the interior of the country. The coalition plan was to fix the bulk of the enemy in the positions where they stood, meanwhile encircling them by a strike from the desert across their rear from west to east.

The plan worked perfectly. On the first day the 1st and 2nd US Marine Divisions and the Arab forces drove into the Iraqi positions immediately west of the Gulf, breaking through trench lines and destroying much enemy armour in tank gunnery battles. Meanwhile the mobile forces on the desert flank were moving north but also swinging east. On the second day the flank forces, positioning logistic resources as they went, swung to threaten the Iraqi rear. On the third day the Marines and Arab forces continued their advance into the Iraqi main position while the mobile forces in the desert steepened their turn inward against the Iraqi rear. On the fourth day the Marines and Arabs largely overran the territory of Kuwait while the desert force cut across to reach the Euphrates river and complete the encirclement of the Iraqi occupation army.

By that stage the principal problem for the coalition was collecting and caring for the prisoners of the war. The enemy had begun to surrender freely as soon as the fighting started, many of them simply out of hunger. By the fourth day surrenders became a flood, the Iraqi conscripts leaving their positions en masse to come forward with their hands up. By 28 February at least 80,000 Iraqi soldiers had surrendered, while another 100,000 had fled into Iraq or actually been withdrawn from

Kuwait in the last days of occupation as the pointlessness of resistance became obvious even to Saddam. Some Iraqi units did fight; elements of the Republican Guard armoured divisions stuck to their positions and exchanged fire with the attackers, until overwhelmed. The disparity in casualties, however, reveals the nature of the conflict. Only 148 American, 47 British, 2 French and 14 Egyptian soldiers were killed in action, against an estimated total of 60,000 Iraqi combat deaths or even more. The British contingent estimated that 2,500 Iraqi tanks, 2,000 infantry fighting vehicles and 2,000 guns had been knocked out. Coalition equipment losses were negligible. The most visible Iraqi losses were suffered during the flight from Kuwait over the Mitla ridge, when coalition air and ground attacks on packed masses of armoured and soft-skinned vehicles produced devastation.

The Iraqi régime had persisted with its diplomacy throughout the war, seeking to arrange interventions by the Soviet Union and to influence resolutions in the UN Security Council. The Soviet peace plan, though it called for the immediate withdrawal of Iraqi forces from Kuwait, was unacceptable to the United States and other members of the coalition because it also demanded the abrogation of all outstanding Security Council resolutions on the situation. The Pope was meanwhile repeating his condemnation of the war; his policy was in part determined by the presence of an historic Christian community in Iraq which he sought to protect. The United States showed no interest in any peace plan which did not insist on instant withdrawal from Kuwait and the payment of reparations to Kuwait for war damage inflicted; Saudi Arabia also demanded reparations.

By 27 February Iraq's military condition was so desperate that its Foreign Minister, Tariq Aziz, a Chaldean Christian and so one of the Pope's flock, communicated to the Security Council Iraq's readiness to accept the resolutions declaring its occupation of Kuwait null and void and its responsibility to pay reparations. His communication was rejected by the permanent members, who insisted on acceptance of all twelve resolutions on Iraqi conduct passed since 2 August 1990. The following day President Bush announced that a cease-fire would be instituted if Iraq would end hostilities and stop firing Scud missiles. Iraq accepted the American offer and a temporary cease-fire came into effect at 0500 GMT.

The crisis had lasted 209 days, of which forty-two had been spent in open warfare. Coalition air sorties flown had reached the total of 106,000. During their occupation of Kuwait and retreat from it, Iraq had set fire to 640 oil wells and damaged another ninety. Iraq had suffered not only heavy loss of life, largely through military casualties, but also severe material damage, to its roads, bridges, electricity-generating plant, telephone and television networks and its infrastructure in general.

At the termination of hostilities, it was also thrown immediately into widespread disorder. In the south many of the Shi'a majority rose in revolt, attacking centres of Ba'athist power and killing state and party officials. The revolt began in Nasiriyah but spread swiftly to Basra, Kut, Hillah, Karbala and Najaf, the last two the holy places of Shi'a belief. Saddam reacted with a mixture of violence and conciliation. To retain the loyalty of his own Sunni supporters, he announced a rapid demobilization of older reservists, distribution of cash handouts and an increase of food rations. To put down resistance, he assembled the armoured vehicles that had survived the army's defeat and concentrated them against the centres of resistance. Confronted by heavy weapons they did not themselves possess, the rebels quickly collapsed. Saddam inflicted crushing reprisals.

In the north the Kurds, who had been in more or less open revolt for many years, seized the opportunity to take possession of the provincial capitals and set up a local administration, hoping for help from neighbouring Iran. The ayatollahs were unwilling to support a movement whose long-term aim was the creation of a greater Kurdistan, partly at Iran's territorial expense. Even less so were the Turks, whose population included a large and troublesome Kurdish minority. Saddam, after suppressing the Shi'a revolt, transferred his internal security forces to the north; a full-scale repression proved unnecessary, however, because the

Kurdish leadership rightly judged that Saddam was open to negotiations, to Kurdish advantage, if the rebellion were curtailed. This redirection of Kurdish policy, strongly underpinned by Western offers of support for the protection of 'safe havens' inside Kurdistan, led to the declaration of a cease-fire on 19 April after which began the return of over a million Kurds who had fled their homes to the mountains or to refuge in Iran and Syria. In the aftermath the Western powers, under UN authority, would impose military supervision over Iraqi forces north of the 36th parallel. Similar limitation of military authority would later be imposed over the Shi'a south.

Yet despite these reductions of Iraqi sovereign power, and the undoubted fact of his overwhelming defeat in war, Saddam refused to admit that he had been beaten or even humiliated. In the face of all the evidence to the contrary, he insisted that Iraq had won the war. In support of that extraordinary assertion, he cited the survival of his own régime and the fact that Iraq remained an independent state. Addressing the nation on 29 July 1991, he announced victory. 'You [the Iraqi people] are victorious because you have refused humiliation and repression and clung to a state that will strengthen the people and the [Arab] nation forever.'

People in the West, leaders and citizens alike, were infuriated by Saddam's denial of what they saw as undeniable fact; they were also bewildered. How could a man, they asked, sitting amid the debris of a military catastrophe he had brought upon himself, in the ruined capital of a country he no longer fully controlled, despised and rejected by his fellow Arab leaders, continue to proclaim a triumph?

There were several elements underpinning Saddam's defiance. Two were salient. The first, easily understood in the Arab world, almost incomprehensible to Westerners, is the power that rhetoric exerts in Arab public life. Arabic is a language of poetry – the Koran itself is the greatest work of Arab poetry – which easily tips into extravagance and then fantasy, without, in Arab consciousness, losing touch with reality. Because of the beauty of Arabic as a language, what sounds right is easily accepted as being right. Thus, when Saddam proclaimed triumph, the sheer extravagance of his words, expressing an idea his audience wished to believe was true, seemed true. When he told his fellow Iraqis that, if they did not feel defeated, they were not defeated, he was believed; undoubtedly he believed so himself.

Simultaneously, however, the practical half of Saddam's mind was supporting rhetoric with calculation. It is a perfectly rational thought that a defeat is only as bad as the victor chooses to make it. If the victor declines to press his advantage to the utmost, the vanquished retains room for manoeuvre, which may win back ground that appears lost. Saddam had led a difficult life, and had been oppressed by many setbacks; by refusing to acquiesce – in the failure of his assassination attempt on President Kassem, of his first attempt to unseat President Arif, of his attack on Iran in 1980, perhaps most of all in the indignity and hardship of imprisonment – he had eventually overcome. Very soon after the rout of his army, he seems to have recovered his resilience again. His enemies gave him cause to do so. They did not demand his removal from office as a condition of terminating hostilities, as the ayatollahs had done; they did not occupy his country; they did not insist on comprehensive disarmament; they even, in an ill-judged concession, gave him permission to fly his helicopters within Iraq, and it was with these that he would reassert a great deal of his power. Saddam may well have discovered their motives: that they shrank from ruling Iraq themselves, particularly from attempting to reconcile Kurds, Sunni and Shi'a; that they continued to regard Saddam as a check on the ayatollahs; that there was no alternative régime to hand; that the Americans in particular wanted no part in a new imperialism.

He may even have guessed that the Pentagon and State Department expected the Saddam problem to be solved within Iraq itself, by assassination or exile, the traditional fate awaiting a loser in that country. It was a reasonable expectation. He took immediate and ruthless steps to see that it was not realized. He ordered exemplary executions of weak and culpable generals. He promoted the harshest of his followers to new responsibilities, making Ali Hassan al-Majid, 'Chemical Ali', the man who had gassed the Kurds, Minister of the Interior. He rearranged other governmental positions, to strengthen the representation of his relatives and tribal brothers from Tikrit. He farther elaborated the measures taken to protect his own security, no longer appearing in public, concealing his places of work and residence and moving frequently and unpredictably to disguise his whereabouts.

Finally and most cunningly he contrived a scheme of apparent co-operation with the United Nations to hide and shelter his weapons of mass destruction. The one ingredient of Saddam's warmaking that had alarmed the coalition was his use of Scud missiles, which threatened both military targets at ranges of 100 miles or more and the extension of the conflict by provoking an Israeli intervention. The Scud risk was heightened by Saddam's known possession of chemical weapons and suspected determination to develop nuclear warheads. Fear of chemical weapons had actually increased civilian casualties in Israel by causing the population to keep out of cellars and bunkers where chemical agents would have been most effective. The United Nations Special Commission on Disarmament (UNSCOM), a body set up largely at American prompting, arrived in Iraq in May 1991 to begin work on identifying the extent of Saddam's unconventional weapons programme, the degree of progress achieved, the location of manufacturing and research sites, and the location and size of stocks held. Saddam acquiesced in UNSCOM's activities at the time because his hands were then fully occupied with suppressing the internal revolts. His acquiescence was secretly conditional, however, on the creation of a programme to delude and mislead UNSCOM's enquiries. Tariq Aziz was put in charge of the deception scheme, designed to conceal weapon sites, disperse forbidden material, hide critical documents and brief essential personnel to deflect penetrating questions. It was not an exercise for which the Iraqis were unprepared. For ten years before 1991 the country had been subject to inspection by the International Atomic Energy Agency (IAEA) and had successfully baffled its investigations. UNSCOM was a more rigorous body, its leader,

Dr David Kay, being a brave and determined man. The nature of his enquiries was so invasive that the Iraqis were forced to destroy much material to prevent it falling into the hands of the inspectors. Ultimately, however, by Saddam's transporting documents and material to numbers of his so-called 'palaces', (Presidential residences he defined as private homes immune from inspection), Kay and his team were frustrated. UNSCOM was eventually unable to certify that it had eliminated all Iraq's forbidden military research and development, a state of affairs which would lead to the dispute over 'weapons of mass destruction' (WMD) that would precipitate the Gulf War of 2003.

5

The Crisis of 2002–03

The 'Fall of the Wall' – the destruction by popular action of the barrier separating West from East Berlin in November 1989 – not only led to the disintegration of the Warsaw Pact and eventually to the collapse of the whole communist system in the Soviet Union and its empire. It also inaugurated, in the stated belief of President George Bush Senior, 'a new world order'.

President Bush's vision foresaw the replacement of a world system, defined by the military antagonism between free-enterprise America and Marxist Russia, by a benevolent commonality of interest between the old power blocs, henceforth dedicated to sustaining the peace of the world through concerted action against aggressors and to eliminating the causes of conflict by fostering democracy and prosperity across the world. His hope of how the new order would work was exemplified by his construction of the coalition of sixty nations, including many former enemies, that punished President Saddam Hussein for his invasion and annexation of independent Kuwait in 1990, by defeating his army of occupation and restoring Kuwait's sovereignty.

Belief in a new world order held tenuous sway throughout the uneasy 1990s. Some signs were positive, others not. Domestic aggression in former Yugoslavia, centre point of the most flagrant violations of respect for human life and political liberty, was eventually checked by international action; on the other hand, organization of the action was too long delayed to avert atrocities that called the effectiveness of the new order into question. Still, grounds for optimism persisted. The setbacks in the Balkans might be seen as growing pains, not disabling weaknesses.

Then, on 11 September 2001, two months short of the twelfth anniversary of the event in Berlin which brought freedom to hundreds of millions, another event in New York made mockery of the whole idea of a world order. Three hijacked airliners, seized by Islamic extremists belonging to the al-Qaeda organization, were flown into the Pentagon building in Washington and the two towers of the New York World Trade Center, causing damage to the one and the collapse of the other, with the loss of nearly three thousand lives. Many died in the most heartrending circumstances, throwing themselves to their deaths in the streets below the buildings to avoid incineration in the inferno inside. A fourth hijacked airliner crashed, killing all on board, after action by brave unarmed passengers against the terrorists.

The events of 11 September – or 9/11 as the day soon became universally known – caused shock throughout the world. In the United States it provoked a revolution, changing national sentiment and redirecting national policy. Before 9/11 the American people, if largely uncomprehending of the outside world, viewed it through benevolent eyes; after 9/11 they saw enemies everywhere. Before 9/11 American governments had, for fifty years, sought to keep the peace by leading a Western alliance of the like-minded; after 9/11 Washington committed itself to the defence of America first and foremost. Thinking Americans, in and out of government, knew that their country still had foreign friends; but henceforth friendship would not be taken on trust. It would have to be demonstrated.

At the turn of the millennium, from twentieth to twenty-first centuries, a new world order was indeed born. It took, however, a form entirely different from that envisaged by the father of the new American President, George W. Bush. Bush senior had foreseen a world continuing to be dominated by the traditional blocs, a First World of rich states, led by America, and a Second World of former Communist states, moving to join the Western system; the evolution of the Third World of poorer states would depend on the success of the first two in disseminating their wealth and ideas to that bloc's peoples. Suddenly such stability had disappeared. The central power of the First World was under attack and would have to put its own security first. The source of the attack lay in the Third World and took forms against which traditional defence, nuclear deterrence and conventional forces organized in international alliances, offered little protection. The attitude of the Second World, for decades the main concern of Western foreign-policy makers, seemed suddenly irrelevant. Armies of experts who had made lifelong careers in the analysis of Marxist politics found themselves at a loose end. The urgent need was for an understanding of militant Islam.

Government officials in the United States were particularly ill-equipped to address the problem, its academic community little better. America has only a tiny Muslim community; Arabic is a language very few Americans, outside a handful of university departments, speak. Historically, moreover, America has little knowledge of the Arab world. A few oil company executives apart, Americans do not live or work in the Arabic-speaking lands or elsewhere in the Muslim world. In that respect, the United States is less well placed to understand Islam than Britain or France, both of which have ruled Arab and other Muslim countries within living memory, and have accepted Muslim immigrants from their ex-colonies in large numbers. British experts, however, struggle to follow the tortuous paths taken by modern Islamic thought. In France, a country with 5 million Muslim inhabitants and a tradition of intellectual involvement with Islam, specialist scholars have led the way in interpreting movements of Islamic thought to other Westerners; yet even the French find difficulty in penetrating the veil. The modern Muslim mind is alien both to Christian and Enlightenment ways of thinking.

What baffles Westerners is why Muslim militants hate Western civilization as bitterly as they do. There is, perhaps, no logical explanation; most modern Westerners would fail to supply a persuasive explanation of the hatred felt between their Protestant and Catholic ancestors in the century of the Reformation. The hatred felt by Muslim extremists is, however, real and it has historic roots. In the years after the Muslim triumph of the seventh and eighth centuries, when Muslim armies conquered the old Christian provinces of the Middle East and North Africa, seized Spain and established a foothold in the Balkans, culminating in the capture of Constantinople in 1453, the ancestors of modern Muslims became, in a sense, the Americans of their age. The system of government they established under the universal Caliphate was an enlightened one which guaranteed freedom of belief to all who acknowledged the Caliph's supremacy, and his scholars were in the forefront of contemporary learning. They rescued Western classical thought from obscurity, they advanced the study of modern mathematics and the practice of medicine and they instituted the systematic study of political sociology.

Until the fourteenth century Islam was the most progressive intellectual force in the world west of China. Then, in a regrettable step, the religious leaders of orthodox − Sunni − Islam decided that its interpretative development, taking account of discoveries in non-theological thought, should come to an end. This 'closing of the gates' spelled an end to Muslim openness. Thereafter, right down to our own day, mainstream Islam found itself confined within intellectual boundaries set by scholars several hundred years dead. Not only was the practice of religious life to be defined by their decisions; so too was public, political and legal life. The law of *Sharia* − 'the path to the waterhole' − thenceforth dictated how pious Muslims should relate to each other, to their business associates, to non-Muslims and to the state. Not that, in orthodox Muslim thought, the state had any existence independent of the religious world that defined it. Until the extinction of the universal Caliphate in 1925 at the behest of the secularist Mustapha Kemal of Turkey, where it had had its seat since the sixteenth century, orthodox Islam made no distinction between worldly and religious authority. One was the other and vice versa.

The interpenetration of the spiritual and the material was, in practical terms, a disaster for Islam. It prevented the separation of theological and pragmatic paths of thought which the Christian West had achieved, if not without a struggle, even before the Protestant Reformation. While, from the Renaissance onwards, Italy, France, Germany, Holland and Britain soared off into the heady altitudes of intellectual freedom that would usher in the Scientific Revolution and the Enlightenment, Islam remained stuck on the path to the waterhole. Its intellectual life decayed, its political institutions, the universal Caliphate foremost, fossilized. In its heyday, from the fifteenth to the seventeenth century, the Caliphate had conquered wherever it turned its steps. By the nineteenth century Turkey, meaning the Caliphate, which still ruled North Africa in name, the Arab lands and the Balkans as colonies, was the Sick Man of Europe. France and Britain fought Russia to prop Turkey up on its deathbed, for fear of the consequences of its final collapse.

Its collapse, when it came at the end of the First World War, gave France and Britain control of what remained of its empire, the Arab lands of which they had not already taken possession. The Arabs proved, however, turbulent subjects, even though promised eventual independence under the terms of the League of Nations mandate which authorized Britain and France to exercise authority over them. Syria, Lebanon, Iraq and in particular Palestine, whose future Britain complicated by offering it as the location of a National Home for the Jews, chafed at the mandate terms. Their populations wanted immediate, not delayed independence.

Independence came. In the meantime, however, developments had occurred that made formal political arrangements a secondary issue. The onetime outposts of the Caliphate's power that had been made French colonies, Tunisia, Algeria and Morocco, achieved independence by secession or armed struggle. Their British equivalents, Egypt and Libya, went the same way, as Iraq and Jordan had already done. Part of Palestine became a Jewish state. Syria and Lebanon achieved separation from France. Inside the Arab world which was comprehended by these states, however, there raged an intellectual ferment which threatened to transcend the idea of mere independence from European rule. In one direction it took the form of an Arab political renaissance, imitating but stressing its separation from European political models; its instrument was the Ba'ath party in Syria and Iraq. In another and later development it reverted to the earliest message of Islam: that the preaching of the Prophet has universal force, that it is his destiny to triumph and that those who oppose the extension of his power over the world are excluded from the promise of compassion that lies at the heart of the Islamic religion.

This perversion of the Prophet's teaching, and that it is a perversion is admitted by the majority of Muslim teachers, was launched on the Islamic world by an Egyptian, Sayyid Qutb, during the period of Nasser's Presidency. Imprisoned by Nasser for membership of the Muslim self-help organization, the Muslim Brotherhood, he moved by stages to an extremist interpretation of Muslim theology. Nasser's essentially secularist version of Islam – though he was an overtly devout believer, his policies emphasized material at the expense of spiritual development in a Muslim society – led Qutb to denounce the Egyptian President as *jahili*, spiritually ignorant. His refusal to moderate his views led to his execution, after a long period of imprisonment, in 1966. Before his death, Qutb had elaborated his new interpretation of Islam to argue – convincingly to many young, frustrated Muslims – that, while the Prophet had undoubtedly preached compassion towards nonbelievers, he had also stressed the primacy of submission to his teachings, which were those of God, and that, until such submission was widely achieved, Muslims were absolved from the duty of showing compassion to those who rejected the preaching of the Prophet's word.

In short, violence against nonbelievers was not sinful. Indeed, and here Qutb harked back to the teaching of Abul Ala Mawdudi, struggle – *jihad* – against the encroachment of the West on the Islamic world was an obligation. Mawdudi, Pakistani by nationality, had called for a universal *jihad* to fight the *jahiliyyah* (ignorance) of the West, just as the Prophet had fought against *jahiliyyah* in pre-Islamic Arabia. He argued that the call to *jihad* was the central doctrine of Islam, exceeding in importance the duty to pray and to give alms. Qutb went farther still. He called on Muslims to model themselves upon Muhammad in their personal lives, then to separate themselves from society and then to wage *jihad* in a violent fashion; an important distinction, since *jihad* can, and indeed should, take the form of a struggle against self. Only when the *jihad* against ignorance – which Qutb identified as the secular modern world – had been won should Muslims revert to the practice of compassion, within what would be a new universal Caliphate.

Qutb's elaboration of Mawdudi's teachings proved enormously influential. It inflamed, rather than inspired, a new generation of Muslims, particularly in Pakistan and Afghanistan, to train for war, to learn the methods of terrorism and to reintroduce into public life the ancient Islamic punishments of stoning and mutilation. It underlay the rise of the Taleban ('students'), products of religious schools where his teaching was passed on. It motivated the assassination of secularist Muslim leaders, notably President Sadat of Egypt. It justified, if it did not directly motivate, the doctrines of al-Qaeda, the perpetrators of 9/11, whose methods are those of universal *jihad* and whose ambitions, the conversion of all to Islam and the establishment of a universal Caliphate, mirror those of Qutb.

The emergence of a new world order according to Qutb was the least expected outcome of the fall of the Berlin Wall; it is most improbable that it could have been foreseen. True, the dissolving of the superpower blocs, what foreign policy experts called the 'bipolar' world, would be likely to result in a measure of instability. Terrifying though the bipolar world had been, with its opposed ranks of nuclear weapons, its nature assured that most states had to belong to one bloc or the other – the 'unaligned' states had no strategic significance – and that the bloc leaders kept their followers in order. Inevitably the collapse of the Soviet Union meant that some of its client states would cease to toe the line determined by the Kremlin, but the presumption was that, at worst, they would resume old quarrels with neighbours. So at first it proved; the Balkan disorders had origins that long predated the Cold War and Saddam's annexation of Kuwait was motivated by a dispute over frontiers that went back to a British disagreement with the Ottoman empire. The international system seemed adapted to coping with such problems. Then 9/11 demonstrated that there were malcontents in the post–Cold War world for whose wrongdoing the international system made no provision at all. The system, whether its roots are traced to the Peace of Westphalia in 1648 or to the creation of the League of Nations after the First World War, is political in substance. It assumes the existence of states and that they will relate to one another in terms of self-interest. The *Salafists* who launched 9/11 – *Salafism* is an Islamic umbrella doctrine embracing all Muslims who reject the concept of the state and seek only a universal kingdom of believers – deny the right of mortals to make policy or frame laws, insisting that all they need to know of public life can be found in the Koran.

This *Salafist* new world order – little known in the West and even less understood – nevertheless indirectly provoked a Western response. In the aftermath of the First Gulf War, which left Saddam in power, a group of Washington foreign-policy makers began to argue that acquiescing in his survival spelled danger to the West. Unaware that there were more dangerous figures active in the Muslim world, they advocated what would become known as the doctrine of pre-emption – striking first to avert a later danger. They included Paul Wolfowitz, then Deputy Secretary of Defense to Dick Cheney, Lewis Libby, also a Pentagon official at the time, and Richard Perle, a defence intellectual omnipresent in post–Cold War Washington. They and many of their associates had begun their political lives on the left of politics. As they moved towards the right, 'rightness' being associated with strategic realism, they acquired the description of 'neo-conservatives'. In 1992, as the first Bush Presidency drew to its close, Wolfowitz wrote a defence policy paper which outlined his view of how a

strategy of pre-emption should work. He argued that, in the face
of calls for a 'peace dividend' following the end of Cold War
hostilities, the United States should spend to maintain its military dominance in Europe and Asia, preserve its strike forces and
be ready to launch pre-emptive attacks against states which, on
escaping the constriction of the superpower system, were setting
up as possessors of weapons of mass destruction – nuclear foremost but also biological and chemical. Those he suspected were
either historically unaligned or pro-Soviet – Iran, Syria, North
Korea, Libya and, of course, Iraq. His paper, though diluted by
bureaucratic process, was eventually published under then Secretary
Cheney's imprimatur as an official document, *Defense Strategy for
the 1990s.*

The succession of President Clinton deprived the neo-
conservatives of direct influence on government. Clinton, though
prepared to intervene abroad, as he eventually did in the Balkans,
preferred to do so in concert with other states and through international organizations, and to proceed with caution. He did not
share the neo-conservatives' beliefs in the necessity of pre-emption
nor in the desirability of régime change in countries overtly
hostile to the United States and able to harm its interests or citizens. Although out of government, the neo-conservatives remained
able to propagate their views, through such publications as the
Weekly Standard and *Commentary,* a major organ of Jewish thought.
Many of the neo-conservatives were Jewish; almost all were Zionist
and pro-Israeli. That was to prove unfortunate for it entangled
their policies for the Middle East, which were generally rational
and enlightened if not always realistic, with their ambitions for
the future of the Jewish state, which were contentious and nation-
alistic. The neo-conservatives believed, in a highly traditional
American cast of mind, that the solution to the world's problems
lay in transforming absolutist, monarchical and autocratic régimes
into free-enterprise democracies. They believed democracy to be
transportable and to have a transforming effect; through its implementation, in societies previously tribal or theocratic or otherwise afflicted by divisive and unrepresentative systems, they

believed populations could be led to become politically enlightened and economically prosperous. They also believed in a 'domino' effect: that the transformation of one society in a region would lead to the same effect in others. They were particularly insistent that 'régime change' in Iraq, the focus of their antipathies, would foster change for the better in its neighbours, including Syria and Iran. Paradoxically, however, several of the neo-conservatives supported extremist politicians in Israel, who rejected compromise with the Palestinians; they wanted a larger and stronger Israeli state, empowered to deal with the Palestinians only on the basis of recognition of its right to exist and to command defensible frontiers. The confusion of policy, for confusion it was and remains – democracy for Middle Eastern Muslims but a particular version of state rights for Israel – weakened and continues to weaken the neo-conservatives' message. To European liberals and leftists in particular, the neo-conservatives appear hypocritical. They interpret the contradictions of neo-conservative policy as an attempt to establish native versions of American democracy in the unreformed Arab states while supporting a selfishly Zionist regime in Israel. Needless to say, that view is widely shared in the Arab world and bedevils American efforts to win friends in the region.

The neo-conservatives farther alienated liberal and leftist opinion in Europe by their devotion to the idea of American 'particularism' – an idea, almost as old as the United States itself, that the country stands for certain superior principles of public and inter-state behaviour – justifying in their view, again a long-established American position, its right to act unilaterally in foreign affairs. From the earliest days of the republic American ideologues have sought to define America as not only detached from but better than the Old World of religious prejudice and political egotism. To the idea of American particularism – Ronald Reagan's vision of 'the city on the hill' – the neo-conservatives conjoined that of 'the American moment'. With the collapse of the Communist system, the neo-conservatives argued, the United States inherited an opportunity, unlikely to be long-lived or to recur, to change by forthright action the world for the better. There had been such a moment once before, in 1918, when the idealistic President Woodrow Wilson had imposed on an exhausted world his plan for a League of Nations that would rid mankind of war. The chance to capitalize on his vision had been missed when his physical collapse allowed less enlightened politicians, some American, to dilute his plans.

With the return of an American moment, the neo-conservatives glimpsed a new opportunity and determined to profit by it. It would not be taken through the medium of the United Nations. An improvement on the Wilsonian conception though it was, with its powers to authorize the use of military force against transgressors of international order, the UN still lacked the capacity for peremptory action. Too many interests had to be placated; too many nationalities were allowed a voice. The neo-conservatives wanted the power to strike, without consultation and without warning. They believed in particular that enemies like Saddam could be disposed of only by unilateral action, with the assistance of such allies as would not quibble and could match American standards of military efficiency. That meant in effect Britain and any British associates, like Australia, that deployed equivalent forces.

Capturing a fleeting American moment required the return to power of a conservative American President. George W. Bush, elected in 2001, was such a figure. At his inauguration he did not seem a neo-conservative choice, though he appointed to office several highly conservative politicians, including Donald Rumsfeld as Secretary of Defense. Dick Cheney, his Vice-President, was also a neo-conservative favourite. The horror of 9/11 set the new President, however, on a neo-conservative path. He was quickly persuaded that the 'war on terror' which he immediately proclaimed was best prosecuted at the outset by attacking al-Qaeda, the perpetrator of 9/11, in its terrorist camps in Afghanistan. Having acquired American bases for the campaign in the ex-Soviet republics in Central Asia, he launched the counter-terrorist attack. By a combination of the commitment of special forces (American, British and Australian), the enlistment of the anti-Taleban forces of the Northern Alliance and the deployment of heavy American airpower, the al-Qaeda units in Afghanistan and their Taleban supporters were quickly overcome. At the culmination of the campaign it was believed that Osama bin Laden, the terrorist mastermind, had been cornered and killed. Later evidence, supplied by video and broadcast tape, dashed such hopes. Nevertheless, he thereafter became a fugitive figure, having scarcely substantial existence, while the material success of the campaign in Afghanistan was undoubted. The country was given a new, plausibly representative administration and the Islamicist régime of the Taleban was dissolved.

With the defeat of the Taleban, which destroyed al-Qaeda's principal platform of support, the Bush Presidency could turn to engage the other main targets of the war on terrorism. Al-Qaeda was reported by American intelligence to have centres of support in as many as fifty countries but the main danger was identified as emanating from Iraq. Saddam, Iraq's President, was indubitably a threat to peace in the Middle East and beyond. During his thirty years in power he had attempted to acquire the capacity to build nuclear weapons – a threat checked only by the Israelis' destruction of the French-supplied Osirak reactor in 1981 – and used chemical weapons both in his war against Iran in 1980–88 and against his own Kurdish citizens. Saddam had also authorized an assassination attempt against the new American President's father, George Bush Senior, who had organized the coalition war against him in 1990–91. Saddam was a wicked man, an aggressor, an oppressor of the Iraqi people and a menace to order in his own régime and the wider world. Whether he was a sponsor of al-Qaeda was more problematic. He had undoubtedly given succour to Abu Nidal, an earlier father of anti-Western terror, and he was generally well-disposed to anti-Western terrorists. His association with al-Qaeda escaped proof. Osama bin Laden was a *Salafist*, a believer in a Muslim world without political institutions. Saddam was an Arab secularist, a type particularly repugnant to Islamic fundamentalists. Had Osama bin Laden attempted to propagate his beliefs in Saddam's Iraq, he would undoubtedly have met the fate of all Saddam's enemies.

Unfortunately for Saddam, official America after 9/11 was uninterested in distinctions between one sort of Arab extremist and another. Osama was violently anti-American. So was Saddam. The decision was taken to eliminate his régime. The steps to that decision were given in two public warnings, President Bush's State of the Union address to Congress in January 2002 and his speech to the graduating class at the US Military Academy in June. In both he denounced Saddam's régime – to Congress as part of an 'axis of evil' – and he threatened pre-emptive action. The decisive moment came, however, on 11 January 2003 when Secretary Rumsfeld ordered the deployment of 60,000 troops, together with military aircraft and warships, to the Gulf; on 20 January Geoffrey Hoon, the British Secretary of State for Defence, commanded the despatch of 26,000 British troops and 100 aircraft; with those already in the area, a quarter of the British army and a third of the Royal Air Force would be present in the zone of operations. Rumsfeld's and Hoon's announcements clarified a puzzling obscurity. Strategic analysts had pondered for months on the territorial difficulties of mounting an operation against Iraq, one of the most inaccessible countries in the northern hemisphere. Its tiny coastline at the head of the Gulf offered scarcely any space for a bridgehead. Saudi Arabia was proving uncooperative. Iran was almost as hostile to the West as Iraq itself. Turkey had suddenly turned contrary. Syria would not breach the Arab front. Jordan seemed too weak to violate Muslim opinion. There seemed no way in. At the last moment, though the Americans had known so for some time, Kuwait was revealed to be willing to offer basing and transit rights. It was a courageous decision, since it isolated the country in the Arab world and carried the risk of terrible retaliation if the coalition operation did not work.

Solving the difficulty of the military preliminaries did not, however, dissolve the political obstacles. The United States could count on the support of Britain and of Australia, which supplied ships, aircraft and special forces (which may have included a New Zealand element). Otherwise it was bereft of allies. Worse; early in the crisis that developed in 2002 and persisted into 2003, right up to the unleashing of hostilities, its traditional European supporters began to object to and even oppose the taking of military action against Saddam. Spain, an unlikely militant, supported President Bush, so enthusiastically that he chose to stage a summit meeting in the Portuguese Azores on 16 March, the very eve of the war. France, however, made strong and increasingly loud protests; so did Germany. Objections by France were to be expected, for many reasons. Historically pro-Arab and pro-Muslim since the seventeenth century, when it had been the Ottoman Emperor's only friend among the Christian powers, and led by the braggart President Chirac, who both gloried in trumpeting his differences with Washington and was deeply implicated in commercial dealings with Saddam's government (dating back to the sale of the Osirak reactor to Iraq at the end of the 1970s), France was an odd man out in the Western world. Germany, by contrast, had always been an American insider. In the days when twenty Soviet divisions occupied the old East Germany, it had been America's most devoted friend on the continent. Liberated, however, from the Soviet threat, thanks to the triumph of President Reagan's policy of bankrupting the Soviet Union by competition in military expenditure, German public and much political opinion yielded to the temptation of seeking the softer way. The defeat of 1945 had altered the German psyche, transforming the most militarist nation in Europe into one genuinely devoted to the principles of peace and the resolution of international disputes by conciliation. The threat of Soviet aggression had forced the German people to embrace NATO and do the military duty membership of the alliance required. The elimination of the Soviet threat allowed German anti-militarism to surface and to predominate. The new German Chancellor, Gerhard Schroeder, a Social Democrat, though lacking Chirac's pro-Arab credentials, shared his anti-Americanism and by 2003 was on equally as bad, if not worse terms with Washington. The Americans were not shocked by Chirac's chauvinism since they had been taught French egoism by the master of the medium, Charles de Gaulle. German ingratitude both surprised the Americans and genuinely hurt; it exemplified de Rochefoucauld's judgement that past favours are never forgiven.

Yet the attitude of France and Germany, shared by some of the smaller Western European countries, was not fully to be explained by personal or contingent factors. Something much larger was at work. Superficially it is easy to say that France and Germany had, during the second half of the twentieth century, become 'European'. The rise of the European Union and the consolidation of its authority had undoubtedly encouraged first France and then Germany to look forward to a rebalancing of international power in the Atlantic world, in a fashion that would equalize the influence of its two halves, American and European. Economically that seemed attainable, for the combined population of the European Union countries exceeded that of the United States and, on the admission of new members, promised to be much larger. It was not impossible either that, with effort and by accepting economic sacrifice, an expanded Europe might eventually match the military capability of the United States. The attainment of economic and military equality, perhaps eventual superiority, depended, however, upon political evolution. At the beginning of the twenty-first century, France and Germany were pressing for the adoption by the states of the Union of a comprehensive constitution, regulating not only economic activity but also defining political institutions and their powers, including the Commission, its executive authority, the council of ministers, the parliament and the European court; the constitution also made provision for a Union president, foreign minister and military authority.

Yet the Europe envisaged by the framers of its constitution – a constitution not in the event adopted, because of the refusal of some of the constituent states to accept it – would not have imitated the United States of America of the Founding Fathers. It would initially have been less but eventually more; initially less because it left to the constituent governments more power than the American constitution left to the states, eventually more because, by accretion, the powers exercised by the Union over its constituent members would have greatly exceeded those of the American federal government. The fathers of the European 'idea', the Frenchman Jean Monnet and the Englishman Arthur Salter, had conceived their vision of Europe's future as officials of the League of Nations, after the First World War. They were inspired by the hope of creating a pan-European system that would render impossible war between its member states. The only way to assure that outcome, they persuaded themselves, was to create a central authority so strong that subordinate governments would lack the means to take independent decisions. Their 'Europe' was therefore to be not 'intergovernmental' in character but 'supranational'.

It was towards that form that 'Europe' gradually evolved in the years after the Second World War. Beginning with a Coal and Steel Community, to which were added an Atomic Energy Community and an Economic Community, with a European court and central bank as adjuncts, and eventually a European currency as a medium of exchange, the European Union was, on the eve of the Iraq War, when the framing of a constitution was at an advanced stage of drafting, almost the supranational body Monnet and Salter had wished to make it. Its executive, the Commission, monopolized the drafting of legislation to regularize its economic life; its parliament had rights only to approve, scarcely to alter, such laws; and the European court had authority to condemn governments in breach of Union legislation. In almost every respect it amounted to a supranational authority, to which the historic governments of Europe were subordinate.

In only one aspect was its authority deficient. It had no power to impose its will, either internally or externally. This was a crippling deficiency, its effect completely unforeseen by the European founding fathers, Monnet and Salter. They, products of an earlier and higher-minded age, were mechanistic in outlook and, believing in the power of economic sanction and collective legal condemnation to regulate misbehaviour, had apparently imagined that treaty and international law would be sufficient to enforce the supranational will. It may be that, in their appreciation of the Union's domestic behaviour, they were correct; the fundamental authority of the Union's institutions has not hitherto been called into question, though the failure of France and Germany to abide by the Union's financial stability pact gives warning of trouble ahead. It is in the Union's external relations, those both of it as a collectivity and of its individual member states, that the weakness is apparent, and never more so than over the crisis with Saddam's Iraq. The crisis of 2002–03 revealed a fundamental breach in foreign policy attitude between 'Europe', both the Union itself and most of the states that compose it, and America. The crisis made it obvious that the United States (originator of the League of Nations idea of collective action that inspired 'Europe', to be enforced at harshest by economic sanction) had been hardened by fifty years of Cold War confrontation to settle for nothing less than bringing transgressors of international order to compliance by military action. The neo-conservatives were merely expressing a national attitude. The Europeans, once so militarist, had by contrast espoused a philosophy of international action that actually rejected action and took refuge in the belief that all conflicts of interest were to be settled by consultation, conciliation and the intervention of international agencies. The conflict of approach between 'hard cop' America and 'soft cop' Europe became manifest in the months that preceded the outbreak of the war.

Iraq's relations with the outside world were governed, following its unsuccessful annexation of Kuwait, by a series of resolutions adopted by the United Nations, eventually to number fifteen altogether. Before the adoption of Resolution 1441 on 9 November 2002, which the United States and Britain were to use as their legal justification for instituting military action against Iraq, the most important of the relevant UN resolutions was 687, adopted immediately after the First Gulf War. Framed to legalize military action if Iraq persisted in the acquisition or development of weapons of mass destruction or their means of delivery – it should be remembered that the results of the First Gulf War had not given the victorious coalition forces the opportunity to inspect weapon sites in Iraq – it demanded unconditionally 'the destruction, removal, rendering harmless of all chemical and biological weapons and all stocks of agents and all related subsystems and components and all research, development, support and manufacturing facilities related thereto; and all ballistic missiles with a range greater than 150 kilometres [approximately 93 miles], and related major parts and repair and production facilities'. Resolution 687 was accepted by international lawyers as reinforcing Resolution 678, that which had authorized the inception of the First Gulf War but which also legitimized all 'subsequent relevant resolutions needed to restore international peace and security' to the region.

Resolution 678 had underpinned the actions of the United States, Britain and other allied nations in enforcing restraint on Saddam in the years after 1991, in particular the 'no fly' principle in northern and southern Iraq. The heightening of Western hostility towards Saddam, following the election of President George W. Bush and 9/11, was at first largely justified by invoking 678, which remained in force. Then, as the new American administration became increasingly concerned by the threat of Iraq's continuing with its development of weapons of mass destruction, 678 came to seem insufficient. In 1999, as the Clinton administration drew towards its close, a new resolution, 1284, had been passed in the United Nations, intended to reinforce the régime imposing inspection measures against weapons of mass destruction imposed by 687. That measure had created an inspection system known as UNSCOM, which had proved extremely effective, far more effective than recognized at the time or afterwards. UNSCOM worked inside Iraq for over seven years, discovering and destroying much of Saddam's arsenal of weapons of mass destruction (WMD). As its agents could use the leverage of denying oil sales in the face of Iraqi non co-operation, its demands for access to WMD sites had usually to be obeyed, to Saddam's disgust. UNSCOM's operational success led eventually to his refusing its inspectors any farther facilities in 1998 and their withdrawal from the country. UNSCOM was replaced by UNMOVIC, an altogether less rigorous régime, under Resolution 1284; even 1284 was opposed by several members of the Security Council, including Russia and France, which were profiting commercially by provisions that allowed Saddam to export oil in return for humanitarian aid (the 'oil-for-food' programme); Saddam, like a Roman emperor of old, had instituted a rationing system to provide dutiful subjects with essentials. In any case, Saddam declined to respect 1284 and refused UN inspectors access.

Saddam's defiance of 1284 inaugurated his downfall. It led the United States and Britain to seek a new UN resolution that would bring him to heel. Washington was less concerned by the need to restrain Saddam under legal authority. The UN Charter, though outlawing military action by one state against another unless authorized by the Security Council, provided, under Article 51, wide latitude for measures of self-defence. The United States had acted under Article 51 to attack the Taleban in Afghanistan in 2002. Britain, however, more influenced by the prevailing European distaste for military action of any sort, unless legally buttressed, was anxious to observe the proprieties. The Prime Minister, Tony Blair, remained committed, however, to supporting President Bush in the war against terrorism, in which Saddam Hussein was identified by Western intelligence as a frontrunner. America was anxious to secure British support in any move against Saddam. During September and October 2002, therefore, American legal officers co-operated with their British counterparts to draft a new resolution for submission to the UN, which would authorize joint military action. Its wording was finally agreed in early November and submitted to the Security Council as Resolution 1441. It stated that Iraq was still in 'material breach' of Resolution 678 of 1990 and all subsequent resolutions affecting its régime. It required the Iraqi government to prove that it no longer possessed weapons of mass destruction and to co-operate with the inspectors of UNMOVIC. It allowed it a 'final opportunity' for co-operation; it warned that, failing such co-operation, 'serious consequences' would follow.

Much has been made subsequently by legalists of the Security Council's failure to adopt its usual form of words, 'all necessary means', to warn of the threat of military action. That seems specious. Resolution 1441 clearly menaced Saddam with severe penalties at the hands of the responsible powers unless he opened Iraq to unrestricted inspection of its military facilities. Should he fail to do so, a repetition of 1991 would follow. Then his forces had been deployed on the territory of Kuwait, proclaimed by him, illegally, to be Iraq's nineteenth province. What he now risked, if he persisted in intransigence, was a direct Western attack on the territory of Iraq proper.

Following the passage of Resolution 1441, there ensued a curious passage of diplomatic dissent by the larger European powers and domestic protest by their populations. The reaction to Resolution 1441 was highly 'European'. The Union's inner circle, France, Germany and Luxembourg, though not Italy, the latter taking unexpectedly a stoutly Atlanticist position, struggled by every means to distance themselves from the decisions of the United States, to put legal obstacles against military measures in its way and to mobilize opposition to its policy in the United Nations. Newer members of the European Union, Spain in particular, gave America wholehearted support, as did recent and aspirant member states in Eastern Europe. Popularly, a European fault line appeared. East of the old Iron Curtain, the European population came out for President Bush. Correctly recognizing Saddam as essentially Stalinist, they supported America's determination to discipline the sort of tyrant who had created the system under which they had suffered for so many of the postwar years. Their governments took a similar position. Poland, which most valued its new status as an American ally through its membership of NATO, actually agreed to send a small military contingent to join the coalition forces. Hungary, Bulgaria and Romania granted vital staging rights to American forces. The Czech Republic and Latvia disassociated themselves from expressions of anti-American opinion. West of the old Iron Curtain, by contrast, popular anti-war majorities appeared. They were large in France and over-whelming in Germany. Even in Britain, whose government proved America's staunchest ally throughout the diplomatic crisis of 2003 and the war that followed, many newspapers declared an anti-American position and demonstrations staged by crowds esti-mated to include over one million people took to the streets.

It was the active opposition of governments formally allied to the United States that most troubled Washington and caused the greatest diplomatic damage. Germany, throughout the Cold War years America's most compliant ally on the European continent, revealed a face to Washington never previously shown. Gerhard Schroeder, its Chancellor, actually campaigned for re-election on an anti-American platform, apparently seeking to compensate for his personal unpopularity by espousing the popular mood of the moment. President Chirac of France went much farther. Chirac had a long personal involvement with Saddam's régime. As Prime Minister in the 1970s he had received Saddam in France, escorted him on a tour of French nuclear facilities and negotiated an agreement by which France sold Iraq the reactors, one containing enough enriched nuclear fuel to construct at least three nuclear warheads. He also agreed to train 600 Iraqi scientists and tech-nicians in nuclear technology. Under farther military agreements France supplied Iraq with $1.5 billion's worth of military equip-ment, including fighters, surface-to-air missiles and air defence equipment. Much of this material was destroyed during the First Gulf War. Iraq paid in oil but also entered into trading arrange-ments with France which, under the oil-for-food programme, resulted in France selling Iraq $1 billion's worth of exports as late as 2002.

Yet neither his long association with Iraq nor the pressure of a major Muslim minority in his country wholly explain Chirac's bitter anti-Americanism in the months preceding the war. What he felt, and it was felt too by many politicians and millions of elec-tors in France, Germany, Britain and elsewhere, was something different and new: a distaste for and hostility towards the use of military action for state purposes. The mood was not one of pacifism but of a changed outlook on the world which might be defined, in a term chosen by Professor Kenneth Minogue, as 'Olympianism'. Olympianism is by definition supranational – the European Union is in essence supranational, not intergovernmental – and seeks to influence and eventually control the behaviour of states not by the traditional means of resorting to force as a last resort but by supplanting force by rational procedures, exercised through supranational bureaucracy and supranational legal systems and institutions. One of the most striking developments in the world since 1945 has been the rise and proliferation of such bodies. The United Nations, deficient as its powers are, is the most obvious; the Hague Tribunal, set up to try war criminals, including those who commit crimes against their own people, and the European Court of Human Rights are others. The most notable, however, is the European Union, a truly Olympian body, since it seeks to supersede the governments of its constituent member states but to do so while lacking any ultimate means to enforce its decisions. Treaties, laws and regulations – millions of regulations – are the media of its power.

To many Europeans the Union provides an example and a vision of how the whole of the world might one day be governed. They are able to believe what they do because, thus far in its existence and development, none of its major decisions have ever been rejected by a member state. The workings of the Union do seem to lend credence to the idea in which Olympians most want to trust: that laws will be obeyed by their mere promulgation and that treaties can be self-enforcing.

The idea is, of course, illusory. 'Covenants without swords are but words' judged the supreme realist Thomas Hobbes and nothing that has happened since the seventeenth century gives reason to expect otherwise. Olympians, and particularly those who live within and are committed to the supranationalism of the European Union, have persuaded themselves differently. As long as 'Europe' continues to make apparent progress towards 'ever closer union' they can persist in the belief that civil servants will eventually displace soldiers and that judges can be supreme commanders.

It was not surprising therefore that the growing prospect of a resumption of war against Saddam should, in the spring of 2003, have brought the crisis that it did in the Western world. All European governments, those recently liberated from Communist oppression excepted, were run by men affected to some degree by Olympianism. The American government, by contrast, was run by men who were emphatically not so influenced. The neo-conservatives, who included in practice the President himself, were old-fashioned believers in the irreplaceable importance of the nation state and in the ultimate primacy of arms as a means of enforcing the national will. Hence the nature of the quarrel that ensued: on one side of the Atlantic the insistence that Saddam should allow unfettered access to Iraq's territory by inspectors authorized to go wherever they choose and see what and whom-soever they desired, under threat of unilateral military action in the event of noncompliance; on the other, an equally powerful insistence that such inspection should not be constrained by a time limit and that, if military action were to be undertaken, a farther UN resolution, beyond Resolution 1441 of 9 November 2002 which threatened 'serious consequences' – the 'second reso-lution' as it became known – should be adopted. In the event, as the dispute hardened, President Chirac appeared to oppose the taking of any military action at all and to be ready to use the French veto in the Security Council to oppose it.

A time limit had indeed been attached to Resolution 1441. Iraq had to declare its acceptance of the resolution within a week of its adoption. It then had thirty days to provide the UN with evidence of what weapons of mass destruction it retained, if any, or of how and when such weapons had been destroyed if that was the case. Besides providing the evidence, Iraq also had to permit the readmission of UNMOVIC, successor to the earlier UNSCOM, which, frustrated by Iraqi non co-operation, had withdrawn from the country in 1999. Not, however, before submitting a final report; UNSCOM had stated that its inspec-tors, who had had access to Iraqi governmental documentation, had been unable to account for 6,000 chemical aircraft bombs, seven Iraqi surface-to-surface missiles and two Russian-supplied Scuds. They had farther failed to account for much chemical and biological weapon material, including that capable of producing 26,000 litres of anthrax and 1.5 tons of VX gas. To exemplify the threat posed by such stocks, UNSCOM noted that 140 litres of VX could kill a million people.

UNMOVIC's inspection teams arrived in Iraq on 25 November 2002. They were led by Hans Blix, a former Swedish foreign minister, not the American or British first choice. The Americans would have preferred the man who had led UNSCOM, Rolf Ekeus, another Swede who had impressed observers by his rigorous methods and his dissatisfaction at Iraqi evasions. Security Council members indulgent of Saddam's pretensions to be a conventional head of state, including France and Russia, had opposed the re-appointment of Ekeus; the United States had opposed the choice of Blix, whom it regarded as 'soft', but without success. The UNMOVIC teams were accompanied by others from the International Atomic Energy Agency (IAEA), led by Mahomed ElBaradei, who would appear with Blix before the Security Council in the weeks to come. UNMOVIC's teams, numbering almost 100 inspectors out of a strength of 270 available, began at once to visit suspect sites in Iraq and to interview Iraqi scientists identified as having knowledge which UNMOVIC needed. Resolution 1441 authorized their transferral to places outside Iraq where they could be debriefed beyond governmental supervision. There was a multiple mismatch between what the Americans and British wanted from the inspection, how Iraq was willing to co-operate with UNMOVIC's methods and what UNMOVIC was trying to do. UNMOVIC sought to survey a country the size of France to declare it clean of WMD; the Iraqi government was concerned to provide paper evidence that it had nothing to hide; America and Britain wanted material verification that all Iraqi WMD had been destroyed. The latter, short of a physical occupation of the country, was impossible to provide; UNMOVIC had set itself an unfeasible task;

Iraq, however much documentation it published, was unlikely to be believed.

So proved to be the case. On 7 December Iraq delivered to the UN office in Baghdad an enormous cache of documents, having previously displayed it to the world media. The forty-three bound volumes, written in English, six folders and twelve CD-ROMs were claimed by General Hassam Muhammad Amin, the Iraqi government's nominated liaison officer with UNMOVIC, to demonstrate that Iraq had already complied with Resolution 1441. 'We are a country', he said, 'devoid of weapons of mass destruction. This fact is known to all countries including the United States of America and Britain and all those concerned.' The delivery of the Iraqi documents to the UN caused a short-lived sensation. The BBC, with an unctuousness that would characterize much of its reporting on the politics of the crisis, declared Iraq to be 'bullish' in the aftermath of the documentary presentation and gave the impression that the prospect of war had receded.

When the documents were delivered for perusal to the competent authorities – UNMOVIC had an office in New York, the IAEA in Vienna – both Blix and ElBaradei announced that it would take weeks to analyse the contents, then months to verify the information in Iraq. President Bush was therefore confronted with the prospect of more delay before bringing Saddam to face the threat of military action if he did not physically demonstrate that he had disarmed. He was frustrated at the prospect and even more frustrated when Blix stated that the Iraqi disclosures would be distributed to all fifteen members of the UN Security Council. The President suspected that some would seek to protract the inspection process farther and that others – France foremost – would attempt to use the material to block resort to military action altogether. As the US had possession of the Iraqi documentation, however, Blix and potential procrastinators could be outflanked. Only the four other permanent members of the Security Council – France, Britain, Russia and China – were given a full set of the papers. The non-permanent members were provided with edited extracts.

Yet the Iraqi presentation, because of its inadequacy, provided the United States with the opportunity it now sought: to demonstrate that Saddam was defying the authority of the UN. The Iraqi papers were a tired collection of old material, disclosing nothing not already known. Hans Blix privately admitted as much. He told some of his UNMOVIC associates, 'Saddam might not like foreigners crawling around his country but if he wants to get out of this mess, he has to engage with us'. Saddam's difficulty, like Blix's, was that the UN's success in securing the readmission of UNMOVIC to Iraq solved nothing. It was posited on the notion, which became an endlessly repeated media catchphrase that somewhere in Iraq there was waiting 'a smoking gun' to be discovered by the inspectors. The 'smoking gun', a particularly vacuous media notion, would have been a cache of chemical weapons, a WMD production facility, a stock of weapons-grade nuclear material or an armoury of missiles capable of delivering warheads to ranges greater than 150 kilometres. Given the size of Iraq relative to that of the inspection teams, and the very small compass of any hiding place in which forbidden weapons could be concealed, Blix's inspectors could have beaten the coverts for years without statistically material hope of finding anything relevant to their investigation. UNMOVIC had been sent on a wild goose chase, as Blix knew and partially admitted in the months following the Iraqi disclosure of 7 December by his begging for time. Saddam knew the same. UNMOVIC had been set the impossible task of proving a negative, that Saddam no longer had forbidden weapons. It was unlikely that, over any foreseeable period, Blix or ElBaradei could prove anything, one way or the other. Saddam was in a comparable fix. He had turned himself into a victim of his own fictions and evasions. Because of his systematic mendacity, he had lost the capacity to persuade anyone that he was telling the truth. Even had he, in the last weeks of free action he enjoyed as President of a sovereign country, had the UN inspectors escorted to the places he knew to be WMD sites, he would not have convinced the powers gathering against him that he had made a full disclosure. The tangled web of deception he had contrived in his last ten years of power was the cause of his own downfall.

President Bush was not prepared to follow Blix or anyone else through the tortuous process of an inspection fated not to produce results. On 19 December 2002, he declared Iraq to be in 'material breach' of Resolution 1441. Colin Powell, his Secretary of State and a known moderate, stated that 'Iraq's non-compliance and defiance of the international community has brought it closer to the day when he has to face the consequences. This declaration [the presentation of December 7] fails totally to move us in the direction of a peaceful solution.'

The policy of direct confrontation with Saddam met with acceptance in the United States. The administration's equation of his defiance of the UN over WMD with its war on terrorism evoked popular support. In Europe the situation proved different. The American government was already aware that in Western Europe it could count only on Italy, Spain and Britain to support its war policy. During the first months of 2003 the British government's difficulty in sustaining commonality of purpose with America became apparent. The beginnings of popular dissent, which were to culminate in large-scale anti-war demonstrations, emerged. Much of the British media, including the BBC, revealed its hostility. Most troublingly for the Prime Minister, Tony Blair, the Labour Party in Parliament, which he had controlled sinuously throughout his first years in power and at the beginning of his second term of government, began to show signs of serious dissent. Labour is a broad church, accommodating many doctrines. Two which have to be placated at all times, however, are anti-Americanism and anti-militarism, particularly if the use of military force is threatened in what might be represented as a neo-colonialist cause. Saddam was an unlikely favourite of Labour's anti-colonialist wing. He was patently a tyrant and oppressor of his own people. He ought also to have been disfavoured by the Labour anti-war party, being one of the most flagrant regional warlords of modern times. Nevertheless, he had credentials which resonated with some Labour ideologues. He was undeniably anti-American; he was also anti-Israeli, a new enthusiasm with some Labour backbenchers; and he made himself appear a military underdog, threatened with the overwhelming force of Western military power.

Many on the Labour backbenches did not like the manifestation of military power in any form; they were, in most cases unwittingly, adherents of the Olympian outlook that believed treaty, legal agreement and diplomatic negotiation sufficient to settle international differences. When, after President Bush's declaration of 19 December 2002 that Iraq was in 'material breach' of Resolution 1441, which threatened 'serious consequences' to Iraq for its failure fully to disclose its WMD state, a declaration falling short of the UN's usual warning that 'all necessary measures' would follow, the dissenters began to demand what became known as the 'second resolution'. They wanted, in effect, the case for military action against Iraq to be taken back to the Security Council and authorized by an additional vote.

There was no such demand in the American Congress, whose members were satisfied that fifteen UN resolutions, including 1441 but originating in 687 of March 1991, which required Iraq to accept under international supervision the destruction of all weapons of mass destruction and their means of delivery, sufficed to justify military action in the face of Saddam's noncompliance. The British Parliament, and a sizeable portion of the British electorate, was soon to show that it dissented. By early February 2003, the anti-war movement in Europe was in full flood. On Saturday 15 February some 100 million protesters in 600 cities took to the streets; perhaps as many as 2 million demonstrated in London. They were not a rent-a-crowd of ageing anti-nuclear protestors or anti-everything dissidents. Many were members of the sober middle class, who had been touched by the Olympian ethic of opposition to any form of international action lying outside the now commonly approved limits of legal disapproval and treaty condemnation. Tony Blair, the 'pretty straight sort of guy', had been hoist with his own petard of decency. Many of the marchers who thronged London's streets were exactly the people whose votes he solicited: Christian, high-minded, internationalist, pro-European.

Worse was to come. The anti-war feeling in the parliamentary Labour Party was strengthening and when on 21 February the chief whip issued an instruction demanding support for a pro-war vote five days later, the dissidents began to organize. An anti-war amendment to the motion was tabled within the hour, getting sixty names underneath the statement that 'the case for military action is not yet proven'. The Labour whips kept calm, believing that, as usually happened, much of the support would fall away on the day. The Prime Minister, his party's chief electoral asset, lobbied hard, inviting the leading anti-war protesters to meet him to discuss their concerns. He had confidence in his own very great powers of persuasion; he also doubted his backbenchers' willingness to weaken his standing. Many of them, however, were in an unreasonable mood. The temptation to indulge deep-seated ideological emotions – anti-Americanism, anti-militarism – was too strong to resist. The Prime Minister told the visiting German Foreign Minister, Joschka Fischer, himself a leading opponent of any war, that he was confident of keeping the number of votes against the motion below 100, perhaps even below fifty. In the event, the tone of the debate was against the government and when the house divided on the evening of 26 February, 121 Labour members voted for the anti-war amendment. It was a deliberate slight to the Prime Minister and a serious setback for his policy.

Yet, strained as he was by the intensity of the crisis and harassed by the disaffection of many he had counted as personal as well as political friends, he retained his resilience and his belief in himself. Tony Blair is that unusual being, a politician sustained by a sense of morality. He believed New Labour, a party he had invented almost single-handedly, was a necessary force for good in his country's domestic life. He also believed that its foreign policy was a necessary force for good in a wicked world. Soon after the vote of 26 February, on a flight to see his European ally, the Spanish Prime Minister, he made to attendant journalists a declaration of faith. Its tone was the opposite of Olympian. It had historical echoes, but not those favoured by his party opponents. He did not hark back, as so many of them did, to the idealist illusions of the appeasers of the 1930s or to the deflated expectations of the supporters of the League of Nations. He took, instead, a Churchillian tone. 'A majority of decent and well-meaning people', he told his little audience in the aircraft, 'said that there was no need to confront Hitler and that those who did were warmongers.' Then, referring to his earlier support for 'progressive war' in the Balkans and elsewhere, 'progressive war' being another of his moralistic inventions, he went on, 'I'm proud of what we've done in Kosovo and Afghanistan, and, in a different way, by supporting the régime in Sierra Leone . . . if you go back now, for all the problems they have got, and you ask if we did the right thing, I believe we did. Those who benefited most from military action had been the people of those countries . . . I believe we have to do this in Iraq, the people of Iraq will be the main beneficiaries.' In a final affirmation of his moral position as the apostle of progressive war, he replied to a questioner who asked why he was so committed to the American President's war policy: 'I believe in it. I am truly committed to dealing with this, irrespective of the position of America. If the Americans were not doing this, I would be pressing for them to be doing so'.

Events in the military sphere were now moving to bring about the outcome he insisted was morally justifiable, as well as politically necessary. By early March most of the forces committed to Operation Iraqi Freedom (Operation Telic in mundane British phraseology) were in place in Kuwait; 170,000 troops were on the ground, dozens of ships on station, hundreds of aircraft deployed for action, some close to the scene of coming combat, some preparing to fly from bases thousands of miles distant. The obstacles to the inception of the operation were few, and all political. Saddam persisted in his refusal to placate his enemies; perhaps after his long years of successful defiance he did not know how. In Britain the Labour Party's dissidents were demanding yet another vote on the transition to war and drawing on popular resistance – 'Not in My Name' was a favourite slogan – to justify parliamentary revolt. At the United Nations, Britain and America – Britain more insistently than America, which scarcely attempted to disguise its loss of faith in the Security Council's commitment to maintaining international order – were pressing for what had become known in Britain as the 'second resolution' for war, to succeed 1441. The working out of these processes would occupy the early weeks of March 2003.

On 7 March Hans Blix made a presentation – his third – of his findings in Iraq. He testified, to American displeasure and British disquiet, that the Iraqis were co-operating more fully with UNMOVIC than they had done in the past, though not to the point of full disclosure. He announced that he had investigated American claims of the existence of mobile biological warfare laboratories and underground facilities but had been unable to authenticate either. Turning to Iraqi delivery systems, he described what he had discovered about the al-Samoud missile. A development of the Russian Scud, itself an improved version of the German V-2 of 1944, its range undoubtedly, if slightly, exceeded 150 kilometres, forbidden under Resolution 687 (that range had been chosen because, subtracting the extent of Kurdish territory from Iraq proper, it would prevent Saddam from launching missiles against Israel); thirty-four al-Samoud missiles had been destroyed, about a third of the number he was satisfied existed. Given more time, at least several months, he could conclude his investigations. More time was precisely not what the Americans wanted Saddam to be allowed. Blix's pedantic manner infuriated the Americans present at this speech; it reinforced their doubts about his suitability as head of UNMOVIC. Their frustration was reinforced when ElBaradei, speaking for the International Atomic Energy Agency, dismissed British intelligence claims that Iraq had obtained supplies of uranium from the African state of Niger. They were based, he said, on a patently forged document. As the British Prime Minister had based many of his arguments for carrying war to Iraq on an intelligence dossier, opened to the public the previous September, Britain even more than America was discountenanced by ElBaradei's announcement. With other matters, it would return to haunt the Prime Minister when the September dossier became the centre point of a major political crisis, focused on the justification for having taken military action, in the aftermath of the war.

Blix's presentation of 7 March and ElBaradei's footnote to it, inaugurated the final passage of political and diplomatic bargaining before the war began. It was not one which involved the Americans, who were now set on war and held firmly to the view that justification for it was provided by the UN resolutions already adopted, beginning with 678 over ten years before and confirmed by 1441. President Bush was concerned by UN politicking only insofar as it would help Tony Blair, his principal foreign ally, to sustain his base of support in his home country. The Prime Minister, by contrast, was desperately anxious for the 'second resolution' in the UN, for what threatened to be a demand for a 'second vote' in the House of Commons and for his legal experts' assurance of the lawfulness of taking military action, in the increasingly complex arena of international law. In the early days of March the British government concentrated on securing the second resolution in the Security Council. Even optimists despaired at swinging the vote. There were fifteen votes, the five of the permanent members – the United States, Britain, France, Russia, China – and those of the ten alternating members. A majority of nine was required. The votes of the United States and Britain were assured. China, during the Cold War aligned with Iraq, was now more concerned to maintain its new Western friendships and would either support the United States or abstain. Bulgaria and Spain would back the Anglo-American position. Pakistan would probably abstain. Germany would be opposed. The 'swing' voters were reckoned to be Mexico, Cameroon, Angola, Guinea and Chile. The position of France, a permanent member, a political if not military member of NATO, a pillar of the Western world, would depend upon the decision of President Chirac. Not truly an Olympian, since he took a characteristically Gallic and realist view of the primacy of national power and armed force, for all his outward commitment to the legalism of the European movement, Chirac's voting choice would be determined entirely by French prejudice.

In the first week of March British efforts to secure the nine votes necessary for adoption of the 'second resolution' giving UN authority to taking war to Iraq became almost frantic. The British ambassador to the UN, Sir Jeremy Greenstock, lobbied his fellow representatives on the Security Council constantly, offering changes of wording and calling on old friendships. He was also daily, sometimes hourly, on the telephone to the Foreign Office and 10 Downing Street. All the news he brought was bad. At one stage he reported that there might be only four votes, besides those of Britain and the United States, for their resolution. Finally, on 10 March the effort to win UN approval was brought to a full stop by Jacques Chirac. In a television broadcast to the French people from his presidential offices in the Elysée Palace, he announced that France would vote against, 'whatever the circumstances'. He seemed to imply that France would use its veto if necessary. Later his officials indicated that he had been misinterpreted: counting voting intentions as they had been declared, he knew that the Americans and British could not win. He was merely aligning himself with the majority.

That was not how his position was viewed by Britain and America. They chose to regard Chirac's declaration as an act of betrayal. The Americans shrugged off the rebuff; they had always been prepared to act unilaterally and anyhow reposed no confidence in France. The Prime Minister was genuinely outraged. However self-deludingly, he had always believed in his personal ability to straddle the Atlantic divide, sustaining the special relationship with America while remaining on co-operative terms with his fellow Europeans, even in the face of Chirac's Gallic nationalism. Now the friendship he believed he had forged with Chirac was shown to be hollow.

The setback was not merely personal. It also objectively undercut his position as a national leader. His personal and press staff swiftly shifted their efforts, to represent Chirac as the cause of Britain's difficulties in winning support for the war. They could not, however, rescue him from his troubles at home. An ungrateful Labour Party, which he had led to two electoral triumphs, was reverting to type, allowing its taste for anti-Americanism and anti-militarism to overcome its political common sense. Unwillingly Blair had promised the party yet another opportunity to debate the justification for going to war and this other 'second vote' now monopolized the energies of the Prime Minister's entourage. Despite Chirac's disabling declaration, diplomatic activity continued at the United Nations. Security Council members were still seeking means to postpone a military showdown. A delay of up to forty-five days was proposed, to give Saddam a final chance to prove his willingness to disarm. Sir Jeremy Greenstock, for Britain, attached to that timetable a list of 'benchmarks' Saddam should be asked to meet, the surrender of all his chemical and biological agents, his mobile WMD production facilities, the destruction of all remaining al-Samoud missiles and the transfer of the thirty most important Iraqi scientists to Cyprus for a UN debriefing. Hans Blix, enthused by the 'benchmark' scheme, went farther. He suggested that Saddam be required to broadcast a statement to the Arab peoples admitting his faults, his evasions of the UN resolutions and his firm determination to comply with the UNMOVIC regime. For a moment the benchmark scheme looked hopeful. Then on 14 March Chile, a non-permanent Security Council member, formally proposed that Iraq be given thirty days to meet the benchmarks. The proposal was immediately quashed by the US ambassador to the UN. 'I was asked several days ago about whether or not the President would be open to extending the deadline from thirty to forty-five days – now you could say that's twenty-six to forty-one days. If it was a non-starter then, it's a non-starter now.' The Prime Minister at once told the President that he accepted the war should begin the following week, that of 17–24 March, but asked that they should have a final meeting to show common cause. The meeting was arranged to take place with the Spanish and Portuguese prime ministers in the Azores, the Portuguese islands off the African coast, on 16 March.

Neither the promise of the Azores meeting nor an American offer to embark on a new attempt to negotiate a settlement between the Israelis and the Palestinians, the 'road map' scheme, were sufficient to palliate the Prime Minister's party troubles. On 17 March, immediately after his return from the Azores, where it had been agreed to give Saddam exactly twenty-four hours to comply with all outstanding UN resolutions if military action were not to begin, one of Labour's most difficult figures, Robin Cook, formerly Foreign Secretary, currently Leader of the House of Commons, appeared at Downing Street to announce his resignation. It was not unexpected and, to his credit as a party loyalist, he indicated his willingness to minimize the difficulty it would cause the government. In his speech to the House later that day, he confined himself to expressing disbelief in the intelligence appreciation used to endorse the need for military action and to explaining his moral reservations. One of the best parliamentary speakers of his era, Cook received a considerate hearing from both sides.

Nevertheless his resignation, together with that of eight other Labour officeholders and of a legal expert at the Foreign Office, did farther damage to the Prime Minister's stance. His inner circle held firm and continued to provide dedicated support. Unlike President Bush, however, who could count on the wholehearted endorsement of his policies by his own circle, by the cabinet, by Congress and by the overwhelming majority of the American people, still in a fervently patriotic mood created by the outrage of 9/11, Tony Blair was in a precarious and exposed position. It was an odd predicament for a national leader. On the threshold of war, Britain usually rallies around its government, whatever its party label. The country had rallied, famously, in 1939–40, when the threat was Nazi aggression. It had rallied during the Korean crisis, distant though that event was, dramatically during the Falklands and once again during the First Gulf War. Only over what was still called 'Suez' in 1956 had the people wavered, and then because the Labour Party in opposition had declared the conflict with Egypt to be neo-colonialist. In 2003 the spectre of

Suez reappeared, with a curious difference. The Labour constituency, the industrial working class, had been pro-war in 1956 as it was in 2003; it was Labour's middle-class constituency which had opposed military action in 1956, while the rest of the middle class had supported the Conservative government. In 2003 wide sections of the middle class, much of it politically Conservative, went the other way. The most unlikely opponents of Labour's war policy emerged, professional people, the comfortably retired, even ex-officers. Tony Blair, a public schoolboy with distinctively officer-like characteristics, found himself suddenly isolated, dependent for control of Parliament on apparatchiks who, if in opposition, would certainly have voted against the policy he was pursuing. The later-twentieth-century, early-twenty-first-century obsession with rights, legalities and the judgement of international institutions, with Olympianism in all its aspects, had touched the great British middle-class. Once sublimely certain of the correctness of how its government acted, middle-class Britain had fallen into doubt.

It was therefore a great relief to the Prime Minister that, in the final days of the prewar crisis, the Attorney General, Lord Goldsmith, entered an opinion that furnished legal support for his decision to join the United States in going to war against Iraq. There were other opinions: Matrix, the legal chambers of his lawyer wife, Cherie Booth, had already announced its view that a resort to war without a second UN resolution would violate international law. Lord Goldsmith, in the aftermath of Robin Cook's resignation, argued differently. Basing his judgment on Chapter VII of the United Nations Charter, which authorizes the use of force for the purpose of restoring international order, he reviewed the effect of the resolutions affecting Iraq since 678 of 1990, which authorized the use of force against Iraq in support of 'all subsequent relevant resolutions needed to restore international peace and security'. He went on to argue that a material breach of Resolution 687, which required the destruction of all weapons of mass destruction and means of delivery, such as missiles, revived authority to use force under 678 and that by Resolution 1441, 'the UN determined that Iraq has been and remains in material breach of Resolution 687, because it had not fully complied with its obligations to disarm under that resolution'. The judgment might have been written at President Bush's dictation. As delivered by Britain's senior law officer, it gave full authorization to the Prime Minister to join with its fellow UN member, the United States, in opening military action against Iraq.

The only impediment to proceeding that remained was the need to win the 'second vote' on a motion for war in the House of Commons. The Prime Minister, anomalously, could count upon the votes of the Conservative opposition. The possibility of defeat was threatened only by his own dissidents, almost all on the back-benches. The 'payroll' vote, those MPs holding senior or junior government office or unpaid but semiofficial positions as parliamentary private secretaries, could be counted on to support the Prime Minister; there were 264 backbenchers, many of whom were loyalists and some, the 'waverers', who might be won over. Hidden in the parliamentary party, however, was a bloc of intransigents who would refuse to be moved. The party managers had been calculating its size on an almost hourly basis, analysing the politics of individuals and targeting those it hoped to win over for person-to-person interviews with senior ministers, sometimes with the Prime Minister himself. In the last resort, however, all turned on the impression Tony Blair would make in the speech he would deliver on the afternoon of 18 March as Prime Minister, leader of his party and spokesman for the nation.

Tony Blair is both a complex character and a complex personality. Upper middle-class in manner and appearance, to the distaste of many in his party, he is populist in sentiment, but ultimately immune to the temptations of popularity. Not an intellectual, though highly intelligent, his centre of gravity is moral; he has deeply held religious beliefs and an unshakeable conviction in the necessity to do what is right. He speaks easily and fluently, too much so at times, succumbing to the seduction of his own voice, and he possesses elements of the actor. An enthusiastic member of his school dramatic society, he was also a highly effective performer in court during his career as a barrister. He has great charm and the priceless political gift of appearing not to be a politician. When, however, the need arrives to speak from the heart, with force and moral conviction, he rises toweringly to the moment. That moment came on 18 March and he was heard by the House with its full attention. A few unworthy attempts at interruption, all from his own side, were ignored or brushed aside. When he moved into his peroration he commanded silence. 'In this dilemma', he said, 'no choice is perfect, no cause ideal. But on this decision [to support war or not] hangs the fate of many things. . . . This is not the time to falter [a Churchillian echo]. This is the time for this House, not just this Government or this Prime Minister, but for this House to give a lead, to show that we will stand up for what we know to be right, to show that we will confront the tyrannies and dictatorships and terrorists who put our way of life at risk, to show at the moment of decision that we have the courage to do the right thing'.

He said more, justifying his policy of alignment with the United States, assuring the House of his commitment to constructing peace between Israel and the Palestinians, referring again to the danger of weapons of mass destruction and arguing for the correctness of President Bush's policy of pre-emption, of anticipating attack by carrying attack to the enemy. Pre-emption and the evidence for weapons of mass destruction formed controversial passages in his speech and touched on the deepest Labour sensitivities. Nevertheless, those passages were outweighed by the fervour of his evident moral conviction. At a most difficult time for his premiership, he showed himself to be a master of the British political process and a fine national leader. When the House divided, the amendment moving that the case for war had not been made was defeated by 396 votes to 217. These included 129 Labour votes, besides those of the Liberals and other smaller parties, but the government had won. The war could now begin, with British as much as American endorsement.

THE EVE OF WAR
Disposition of Iraqi and Allied forces

Black Sea

GEORGIA

RUSSIAN FEDERATION

Caspian Sea

·Tbilisi

ARMENIA

AZERBAIJAN

·Baku

TURKEY

·Yerevan

Van Golu

·Diyarbakir

·Tabriz

Lake Urmia

·Mahabad

·Zakho

3 ‖‖ 10

IRAN

Mosul B XX Adnan

·Rawanda

Northern no-fly zone

·Kirkuk

·Sanandaj

Dayr az Zawr

XX B

SYRIA

R. Euphrates

·Tikrit

·Bakhtaran

Abu Kamal

Hadithah·

I   R   A   Q

·Khorramabad

B XX Baghdad

3 X s Southern no-fly zone

B XX B XX

JORDAN

Karbala·

·Hillah   Kut

·Dezful

·Najaf   C

Samawah·   C XX

A ‖

·Amarah

XXX A

·Ahvaz

20 March 2003
IRAQI FORCES
A   Regular army
B   Republican Guard
C   Irregulars
COALITION FORCES
1   US Army
2   US Marines
3   Special forces
4   British forces
▬   Armoured units

Areas under Kurdish control

A XX

Nasiriyah·

Kurnah·

C A   51

Basra·

Safwan

2 XXX XX 4

1MEF

1 XXX V

KUWAIT

·Kuwait City

The Gulf

N

0   100   200 miles
0   100   200   300 km

SAUDI   ARABIA

6

The American War

History repeats itself, though no two historians agree quite how. Those who reported the First Gulf War of 1990–91 had an almost eerie impression of events replicating themselves between Iraq and its enemies twelve years later but, once the campaign began to unfold, it was the differences rather than the similarities which commanded attention and demanded explanation. In February 1991 a very large and high-quality Western army confronted an equally large but low-quality Iraqi army and, following six weeks of intense aerial attack, destroyed its military capability in four days of fighting. In March 2003 a much smaller but even higher quality Western army confronted an Iraqi army degraded and ennervated by its earlier defeat and by twelve years of isolation from its foreign sources of supply and, during three weeks of high-speed advance over long distances, brought about not merely its disintegration but its apparent evaporation from the field of battle. By the beginning of April the evidence of defeat strewed the Iraqi landscape, discarded small arms, shot-riddled military vehicles, burnt-out tanks and the pathetic, ragged bodies of Iraqi dead; yet not only had Saddam's army disappeared from view. The signs lacked that it had ever been there. There were no columns of surrendering prisoners, no senior officers offering their capitulation. The war was over but where was the defeated enemy? For all the millions of rounds of ammunition expended, for all the thousands of tons of high-explosive delivered to targets, it was as if the Iraqi army had not existed in the first place. American and British soldiers could testify to the undoubted experience of combat, often at high intensity; but when the shooting stopped, their enemies had vanished.

Yet the Iraqi army had undoubtedly existed before the shooting began. Coalition intelligence had a clear picture of its order of battle and had drawn up detailed situation maps of its deployment on the ground. The Iraqi forces consisted of three elements. Militarily the most significant was the Republican Guard, founded by President Arif in the early 1960s as his régime's praetorian guard to protect it against coups and officered and to a considerable extent recruited from Arif's al-Jumaila tribe, who live in the al-Ramadi region on the Euphrates west of Baghdad. Originally only of brigade size, though with an integral tank regiment, it was progressively expanded under Arif's successors. Saddam raised it to a strength of six divisions, recruited and officered from men identified for their loyalty to himself personally and to the Ba'ath party. At the outbreak of war in 1991 it consisted of the Adnan Mechanized Division, the Baghdad Infantry Division, the Abed Infantry Division, the Medina Armoured Division, the Nebuchadnezzar Infantry Division and the Hammurabi Mechanized Division. Saddam also raised a Special Republican Guard of three brigades as an inner security force, commanded by his son Qusay, but it was not organized for combat. The Republican Guard retained its strength of 60,000 men in 2003, though its equipment, like that of all formations in Iraq, was badly serviced and short of spare parts. The Adnan, Baghdad and Abed divisions were stationed north of Baghdad, the Nebuchadnezzar and Hammurabi to the south and the Medina on the outskirts of the capital.

The so-called regular army had greatly shrunk in size since 1991. Then its paper strength was over forty divisions. By 2003, because of the losses suffered in the First Gulf War, of desertions and of inefficiencies of administration, the number of divisions totalled only seventeen: six infantry and two mechanized divisions in the north, one armoured and two infantry divisions in

US Secretary of State Colin Powell (*left*) talks with British Foreign Secretary Jack Straw (*centre*) and other officials, as US National Security Advisor Condoleezza Rice (*far right*) looks on, before a news conference by Prime Minister Tony Blair and President George W. Bush at Camp David, Maryland, 27 March 2003.

General Tommy Franks speaking to reporters at a press conference in the media centre at Camp As-Sayliyah, outside Doha, Qatar, 30 March 2003.

Iraqi Information Minister Muhammad Saeed al-Sahhaf speaks during a news conference in Baghdad, 22 March 2003. Sahhaf, who earned the nickname 'Comical Ali' during the Iraq War, handed himself in to US forces but was released after questioning.

The US military's Central Command (CENTCOM) personnel sit behind rows of networking computers in the Joint Operations Centre (JOC) as they process information relating to regional operations at Camp As-Sayliyah, Qatar.

The Coalition Land Forces Component Commander (LFCC) Lieutenant-General John McKiernan who was based at CENTCOM during the war.

A USAF B-1 bomber from the 405th Expeditionary Air Wing pictured minutes after being refuelled by a KC-135 Stratotanker over the skies of Iraq on 25 March 2003 during Operation Iraqi Freedom.

Captain Tom Bryant of V Corps walks ahead of his Humvee during a fierce sandstorm as his unit heads into Iraq during the early days of the assault by coalition forces.

Cobra helicopter (US Marines) fires missiles in support of 1st Light Reconnaissance Battalion during a battle with Iraqi forces in northern Iraq. The 1st Light Recce Battalion is part of the 1st Marine Division.

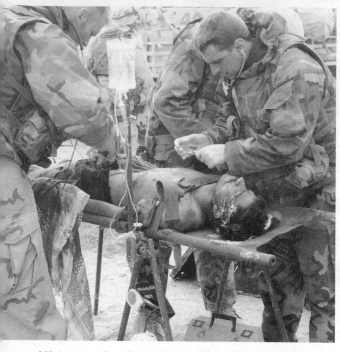

US Army medics of the 2nd Brigade provide treatment to an injured civilian during the early days of the conflict. This image was taken on 31 March 2003.

US special forces pictured in northern Iraq with members of the Kurdish fighters on the northern border where US special forces spearheaded the advance with the Kurds.

Chinook helicopter crewmen enjoy a quick break during operations in northern Iraq. The aircraft believed to be fitted with long-range fuel tanks for special forces operations were working in support of US airborne forces (173rd Airborne Brigade) that parachuted into northern Iraq from Aviano in Italy.

A US Airborne soldier drops into northern Iraq during the northern phase of the coalition advance.

A river crossing in northern Iraq. Marines of Delta Company 1st Light Armoured Reconnaissance Battalion of the 1st Marine Division drive across a bridge built by US Army engineers.

US Army M1-A1 Abrams of the 1st Tank Battalion, 1st Marine Division, pictured at An Nasariyah as it provides fire support for American troops entering the area.

Australian special forces Land Rover is packed into a US Chinook helicopter. The Australians played a key role in the coalition special forces, which deployed to the western desert.

US Army tanks and Bradley fighting vehicles with the 3rd Infantry Division Task Force 1-64 move north near Karbala in central Iraq, 2 April 2003.

The A-10 ground support aircraft known as the Warthog. This aircraft can fly high and fast or low and slow and is ideal for providing fire support to infantry troops. Sadly during the war an A-10 crew fired on a British armoured vehicle.

An Apache helicopter which crashed during preparation at Assembly Area SHELL on 30 March. The Apache came up against stiff resistance in Iraq and it is believed that at least one was shot down in northern Iraq.

US Naval special operations units pictured south of Basra. The rigid inflatable boats (RIBs) are equipped with 50-calibre machineguns and were used by the US teams to support advance force operations.

US Marine Sergeant Dan Lockward leads his fire team of Gun Two Lima Battery 3/11th Marines as they fire their M198 towed Field Howitzer during a fire mission on 13 April 2003.

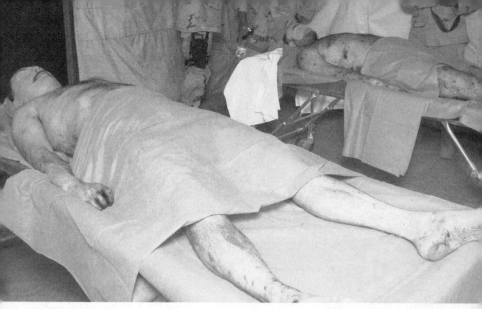

Saddam's sons Uday and Qusay pictured in the mortuary after they had been hunted down in northern Iraq by US special forces. The brothers refused to surrender and died in the fire-fight with coalition forces.

A British Royal Marine from 42 Commando fires a Milan wire-guided missile at an Iraqi position on the Al Fao peninsula, southern Iraq, 21 March 2003.

British gunners from 7 Parachute Regiment Royal Horse Artillery fire their 105mm light gun during the artillery bombardment on Iraqi positions in the early weeks of the war.

British soldiers of the 1st Battalion the Parachute Regiment pictured in Land Rovers specially fitted with 50-calibre guns during operations inside Iraq.

The lead elements of the 3rd Battalion the Parachute Regiment advance into the northern part of Basra. The man on the left is part of a specialist sniper team.

A British Army Warrior vehicle passes a destroyed Iraqi T-55 tank south of Basra, 2 April 2003.

A convoy of Humvees of the 5th Marines pictured on 26 March 2003 during a sandstorm in the drive towards Baghdad. The vehicles are equipped with TOW (Tube launched Optically tracked Wire guided missile). The Marines were part of the 1st Light Armoured Reconnaissance Battalion.

A US Army 3rd Division tank rolls across the tarmac of Baghdad International Airport during an allied advance on the Iraqi capital on 4 April 2003. US and Iraqi forces exchanged heavy fire throughout the day as they battled for control of the strategic facility.

US Marines from Charlie Company, 1st Battalion, 5th Marines fight their way through the streets as they make their way towards Saddam's Presidential Palace on the banks of the Tigris in Baghdad.

A statue of Saddam Hussein falls into the lower level of the main entrance to Saddam's palace grounds in Tikrit, around 100 miles northwest of Baghdad, 18 July 2003. The US army used explosives to remove the statue.

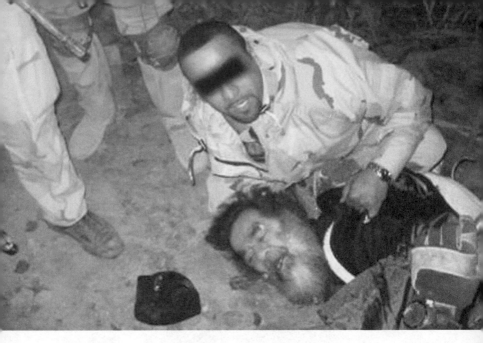

Saddam Hussein being dragged by US troops on 13 December 2003 out of an underground hole at a farm in the village of ad-Dawr, near his home town of Tikrit in northern Iraq. A unit from the 4th Infantry Division found him hiding in a small man-made cellar, along with a series of secret papers and several hundred thousand dollars.

The former President pictured minutes after capture.

the centre, deployed on the border with Iran, and in the south two armoured, one mechanized and three infantry divisions. All were undermanned. Even the Iraqi government seems to have lacked a clear picture of the army's strength: perhaps 200,000 at most or as few as 150,000. Its equipment stocks had also fallen disastrously low. In 1991 it had over 5,000 tanks, but in 2003 it had only 2,000; nearly 7,000 armed personnel carriers in 1991, in 2003 less than 2,000; self-propelled artillery equipment 500 in 1991, 150 in 2003; towed guns 3,000 in 1991, under 2,000 in 2003. Most of the Iraqi equipment, moreover, largely Soviet but some French in origin, was old, even antiquated; its T-55 tanks were a fifty-year-old model, worse than obsolete, actually death traps if pitted against modern Western tanks. Everything – tanks, personnel carriers, artillery pieces – lacked spare parts and was badly serviced. The same was true of the anti-aircraft equipment; before 1990 Iraq had operated an extensive, integrated air-defence system, with many radars linked by fibre-optic connections to control centres. In the interwar period, 1991–2003, when America, Britain and their allies enforced the 'no-fly' zones over northern and southern Iraq, much of this equipment was destroyed by radar-seeking missiles, the result of Saddam's having ordered the allied aircraft to be attacked or targeted despite the inevitably harmful consequences. The only effective equipment in the Iraqi armoury were a few surface-to-air missiles, including some shoulder-fired systems – but these were useful only against heli-copters and low-flying aircraft – and the South African-built 155mm G5 gun.

A third category of Iraqi armed force, beside the Republican Guard and the regular army – a misnomer, since the soldiers were conscripts, not long-service enlistees – were the irregulars, who were often to prove the most dedicated fighters. There were several varieties of irregular units. Loosely and collectively known as *fedayeen* ('martyrs'), after the Islamic fighters who opposed the Soviet army in Afghanistan, they included members of the Popular Army founded by Saddam in the 1970s as a political counter-weight to the army itself, Ba'ath party faithful and a considerable contingent of anti-Western fanatics from other Islamic countries, Syria, Egypt, Saudi Arabia, Algeria, Morocco and Pakistan foremost. Their number was hard to calculate. As the British complained at the beginning of their efforts to administer the mandate in 1921, the Iraqi countryside was awash with weapons; almost every Iraqi male possessed a rifle and was ready to use it, in tribal, inter-village, family or personal dispute. The situation was not different eighty years later.

Air power was the only element of Iraq's defences with which the coalition did not have to reckon. In 1991 the Iraqi air force, equipped with several hundred Soviet and French aircraft, was still formidable, even if unequal to a full-scale confrontation. In the event it declined the challenge; after suffering heavy losses in the opening days of the campaign, it decamped *en masse* to Iran, where it was given refuge until the war was over. In 2003 only a remnant of Iraqi air strength survived. It made no effort to contest the issue once the invasion began and much of its surviving equipment was discovered hidden in a remote location as the coalition forces advanced.

The force that the coalition opposed the Iraqis, though wholly outweighing it in quality, was altogether smaller than that which had fought the First Gulf War. Then the alliance had deployed eight American divisions (seven army, two marine), a British armoured division, a French light armoured division, two Egyptian and one Syrian divisions and contingents of varying size from Pakistan, Saudi Arabia and twelve other countries, totalling nearly 750,000 troops. They had been assembled through the relentless telephone diplomacy of President George H. W. Bush, who had also persuaded the coalition he created to add significant air and naval components to the troops General Schwarzkopf eventually commanded. President George W. Bush went to war with a considerably smaller deployment. The British, as before, sent a division and other naval, air and ground troops. Australia, which had sent a naval force to the 1991 war, again sent ships, together with aircraft and special forces. Otherwise the strength was exclusively American, the allies of 1991 having declined to lend support.

The American armed forces of the late twentieth century had emerged from a difficult past. Tiny before 1941, as befitted those of a country that eschewed involvement in world affairs, they had grown during the Second World War to become stronger at sea and in the air than any other and to include a large army of formidable fighting power. Sharply reduced in size during the peace that followed and in the belief that possession of nuclear weapons made larger conventional forces an expensive redundancy, they had been rapidly expanded to fight the Vietnam War of 1965–72. Its human costs and the political turmoil it engendered had cast the United States Army, in particular, into disarray. Belief in the value of the military vocation was compromised, morale and discipline were eroded. Much of civil society ceased to give support and the forces risked losing belief in themselves and their mission.

They were rescued by the emergence of a new generation of young officers who resolved to rebuild the military ethos from within. Gradually, under the patriotic Presidency of Ronald Reagan, the military regained its morale; President Reagan's extravagant spending on defence trumped the Soviet Union's ability to sustain the Cold War; new military doctrines and capabilities persuaded army, navy and air force that they had the capacity to meet any challenge the post-Cold War world would present. The test of their revived self-confidence came in 1991, when truly post-Vietnam forces took the field and achieved victory in a brilliant display of professional competence.

The expeditionary force of 2003 had put doubt behind it. Its officers and enlisted men, army, navy, air force, marines, knew that the Iraqis who opposed them did not match their quality, however measured. In terms of equipment, personnel, organization or military practice, they were better than any in the field and matched by only a tiny handful of close allies.

The force was commanded at the top by Central Command, created in the Reagan years to oversee operations beyond the continental United States and tri-service in composition. Inter-service rivalry had bedevilled American military activity throughout the Cold War, and inter-service rivalry had been farther compounded by demarcation disputes between the regional commands of the single services. The Central Command system, designed to place unified tri-service forces in any chosen theatre of operations, working under a commander having authority over all assigned components, had first been tried in the Gulf in 1990–91. The system had proved itself, though with need for refinement. The First Gulf War commander, Norman Schwarzkopf, an army general, had exercised his authority directly and with little regard for personal sensitivities. General Tommy Franks, the Central Command commander in 2003, was to work in a different way. Because he was also responsible for the continuing operation in Afghanistan, he could not directly control the land battle but had to delegate authority to the Third Army commander, Lieutenant General David McKiernan. Franks, moreover, was a markedly different character from Schwarzkopf, less of a showman, less overbearing and more thoughtful. By origin an enlisted man, he had begun his career in the artillery but made his way upwards in the armoured cavalry, itself an inter-arms organization comprising artillery and infantry as well as armoured components. He thus understood several different military disciplines and had also acquired an openness to the armed forces of other countries that was to be of the greatest value in an operation in which he had to control British and Australian as well as American forces. Perhaps because he had not been through the rigid processing of West Point, he has an enquiring mind, an ability to think on his feet and a remarkable freedom from the doctrinaire approach so often characteristic of the products of Sparta-on-Hudson. He is an attractive character, with a touching gratitude for the opportunity his army has given him to rise from his origins as a 'trailer park kid' to the rank of four star general.

In the expeditionary force the chain of command led from General Franks via General McKiernan to two subordinate formations, V Corps, part of Third Army, and the 1st Marine Expeditionary Force. V Corps consisted of 3rd Infantry Division, parts of 101st Airborne Division (Air Assault), a brigade of 82nd Airborne Division, to which was later added 173rd Airborne Brigade and parts of 4th Infantry Division. The 1st Marine Expeditionary Force was composed of 1st Marine Division, Task Force Tarawa, which was a reinforced marine brigade, and 3rd Marine Aircraft Wing.

An infantry division is an armoured division in all but name, fielding 270 Abrams tanks as well as self-propelled artillery, a large infantry component mounted in Bradley fighting vehicles and an integral unit of Apache helicopter gunships. It has the ability to form itself rapidly into battle groups – typically a Bradley battalion and a tank battalion – for tasks demanded by the changing tactical situation, and to subdivide its artillery to provide battle group support. Its helicopters are trained to operate on the 'cab rank' principle, answering calls to provide overhead support at short notice. The division could also call on air support from air force or navy squadrons, though those were not under command.

The Marine Expeditionary Force was organized differently, achieving a high degree of integration between its ground and air components. A marine air wing's aircraft are flown by marine pilots; wing and division are permanently associated. Marine divisions have long histories; 1st Marine Division had fought in the First World War and taken part in most of the great island battles of the Pacific War of 1942–45, as had its sub-units, 1st Marines, 4th Marines, 5th Marines and 7th Marines. These Marine regiments, like old-style British infantry regiments, have several battalions, with long and distinguished histories. 1st Battalion, 3rd Marines, for example, had fought at Guadalcanal and Pelelieu, bitter struggles with the Japanese in which it had won cherished battle honours. 1st Marine Division's infantry battalions were organized into three regimental combat teams, 1, 5 and 7 RCT, comprising 3rd/1st, 1st/4th and 2nd/23rd Marines, 1st, 2nd and 3rd/5th Marines and 1st and 3rd/7th Marines and 3rd/4th Marines. Each RCT also included a tank and a light armoured reconnaissance battalion and amphibious armour (Amtracs) from 2nd and 3rd Assault Amphibian Battalions. The divisional artillery was provided by three battalions of 11th Marines and combat engineers by 1st Marine Engineer Battalion.

It is the uniformly 'Marine' character of the three United States Marine Corps divisions that give them their formidable fighting power. Even in the highly cohesive modern US Army, slight fault lines exist between infantry, armour, artillery and helicopter units; they are recruited separately and trained separately, at camps owned by the branch to which they belong. Marines, by contrast, all join together and train together and are Marines before they are infantry, armour or artillery. The mythology of the Marines, expressed in the Marine Hymn and the motto, *Semper Fidelis* (Always Faithful), together with a litany of Corps slogans – including 'A Marine Never Dies' – has poetic truth. If a recruit chooses to think otherwise, he will be put straight by the long-service NCO of the Corps, gunnery sergeants and sergeant-majors, who are tradition's ultimate guardians. Marines are admired throughout the American armed forces and beyond, particularly by the British army and Royal Marines, who served with the USMC in Korea and the First Gulf War.

The 1st Marine Division and the 3rd Infantry Division provided General Franks with his main force for the drive on Baghdad. There were ancillary units. Some came from the 82nd Airborne Division and the 101st Airborne Division (Air Assault). The two are sister formations. Raised during the Second World War as parachute divisions, with a complement of glider infantry, they had dropped on the night of 5–6 June 1944 on the western flank of the Normandy bridgehead to open the invasion of Europe. Subsequently their glider infantry battalions had been disbanded, gliders proving too vulnerable to ground fire, and the 101st had eventually given up parachuting to become entirely heliborne, with a heavy complement of gunships to cover infantry landing at the point of assault. For the Iraq War the 101st deployed as a nearly complete formation, the 82nd provided a brigade. Also deployed was the 173rd, a 'separate' parachute brigade which dropped into Kurdistan to provide conventional support to the *peshmerga* guerrillas.

The other large formation available to General Franks was the British 1st (UK) Armoured Division, a hastily assembled formation consisting of the 7th Armoured Brigade, which had fought in the First Gulf War, the 16th Air Assault Brigade, composed of parachute and helicopter units, and the 3rd Commando Brigade of Royal Marines. Because the Commandos are a light force, trained and equipped for intervention operations, General Franks attached to them the 1st Marine Expeditionary Unit, which fielded tanks and helicopter gunships.

The plan for Operation Iraqi Freedom began to be drawn up as early as 1995, when Saddam's combination of deviousness and intransigence persuaded Washington that it might not be possible to avoid a military confrontation if his determination to develop and deploy weapons of mass destruction were to be quashed. The original problem was to choose a point of departure. Iraq is a difficult country to attack. Though it was, under Saddam, on bad terms with all its neighbours – Iran, Saudi Arabia, Jordan, Syria, Turkey and Kuwait – all might have reasons for wishing to deny Western governments basing or transit rights. Iran was still, under its ayatollah régime, implacably anti-Western. The monarchical government of Saudi Arabia, closely allied to a puritanical Islamic clerisy and in fear of provoking an anti-Western reaction in its population, was unlikely to offer the same operational facilities as it had done in 1990–91, when Saddam's invasion of Kuwait had confronted it with the direct threat of Iraqi aggression. Syria, accused by the United States of sponsoring international terrorism, was too hostile to be drawn into an anti-Saddam coalition despite its troubled relations with Iraq. Jordan, though pro-Western, feared for its credentials as an Arab state if it co-operated too closely with a Western incursion into the Middle Eastern world though it would do so covertly. By a process of elimination, therefore, only three points of entry remained. One was Iraq's own sea coast, a short, constricted and swampy stretch of shoreline at the head of the Gulf; a second was across the Iraqi–Turkish border; and third, the territory of Kuwait. Kuwait, the weakest of all Arab states, was the most likely provider of basing and transit facilities. Not only had it suffered invasion and occupation in 1991, its very right to exist as an independent sovereignty was denied by Saddam, as it had been by several of his predecessors.

It might nevertheless have been feared that Kuwait, for reasons of timorous self-protection, would shy from providing a Western coalition with a *place d'armes*. It was one thing to host a force that would achieve a victorious blitzkrieg, disposing of Saddam the aggressor forever; another thing altogether to provide military facilities for a crisis that might be settled by negotiation, leaving Saddam still in power, chastened but capable of taking his revenge at some later date when the West's attention would perhaps be diverted by trouble in another region of the world altogether. It was greatly to Kuwait's credit that it chose to align itself with the Western coalition from the start and to abide by its choice unflinchingly.

The enigma in the pre-war planning process was Turkey. Though the Turkish population is exclusively Muslim, the state is doctrinally secular and so anti-Islamic, a national ethos determined by the country's founder, Kemal Ataturk, who had rejected Ottomanism, pan-Turanianism (a movement seeking to unify all Turkic-speaking peoples in and outside the boundaries of modern Turkey) and the Muslim Caliphate. Kemal chose what he identified as the path of nationalism: that his Turkey would impose separation of mosque and state and pursue the path of modernization, which to him meant Westernization. Kemalist Turkey was the only true success among the new states to emerge from the postwar settlement of 1918. It evolved swiftly into a stable polity, free of internal racial or religious conflicts, neutral between the great power blocs yet open to influence from the West and committed to economic development and the education of its people. Kemal entrusted the protection of this system and philosophy to the institution within which he had grown up and come to power, the Turkish army. The army was Kemalist through and through, suspicious of any form of political extremism, even more suspicious of Islamic influence in public life and ready, if it detected any destabilization of the Kemalist settlement, to seize power and restore the balance. The army has exercised political power several times in recent Turkish history but always, when it was satisfied that Kemalist normality had been re-established, has returned to barracks and resigned control to civilian politicians.

Even in secularist Turkey, however, the Islamic mood sweeping the Muslim world had had its effect. While the army and the official class remained faithful to the Kemalist legacy, a religious revival had been gaining ground in the provinces for twenty years. A mosque-building boom had raised new minarets in many towns and villages and Muslim dress, outlawed by Kemal, had re-appeared. In November 2002 an overtly Islamic party, led by Recep Tayyip Erdogan, had gained power at the general election. It had new priorities. For fifty years Turkish politics had been dominated by issues scarcely different from those engaging the political class throughout Europe or America: economic advancement, anti-Communism and, more recently, inter-state relationships within the context of continental co-operation. Turkey had early set its sights on securing admission to the European Union, in which it was supported by the United States, grateful as it was for Turkey's loyal membership of NATO. Only the historic antipathy of Greece to normalizing relations with its former imperial master appeared to stand in the way and even the Greeks seemed persuadable. The election of Erdogan's party imposed an abrupt change. While the Kemalists would never have done anything to damage relations with Washington, Erdogan was concerned, as an Islamicist, to show his readiness to oppose the United States in a matter involving another Muslim country.

Washington, anticipating difficulty, decided to resort to inducement. Its initial planning for the invasion of Iraq laid heavy emphasis on the need for Turkish co-operation, which it had fully enjoyed in 1990–91. It needed the use of Turkish airspace, which it had had during its operation of the northern 'no-fly' zone in the 1990s. It even more urgently needed transit rights through Turkish territory into northern Iraq, for the passage of a major military force able to engage Saddam's army from a second direction. A division, the 4th Infantry, had been earmarked for the intervention and had been brought by sea from the continental United States to the eastern Mediterranean. Without the Erdogan government's co-operation, however, it could neither be landed at a Turkish port nor staged southward through Turkish territory. The Erdogan government's consent would, it was known, be difficult to secure. There was not only the question of its Islamic sympathies. There was also the issue of Turkish attitudes, quite separate from any religious ingredient, to Kurdish politics. The 4th Division's deployment area would be within Iraqi Kurdistan. The Kurds, ethnically an Iranian people, Muslim but not Arab, were in the unfortunate position of having a strong sense of national identity but no national territory; their habitat straddled the borders of at least four countries, including Iran, Iraq and Turkey. Within Turkey they were categorized not as a separate minority but as 'mountain Turks' and the Ankara government was resolute in treating them, numerous as they were, as ethnic Turks. It feared all developments that would encourage Kurdish separatism, particularly any move to establish Iraqi Kurdistan as a political entity. An American military intervention in the region, which would inevitably entail American military co-operation with the Kurdish guerrilla forces fighting the Baghdad central government, threatened what Turkey most feared.

In the circumstances, it was understandable that the American government should be willing to pay for Ankara's co-operation. So it showed itself to be; it offered $6 billion in aid as a recompense for the Turkish parliament's agreement to allow the 4th Infantry Division and other American forces to enter Turkish territory. The inducement was not large enough; perhaps none could have been. The Islamic majority in the new Turkish parliament apparently placed religious affinity above historic political association. On 1 March 2003, the American proposal was rejected. Rather than appear anti-Islamic, the new Turkish parliamentarians were prepared to risk alienating the United States, the defence it had offered through NATO against Soviet Russia, Turkey's oldest and most formidable enemy, and the support it provided for Turkey's effort to enter the European Union.

Frantic diplomatic activity was to follow the rejection of 1 March; British as well as American diplomats attempted repeatedly to change the Turks' minds; but without success. It became clear that if there was to be a northern front to the attack against Saddam it would have to be opened by other means. One was to encourage the *peshmergas* – divided into two main political groupings – to intensify their attacks; a second was to support them with special forces; a third was to bring more conventional intervention forces into the region – both the insertion of special forces and other troops would require the creation of an 'air bridge', a difficult logistic and delicate diplomatic task; a fourth was to use subversive means to persuade Saddam that the Turks would eventually fall in with the Americans after all.

The story of the creation of the *peshmerga*-cum-special forces-cum-intervention units front belongs later in the story. The subversive campaign was part of the preliminary planning. General Franks told me that, when it became clear that the Turkish parliamentary position could not be shifted, his headquarters turned to poisoning channels of communication it had with the Iraqi high command. Through intelligence networks, the Saddam leadership was informed that the American military had activated its own contacts with the Turkish army and was confident of the generals bringing the parliamentarians to see sense. This was an intrinsically convincing and persuasive story. Historically the Turkish army had always had the last word in the Kemalist state; its leadership was strongly pro-American (though less pro-British) and pro-NATO; it also retained something of its old imperialist attitude to its former Arab subjects. The Arabs, for their part, held the Turkish army in healthy respect; they recognized its formidable fighting power and were highly conscious of its ability to bring politicians to heel when that was thought to be in the national interest. Indeed, under Nuri al-Sa'id, who embodied Ottoman military tradition, they had had first-hand experience of the interventionist power of generals in state affairs. As a result the subtle subversion of intelligence channels paid off. American intelligence peddled the story that, if only at the last moment, the Turkish parliament would bow to military pressure and agree to grant transit rights to American troops; and, as a result, Saddam judged it too dangerous to withdraw his regular forces from Kurdistan, thus assuring indirectly some if not all of the effect that would have been achieved by positioning 4th Infantry Division in the north.

Nevertheless, General Franks's Central Command headquarters, located for the coming operation at Doha in Qatar, had to plan the invasion of Iraq as a one-front operation, with the attacking forces launched into Iraqi territory from the extreme south. Thanks to the steadfast co-operation of the Kuwaitis, the two large American formations, 1st Marine Expeditionary Force and 3rd Infantry Division, could be positioned to cross directly into Iraq over the Iraqi–Kuwait frontier, as could the heavy part of the British contingent. The other part, the British 3rd Commando Brigade, would land by sea from the Gulf onto the Fao peninsula south of Baghdad, together with American troops, all tasked to seize the port of Umm Qasr and capture the rich Rumaila oil fields before the wells could be set afire. The British contingent, heavy and light elements together, would then advance to seize Basra, Iraq's second city, while the American Marines and 3rd Mechanized Division set out northward to defeat the Iraqi army and seize the capital of Baghdad.

There lay the second problem. Not only is Iraq a difficult country to invade from the south, because of the narrowness of the point of entry, it is also a difficult country to conquer, because of the distance from the point of entry to Baghdad, over 300 miles to the north. Not only is distance an obstacle; so too is the intervening geography. Iraq – or Mesopotamia, the land between the rivers – is both encircled and defended by the waters of the Euphrates and Tigris, which combine at Basra to form the Shatt el-Arab estuary. The rivers meander, spill out into the floodplain and collect tributaries, so that any invader making his way northward is confronted by the need either to capture bridges if he is to advance or to bridge himself if the permanent bridges are destroyed. The two main highways northward, Routes 1 and 7, follow the Euphrates and Tigris respectively, but an invader must also get control of the interconnections, Routes 17 and 27, and such parallel highways as Routes 8 and 9. The land is almost completely flat; between Baghdad and Basra it descends only 34 metres in 338 kilometres (112 feet in 210 miles). The flatness of the river plain theoretically permits speed but also exposes the invader to defensive fire at long range whenever a built-up area impedes the advance.

One method of ensuring rapidity of advance was to repeat the pattern of the First Gulf War and precede ground operations by a prolonged and crushing air offensive. There were good reasons to judge such an operation undesirable. In 1991 the Iraqi army had been deployed by Saddam beyond the borders of his own territory in unvegetated and uninhabited desert. Its positions were clearly marked to observation by overflying coalition aircraft by the entrenchments, including high sand berms, thrown up by the Iraqi invaders of Kuwait. While they invited bombardment, they provided little protection to their occupants. The result was that between 17 January and 24 February 1991 the Iraqi invaders were devastated by a relentless campaign of heavy bombing, supplemented by point attacks on exposed equipment by strike aircraft. Enormous damage was inflicted on Iraqi military personnel exclusively, without any 'collateral' effect on civilian targets.

In 2003 the air forces, particularly the USAF, argued energetically for a repetition of the 1991 air campaign. General Franks opposed the scheme. He had several reasons for so doing. First was the geographical factor. Though in 1991 the air campaign undoubtedly so softened the defences that the ground forces thereafter had little to do, its effect was enhanced by the concentration of the Iraqi army in a confined area. In 2003, by contrast, the Iraqi forces were dispersed widely across Iraqi national territory, did not present a 'target-rich' strike pattern and invited 'collateral' damage to civilian targets that would have ensured a hostile media reaction. Second, there was the time factor. A prolonged preliminary air campaign would have given Saddam room to mobilize Middle Eastern and Third World opinion against the war, as well as the opportunity to sabotage his own oil facilities and cause widespread ecological damage by flooding the Gulf with emissions of crude oil. Third, an air campaign protracted in time would have put the Iraqi army on alert, heightened its responses and perhaps made the subsequent ground campaign less rather than more easy to win. Finally, by opening the war with a time-consuming air campaign, while the ground troops remained massed in the constricted area of Kuwait, Saddam would be given both opportunity and cause to use weapons of mass destruction against them. Belief in Iraq's weapons of mass destruction not only provided the motivation for the war but, in the preliminary stages, heavily influenced the strategy by which it would be fought.

The strategy eventually chosen, therefore, was for a brief air campaign timed to coincide with the initial ground attack. Its distinctive characteristic – and the justification for its brevity – was to be the very precision of the weaponry delivered. Since 1991 there had been a revolution in accuracy, promising the results sought by air forces since the dawn of strategic bombing but only rarely achieved. In the First Gulf War only ten per cent of the munitions delivered by air, whether air-dropped bombs, air-launched missiles or sea- or land-launched cruise missiles, had been 'smart'. In the Iraq War, the proportion was to be seventy per cent, the majority guided either by laser or by Global Positioning Satellite (GPS). The first system requires the target to be identified by laser illumination, which the munition detects, the second is directed very precisely to a chosen spot on the ground. An important development since 1991 was that of fitting guidance systems to munitions which lacked propulsion, thus turning a 'dumb' bomb into a weapon as accurate as a cruise-missile at a fraction of its cost. One was the Joint Stand Off Weapon (JSOW), another the Joint Direct Attack Munition (JDAM). A third weapon, CBU-97 WCMD (Cluster Bomb Unit 97 Wind Corrected Munitions Dispenser), ejected armour-penetrating bomblets from a height, which then guided themselves onto the thin upper armour of vehicles within their search area. The ready availability of such high-precision weapons, delivered by aircraft as diverse as the B-2 Stealth Bomber, the B-1 and the veteran B-52, averted the need to stage blanket bombardments which had preceded the First Gulf War or to attack civilian infrastructure targets, such as power stations, a programme that had attracted a bad press during the anti-Milosevic operations in Bosnia and Kosovo in the 1990s. The air war could be, and was, directed almost exclusively at military targets, though in the opening stage, widely described as that of 'shock and awe', the headquarters and administrative buildings of the Iraqi government and Ba'ath party were deemed to be military targets. General Franks, in the aftermath of the war, denied to me that he had ever sought to create 'shock and awe' or include those effects in his strategic plan.

The plan foresaw the disarming of Iraqi forces by air action while the ground offensive was in its early stage of development. Even before the ground forces had begun to move, however, General Franks had begun to neutralize Iraqi resistance by subversive activity against the command structure of the Iraqi divisions directly opposed to the coalition forces across the Iraq–Kuwait border. Intelligence agents had got into contact with the commanders of the six Iraqi divisions deployed furthest south, including the 51st Mechanized, and the 11th Infantry, and had urged them not to fight – with, according to General Franks, some success. Certainly, once the coalition began to push forward, the Iraqi divisions in the south melted away without offering serious resistance.

General Franks meanwhile was also inserting special forces through the frontier defences with orders to reach and neutralize the key bridges across the rivers. He assigned forty-eight special forces groups to these and other tasks, the majority American but including British and Australian units also. Special Operations Task Force 20, supported by an American Ranger regiment, and numbering 4,000 men, operated in the Iraqi desert west of the Euphrates, with the aim of cutting Iraqi routes into Syria and

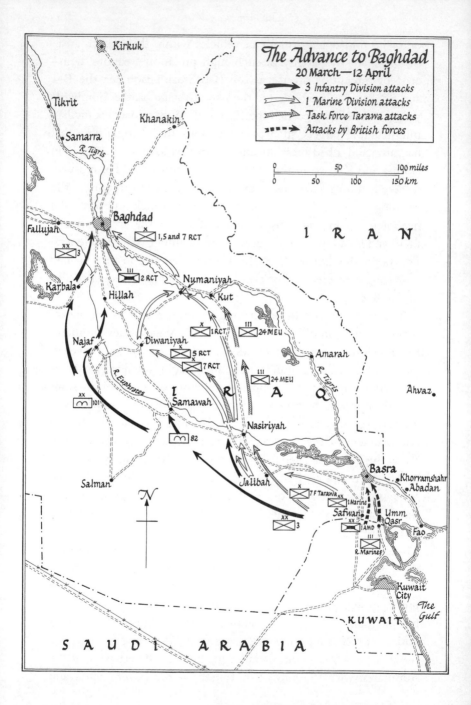

The Advance to Baghdad
20 March — 12 April

3 Infantry Division attacks
1 Marine Division attacks
Task Force Tarawa attacks
Attacks by British forces

0   50   100 miles
0   50   100   150 km

Kirkuk

Tikrit

Samarra
R. Tigris

Khanakin

Fallujah

Baghdad

XX 3

Karbala

Hillah

Najaf

Diwaniyah

R. Euphrates

Samawah

Salman

Jalibah

X 1,5 and 7 RCT

III 2 RCT

Numaniyah
Kut

X 1 RCT

III 24 MEU

X 5 RCT

X 7 RCT

III 24 MEU

XX 101

XX 82

Nasiriyah

Amarah

R. Tigris

Ahvaz

I R A N

I   R   A   Q

X 7 F Tarawa

XX 1 Marine

XX 3

Safwan

XX 1 AMD

III R. Marines

Basra

Khorramshahr
Abadan

Umm
Qasr

Fao

Kuwait
City

The
Gulf

KUWAIT

S A U D I   A R A B I A

N

taking possession of the 'Scud pans'. The Scud, though a mobile system, needs to be erected on an area of hard ground against which its rocket gases can push. Such 'pans' are comparatively few and widely scattered in the desert area. During the First Gulf War special forces attempted to attack the Scud threat by finding and eliminating the launchers themselves, a frustrating task given the ease with which they could be moved and hidden. The decision, in the Iraq war, to focus attention on potential launch sites proved much more fruitful. Very few of Saddam's surviving Scuds were launched against coalition targets and none against surrounding countries, such as Israel.

The conventional offensive had more substantial objectives. There were to be two main thrusts, by 3rd Infantry Division out of Kuwait up the Euphrates valley, with the division's vehicles covering ground across the desert before swinging back to join the main roads and advance on Baghdad via Karbala. The 1st Marine Expeditionary Force would simultaneously push up from Kuwait along Route 1, via Jalibal and Nasiriyah, between the Euphrates and Tigris, but send one of its regiments to reach the Tigris at Kut (scene of a British military disaster at the hands of the Turks in the First World War) before taking Route 6, also to arrive at Baghdad. Task Force Tarawa would shadow 1st Marine Expeditionary Force to secure the southern towns. Troops of the 82nd Airborne and 101st Air Assault Divisions would intervene to secure objectives short of Baghdad. In a separate operation altogether, the British 1st (UK) Armoured Division, with its air assault and commando brigades, would seize and secure the lower waters of the great rivers and capture Basra, Iraq's second city. The operations were planned in great detail, a key element being the preparation of re-supply. American forces excel at logistics. The advance of both 3rd Infantry Division and 1st MEF was predicated on the principle of their advancing at the highest possible speed, brushing aside resistance and halting to fight only when absolutely necessary, but pausing at regular intervals of a day or two for the logistic train of fuel, ammunition and re-supply vehicles to make good their wants in a rapid disgorging of necessities. British observers who travelled with the Americans have testified to the awesomeness of the spectacle. 'The armour had halted,' a British colonel described to me, 'dozens of vehicles abreast in the first line and dozens more in the lines behind them. Suddenly out of the dust appeared every logistic vehicle you can imagine, tankers, water bowsers, ammunition trucks, mobile repair workshops, ration trucks. As they stopped, crews began connecting up hoses, hoisting pallets, throwing off crates. The contents were seized by the combat troops and disappeared inside the fighting vehicles as fast as they could be stowed. Sooner than you could imagine the combat echelon was re-supplied and ready to move forward again.' Re-supply, quite as much as firepower or air support, was to be the secret of the coalition's overwhelming of Saddam's forces.

The first objective of the coalition attack, however, did not require any large logistic effort to be reached, for it lay just inside Iraqi territory from the coalition concentration area in Kuwait. It was the Rumaila oil fields, after the great Kirkuk–Mosul fields in Kurdistan the richest in Iraq: about a thousand wells, occupying an area fifty miles long below Basra and parallel to the border with Iran. The most valuable of the fields pumped over two million barrels a day from over 300 wells, through twelve gas-oil separation plants, to a main pumping station at Zubayr, from which it was sent to the terminal in the Fao peninsula. It was vital to seize the gas-oil separation plants and the pumping station undamaged, since the postwar reconstruction of Iraq would require their output, which earned $40 million a day.

A team from 1st Battalion 7th Marines (1/7) was chosen to seize the installations and a detailed reconnaissance carried out, providing the attackers with a computer-simulated picture of the layout of the objectives and satellite photographs of the surroundings. The British provided a team of experts from the oil companies which had installed the machinery in the 1950s to take over as soon as the buildings were seized, check the machinery for sabotage and put it back into operation as quickly as possible.

On the day of the attack, 20 March, advanced 24 hours because of a last-minute decision to open the air attack on Baghdad early, 1/7 crossed the sand barriers marking the border between Iraq and Kuwait and, in the centre of an extended line of fifty battalion-sized units, moving on a front of fifty kilometres (31 miles), raced towards the Rumaila fields. To the marines' left was 3rd Infantry Division, to their right 1st (UK) Armoured Division. By early afternoon of March 21, 1/7 were in an attacking position, sixty kilometres inside Iraq and five short of their objective. They had met sporadic resistance and seen some knocked-out Iraqi armour but had not been seriously opposed. Suddenly, round a corner, the pumping station appeared to their front. The commander of C Company, 1/7, the sub-unit charged with the actual capture, halted his men while he made an appreciation. It was crucial not to start a fire-fight which might detonate tons of highly flammable oil and gas in the pipes. Ordering his vehicles' engines to be switched off, he listened. All he could hear was shouting from inside the perimeter wall and all he could see were civilian workers milling about. Realizing with a flash of inspiration that they had shut the pumping equipment down, averting the risk of inflammation, he gave the order to assault. An engineer team blew a hole in the perimeter wall, his riflemen poured through. Another gap was opened in a wire fence. Within minutes the riflemen had seized the buildings inside and begun to round up the civilian workers. There were no military defenders. The British industrial experts were brought forward to examine the machinery. They reported that there had been some amateur sabotage but nothing that could not be easily repaired. Half an hour after the assault had begun the position was secured.

Later, at a short distance from the objective, 1/7 found twelve T-54 tanks and a collection of Soviet-supplied armoured fighting vehicles. They were securely dug in but had not fired their guns and had been abandoned by their crews, some of whom came out of hiding to surrender to the marines. It was an augury of the character of the fighting that was to unfold in the following days. Smoke rose from a few wellheads that had been torched but the oil fields and their vital machinery were intact. The operation to capture what had been christened 'the Crown Jewels' had been an outstanding success.

On 22 March the great ground armada proceeded north. The plan was for the British, with objectives in the Fao peninsula and then the prime aim of taking and occupying Basra, to wheel right, while 1st MEF and the army's V Corps, of which 3rd Infantry Division was the main element, struck towards Baghdad. The enemy opposing the coalition forces were estimated at eight divisions. One, the 51st, had been destroyed or had disbanded itself during the fighting in the oil fields. By American estimation, its personnel had largely deserted. Desertion was thought to have occurred in two waves, encouraged by intelligence contact with the divisional commander. The first wave of desertions had been prompted by fear of coalition air attack and had happened despite its absence. The second wave, among the more stalwart, had begun when the sound of approaching American tanks was heard. The Iraqi soldiers, who were from the locality, had simply dropped their weapons, shed their uniforms and fled home.

After the collapse of 51st Division, five others remained in the south, stationed along the Tigris river. The marines were to stage a feint in their direction, a feint supported by the British move on Basra, and then to turn west into the central plain, leaving the Iraqis bypassed while 1st MEF and Task Force Tarawa pressed on towards Baghdad. The lead elements of 1st MEF were to concentrate against the town of Nasiriyah, where they would cross the Euphrates and proceed north to engage the two Republican Guard divisions defending the capital.

Nasiriyah is an important crossing place over the Euphrates. A combat historian travelling with 1st MEF described it as 'a dingy, neglected collection of one- and two-storey cinder-block and mud houses sandwiched in square city blocks between the river and the Saddam Canal to the north. In essence an island two and a half miles square, Nasiriyah had bridges on its north and south ends: two on Route 7 through the heart of the city, and two on Route 8 – called Route Moe by Task Force Tarawa

– that skirted the city's eastern border.' The plan to take and secure Nasiriyah had been made aboard ship by the staff of Task Force Tarawa, commanding 2nd and 8th Marines, before the deployment began. It required 1st Battalion 2nd Marines (1/2) to pass through the eastern edge of the city and seize one of the northern bridges. It was to be followed by another battalion which would secure the city allowing the 1st MEF – comprising the three regimental combat teams formed from 1st, 4th, 5th and 7th Marines – to pass through and continue the advance northward. There was to be plentiful helicopter and artillery support, and armour would also be available.

Careful planning failed, in circumstances fortunately unique during the Iraq War, to deliver the desired result. There was to be an unforeseen battle for Nasiriyah and it was to take a messy and costly form, seized on gleefully by anti-American elements in the Western media to demonstrate that the war was not going the coalition's way. The Marines had anticipated trouble in Nasiriyah. They had even coined the term 'Ambush Alley' to describe what they expected there. Trouble came but not of the sort anticipated. The defending division, the 11th, deserted, as predicted. What the Marines had been led to believe was that the population was pro-Saddam. That was not so; they had risen against him in 1991, had been severely punished and had learnt prudence. Just as bad, however, was what occurred instead. Nasiriyah was chosen by the Ba'ath party and Saddam's various militias as a productive place in which to stage resistance. During 22–23 March, *fedayeen* fighters began to arrive in the town by private transport – cars, motorcycles, taxis – and in Ba'ath party commandeered buses. Many of the fighters were not Iraqis but extremists from other Arab countries, poorly trained but anxious to die in a war against the West. They brought their usual paraphernalia – RPG-7 grenade launchers, Kalashnikov assault rifles and explosive charges.

Neither side was properly organized to conduct the battle that ensued. The Iraqi fighters were outsiders and lacked the local knowledge necessary to put Nasiriyah into a state of defence. On the other hand, the Americans had no desire to capture Nasiriyah. They merely wished to pass through as quickly as possible, seize the bridges and clear routes for the convoys following in their rear. It was a recipe for confusion and confusion quickly followed.

Three concentrations of American forces were converging on the Nasiriyah area: the 3rd Infantry Division in the lead, with its long logistic tail following; the 1st Marine Expeditionary Force; and Task Force Tarawa. They got intermingled. In darkness and swirling dust, a supply unit of 3rd Infantry Division, 507th Maintenance Company, missed a turning, drove into Nasiriyah towards the eastern bridge over the Euphrates and was shot up. Nine soldiers were killed and six captured. One was a woman, Private Jessica Lynch, who was to become an unwitting heroine of the Iraq War.

The news of 507th's misadventure filtered back to Task Force Tarawa, still south of the city, which despatched 1st Battalion 2nd Marines (1/2) with a tank company to rescue the 507th's survivors. It quickly got involved in street fighting, which slowed its progress, and its companies got separated. Five servicemen of the 507th were found alive, however, and later the burnt-out remains of their trucks. It was by then noon and 1/2's commander, under pressure to hasten the advance from higher command, gave orders to rush the eastern bridge. His A Company seized it and B Company passed across but itself took a wrong turning beyond, found itself in a firefight with *fedayeen* and bogged several of its vehicles in soft ground. Meanwhile C Company tried to secure a farther bridge across the Saddam Canal. Half the company got across but a hit by an RPG set a vehicle in the centre of the column afire, leaving four of its amphibious tractors on one side, seven on the other. A large party of *fedayeen* appeared and began firing automatic weapons and grenade launchers at the stalled unit, killing several and wounding more. As officers and sergeants tried to organize a return of fire and evacuate the wounded, an American A-10 anti-tank aircraft passed overhead, shooting up several marine vehicles and wounding an already wounded marine; A-10 pilots had caused several serious 'friendly fire' incidents involving British troops during the First Gulf War but they had hitherto avoided attacking their own. Soon after the A-10 pass, two more amphibious tractors were blown up, apparently by Iraqi fire, and shooting continued throughout the afternoon. Not until five o'clock, when A Company appeared with tank support, did the fighting die down. It had been a horrible day for 1/2, an episode of military confusion almost at its worst. There was little blame to apportion, and the Iraqis could take no credit for their success. Their resistance was not planned or co-ordinated. They had merely profited from their enemy's ignorance of local geography and choice of wrong turnings. The battle of Nasiriyah was a catalogue of errors.

The flavour of the fighting was caught by the account of Evan Wright, *Rolling Stone*'s reporter with 1st MEF's reconnaissance battalion.

Just after sunrise our seventy-vehicle convoy rolls over the bridge on the Euphrates and enters An Nasiriyah. It's one of those sprawling Third World mud-brick-and-cinder-block cities that probably looks pretty badly rubbled even on a good day. This morning, smoke curls from collapsed structures. Most buildings facing the road are pockmarked and cratered. Cobras (helicopters) fly overhead spilling machine-gun fire. Dogs roam the ruins . . . A few vehicles come under machine-gun and RPG fire. The [Marines] return fire and redecorate a building with about a dozen grenades fired from a Mark 19 [automatic grenade launcher]. In an hour we clear the outer limits of the city and start to head north. Dead bodies are scattered along the edge of the road. Most are men, enemy fighters, still with weapons in their hands . . . . There are shot-up cars with bodies hanging over the edges. We pass a bus smashed and burned, with charred remains sitting upright in some windows. There's a man with no head in the road and a dead little girl, too, about three or four, lying on her back. She's wearing a dress and has no legs.

Another reporter, Andrew North of the BBC, described the last evening of the fighting,

[We're] on the city's southern outskirts, near a fly-infested rubbish dump. Suddenly there was a screeching sound and four bright dots in the sky – Iraqi rockets heading our way. 'Get down!' someone shouted and everyone scattered, looking desperately for cover. Machine guns opened up as more rockets landed. When it was over, thirty marines had been injured, many in friendly fire because of the confusion. The Iraqis had used the cover of a sandstorm to get in close and mount another surprise assault.

'Assault' is a misnomer, a typical misuse of military language by a media man inexperienced in the events of warfare. An assault is a combination of fire and movement, culminating in an attempt to capture a position by troops pressing to close quarters. Assault was not the Iraqis' style. Almost always they kept their distance, loosing off rounds haphazard and unsighted, dodging in and out of cover and hoping to inflict casualties by luck rather than skill.

The Marines, by contrast, did assault frequently once it had become clear, on the second and third day of the battle, that the city would have to be captured if its streets were to be secured for the passage of supply columns. In retrospect it would have been better to bypass Nasiriyah rather than allow it to become a bottleneck, by bridging the Euphrates below or above the position it occupied on the river. The bridging equipment was available, brought from the United States by specialist National Guard units from the southern states, where they practised the skills on the enormous waterways of the Mississippi and its tributaries. Whilst bridges were available, however, roads were not. The hard fact of the matter was that the roads north led through Nasiriyah and had to be taken if the speed of advance were to be maintained at a pace that would guarantee the rapid fall of the Saddam régime. So during 23–24 March Task Force Tarawa established a cordon around the city to prevent the infiltration of fresh bands of fighters and set about finding, capturing or killing the *fedayeen* and Ba'athists who were sustaining the resistance. As Task Force Tarawa passed into the city and began to demonstrate an American presence, its task was eased by the garnering of local intelligence. As snipers killed *fedayeen* in ambush positions, and special forces accompanying the task force seized control of dominant buildings and city blocks, the Shi'ite residents, who had no reason to love the Ba'ath or Saddam after his brutal repression of their community, began to supply information about the location of *fedayeen* positions and supply stores. The Marines on the ground were supported by Marine helicopter and aircraft crews in the air overhead. Piece by piece, the Iraqi control of the city started to collapse.

An encouraging and instantly celebrated benefit of Task Force Tarawa's action was the recovery of Private Jessica Lynch from captivity. A very brave Iraqi, discovering that she was being held in a local hospital, where she had been taken wounded, visited the building to assess how closely she was guarded and then informed the Americans of what he had found. A snatch squad of marines, Navy SEALs (sea-air-land commandos) and army Rangers was formed, which successfully surrounded her place of captivity, staged a diversion to draw off her captors and extracted her to safety. The rescue was a model of how a small-scale military operation should be conducted. The same could not be said of media treatment of the event or of her story. Private Lynch was transformed into a Hollywood heroine, who had fought to the last round and then been barbarically mistreated. The truth was that, though she had undoubtedly defended herself and been badly wounded, she had little memory of her ordeal and her captors had treated her with care and consideration. The real hero of the episode, the Iraqi who had been instrumental in saving her, received little of the media credit he was due.

Not until the last days of March did Task Force Tarawa succeed in suppressing all resistance in Nasiriyah, securing the city and making it safe for the long supply columns following the marine spearhead racing towards Baghdad to transit safely. The local element of the spearhead, to which Task Force Tarawa was acting as 'force protection', was 1st Marines, the main element of 1st Regimental Combat Team (RCT 1). Its mission once clear of Nasiriyah was to push on up Route 7, the main highway through the central valley, as far as Kut, on the Tigris, where it expected to find the Baghdad Division of the Republican Guard. After defeating or otherwise disposing of that division, it was to regroup for the final drive on the capital. Beyond Kut it would be rejoined by 5th and 7th Marines (RCT 5 and 7), which were scheduled to proceed in parallel to its left, up Route 1 until, beyond Dinaniyah, they would, at a point denoted as 'the Elbow', leave Route 1 and cross the central plain on Route 27 to concentrate with RCT 1 and advance on Sabat. Simultaneously the 3rd Infantry Division would move on the marines' left up the Euphrates to reach the 'Karbala gap' between that city and Route 8, from which it would also launch its assault on Baghdad.

Nothing in war is predictable. Two factors now intervened to set back the timetable. One was the weather. The other was a shortage of supplies reaching 3rd Infantry Division. The supply shortage was subject to human correction. The weather was not. During the fight for Nasiriyah a dust storm – a *shamal* – began to blow, turning daytime to dusk and interfering with observation. As the lead elements of 1st MEF left the city and headed up Route 7 towards Kut, the *shamal* grew in strength. Iraq's central valley, between the rivers, is an alluvial plain, its fertility renewed each year by silt brought by the snowmelt off the northern Zagros mountains. Immediately after winter much of the surface disappears under water, which lies in huge, shifting, shallow lakes. As the lakes disperse and dry, the silt lies loose on the surface, ready to be whipped up and driven in cutting clouds by the spring gales. All the invaders had suffered from dust clouds – sand in the Kuwait desert – as soon as they began to move. They had wrapped cloths around their heads to keep it out, to little effect. The sand, then the airborne silt, had penetrated everything, clogged mouths and lungs and caused an epidemic of coughing and spitting. The silt was worse than the sand. Because it carried a high concentration of decayed vegetable matter, it caused the soldiers to suffer low-grade fevers which lasted for several days until the sufferers adapted. The machinery did not adapt, nor did night-vision devices. Machinery clogged, sights could not penetrate the gloom. The march north from Nasiriyah was a misery, slowed by the dust storms which at times turned wet and cold as sleet and hail mixed in. At one stage, just north of Nasiriyah, the *fedayeen* profited from the conditions to stage a blocking attack. The high command in Baghdad had apparently heard of the marines' difficulties in the city and organized reinforcements to join the battle. Arriving in civilian transport, and too late, they were stopped on Route 7 but manfully debussed, deployed and conducted one of the few genuine fire-and-movement engagements the Marines encountered anywhere in Iraq. It lasted two hours and left all the *fedayeen*, almost sixty in number, dead.

Even in the dust storm the three marine regimental combat teams pressed on, RCT 1 up Route 7, RCT 5 and 7 up Route 1 to its left, while the 3rd Infantry Division was moving with RCT 5 and 7 towards Karbala and the Baghdad outskirts. On 26 March, however, the command of 3rd Infantry Division, which had overextended its resources, decided that it would have to halt for resupply. The Marines, who have a tradition of travelling lighter than the army, did not need to pause. The divisional commander, Major General James Mattis, had arranged for C-130 tactical transport aircraft, carrying, 5,000-gallon fuel bladders, to land on the hard surface of Route 1, allowing the division's vehicles to top up on the line of march.

The advance had, however, to be co-ordinated. Army and marine formations could not get out of phase. The capture of Baghdad could be guaranteed only if the two main formations, 3rd Infantry and 1st MEF, arrived at the final line of departure simultaneously. Feeble though Iraqi resistance was, the better Iraqi divisions, the Republican Guard, still lay to their front. They must not be offered the opportunity to engage the American forces in sequence, but must be forced to fight a solid concentration, and to do so under heavy air attack by the coalition air forces. A pause was necessary.

It was arranged on Thursday 27 March at 1st MEF head-quarters by General James Conway, its commanding general, General William Wallace, commanding V Corps (3rd Infantry Division and attached army brigades) and General McKiernan (overall ground commander). Because the Marines were not short of supplies, they were reluctant to break the momentum of their advance. In the master plan, however, they were supporting V Corps, not conducting an independent mission. It was there-fore agreed that they should pause, so as not to lose contact with 3rd Infantry Division, and that their lead element, RCT 5, should actually retrace its steps for twenty-three miles, having got too far ahead. There was an underswell of complaint among the Marines. They had heard that Wallace and McKiernan were both close friends and logistics experts, and suspected that they preferred to work by the book. The Marines knew that the USMC and the army worked by different rules. They regarded their own, which pared supply scales to the bone and ultimately allowed only for the movement of fuel, ammunition, food and water, as superior. They were also alarmed by rumours that the pause might last longer than the seventy-two to ninety-six hours officially forecast. Hints picked up from the BBC and American domestic radio suggested a pause of as much as eighteen to twenty-one days. To the Marines, who had made exceptional progress despite having to overcome resistance, and who felt the way ahead to be open if pressure were maintained, the prospect of a pause was highly unwelcome. Their commanders felt the same, seeing that the plan might be changed to make their thrust the main effort, with V Corps assuming the support role.

Changing plans in mid-campaign is not, however, to be recom-mended, unless there is an overwhelmingly powerful reason. At that stage of the Iraq War, there was no such reason. The enemy was not exerting significant resistance and was still vulnerable to the offensive effort General Franks had planned at the outset. It was therefore decided to proceed as foreseen, with the following differences. First, it would be necessary to clear up the tactical situation along the line of advance, reaching back to Nasiriyah; to do so, V Corps would deploy its reserves, 2 Brigade of 82nd Airborne Division, 2 and 3 Brigades of 101st Air Assault Division, to fight local battles at towns along Route 1. Second, the logistic organization would dump forward 3–4 days' supply. Third, the divisions would have to organize reconnaissance in force, ahead of the main columns, to establish the strength and whereabouts of the defenders of Baghdad.

The 3rd Infantry Division, travelling partly on hard desert rather than paved roads to the west of the Euphrates, had already outstripped the 1st MEF to reach Najaf, short of its penultimate objective, the Karbala gap, between Karbala and Lake Razzazah, from which the route lay towards the capital. It had had difficulties, particularly during an attack by 11th Helicopter Regiment, supporting 3rd Infantry Division, on the supposed positions of the Medina Republican Guard Division near Najaf. Flying in appalling weather, the precursor of the great *shamal*, the 11th Helicopter Regiment had also had difficulty in refuelling and difficulty with its communications, having to rely at a critical stage on a single satellite radio link. As a result, the number of missions to be flown had to be reduced, as did the number of designated targets to be attacked. In the circumstances it was not surprising that the American helicopters flew into trouble, being engaged by heavy ground fire from the Medina Division's positions; what was surprising was that only one of the thirty-two attacking Apache helicopters was shot down; many others, however, were hit and damaged.

The brigades of the two airborne divisions, 82nd and 101st, had great success in their mission to clear the left flank of the advance and suppress resistance in the towns, particularly Samawah and Najaf, on 3rd Infantry Division's right. The advance elements were supported by the 69th Tank Battalion and the famed 7th Cavalry, Custer's regiment at the Little Big Horn. The best reported of the engagements, however, was that of 325th Regiment, 82nd Airborne Division. The 325th had originally been glider infantry and had landed on the Cotentin peninsula on D-Day in 1944. Going to battle by glider had, even by the end of the Second World War, been recognized as too dangerous a means of transit to combat to be continued; the role of the glider infantryman was seen to be hazardous at best and little short of suicidal at worst. The glider regiments of 82nd and 101st Divisions, while keeping their numbers, were found other roles, either as parachute or heliborne units.

The 325th had begun the campaign on 25 March in Kuwait, then advanced, some of its personnel by road, some by helicopter, first to Tallil military air base inside Iraq and then to Samawah on the Euphrates, north-west of Nasiriyah. Halted short of Samawah on 27–28 March while the brigade plans and executes operations against the town, commanders and staff officers, observed by Karl Zinsmeister, an embedded journalist from *American Enterprise* magazine, discuss the appropriate degree of firepower to unleash. They are working on intelligence supplied by the CIA, which has local contacts, and reports that a meeting between two high-level Ba'ath party officials, organizing Samawah's defence, is about to take place in a building to their front. The brigade intelligence officer and its judge advocate general, the legal officer responsible for enforcing rules of engagement, review the issues. 'We've learned from [our] source that Muhayfen Halwan, the number-one Ba'ath party official in the Salwan region down on the Saudi border has come up to meet with Sultan Al-Sayf, the number-two guy in this region. As of 0915 this morning they were planning future ops in this compound.'

Intense discussion follows. There is a school 145 yards from the target, others within 220 yards. The CIA officer believes the schools are empty. Nevertheless the operations officers controlling the attack aircraft to be employed, fixed-wing strike aircraft and helicopters, fall into anxious debate about what weapons to employ. Should they be strike aircraft, delivering a 500-pound bomb, or attack helicopters, delivering an 18-pound Hellfire missile? The fire support officer states that 'the smallest Air Force precision bomb has a five-hundred pound warhead, versus eighteen

pounds of high explosive on a Hellfire. If we're looking to minimize risks of destruction overflow, maybe that's enough.' The
judge advocate counters that, 'On the other hand, there's a big
political and psychological component to this strike, and if we're
trying to send a message, a bigger boom is better – so long as
we're comfortable we're not gonna get unwanted collateral
damage.' While the debate continues, General Wallace, the
commanding general of V Corps, appears at the conference to
be briefed. While he listens, a forward air controller in one of
the large overflying AWACS aircraft intervenes. He seems to be
arguing for the use of a 2,000-lb satellite-guided bomb. Then he
modifies the order, apparently as a result of discussion with
Central Command. The decision now is for a Hellfire strike.

Half an hour after the conference began, the helicopter pilots
report that three missiles have been fired. Their high-definition
sensors report the results. The target building has been holed but
is still standing and a truck with three occupants has made its
escape. The conclusion is that the 'bad guys' may have got away.
Zinsmeister, a close observer throughout the tactical conference,
is impressed by the care taken not to do more damage than is
necessary and to avoid causing civilian casualties. Next day, 2 April,
he gets first-hand reports of contrary efforts made by the *fedayeen*
to involve civilians. Some use an ambulance to mount an attack
on an American post, others seize women and children off the
street to protect a target about to be attacked by an American
aircraft. In retrospect he reviews 325th Infantry Regiment's work
in Samawah during the week: 'basic infantry blocking and tackling, but much of it is the more delicate and tricky work of urban
warfare – clearing intersections and buildings, taking and holding
bridges, draining sniper's nests, smashing mortar and machine-gun
sites hidden in residential neighbourhoods.'

The care taken to avoid causing hurt to innocents is not casual.
Before the first assault to clear Samawah of *fedayeen* and Ba'athists,
Zinsmeister witnesses 325's 'rock drill', a tactical conference on
the coming battle, so called because pieces of rock are used to
mark key points on a tent floor, with parachute cord, stretched

to show map grid lines that would show up on GPS indicators. Pieces of cardboard, bricks and piles of sand were added to the improvised map to stand for other features and locations. When the improvised model – familiar from classroom seminars in all officer and NCO training schools – was ready, the platoon and squad leaders clustered round, to be talked through the operation that would shortly unroll on the real terrain it represented.

During the rest of 3 April and the beginning of the night of 4 April the preparations for the final advance and capture of Samawah continue. Intelligence reports indicate that Karim Handany, a member of Saddam's inner circle and a four-star uniformed general in the Republican Guard, had come down from Baghdad 'to organize the local resistance. Street intersections had been built up with fighting positions. Machine-gun units were dug in and sandbagged in many locations. RPGs and ammunition were stashed in scores of buildings across the northern neighbourhoods', which had not yet been taken. The troop leaders give their last orders:

> Hot spots, check points and problem buildings are identified. Decisions are made on which squads should attack each. Snipers are assigned positions on high buildings. There is heavy emphasis on the rule of engagement, on fields of fire and physical operational limits, all of which are carefully calculated to avoid fratricide or collateral civilian damage.

At 0435 on the morning of 4 April the final assault on north Samawah begins.

> The alleys are narrow, and dark windows and doors threaten from every direction. The squad clings to opposite sides of the street, scanning the rooftops and windows through gunsights as they make their way toward the river. A machine gunner is posted at each intersection. Gradually the troops clear out critical buildings. First the door is blown off with a shotgun, or the door is blasted open with C4 explosive. Then each room

is swept at riflepoint. Most structures seem empty, but some have young men or families in them, who are gathered up for relocation to a safer quadrant farther back, and in some cases for questioning. Nearby, booms and machine gun bursts as adjoining squads encounter fire.

So, painstakingly, block by block, house by house, north Samawah is cleared. The infantrymen of 325th are alert to the appearance of 'technicals', a term learnt in Somalia, signifying a pickup truck carrying automatic weapons. There are other enemy mobile units, including taxis and civilian buses. By the afternoon of 4 April, however, Samawah has been emptied of hostile fighters, at a cost to the 82nd Airborne Division of one American soldier dead and twenty wounded. Zinsmeister is encouraged to hope that the rest of the campaign in Iraq, leading to the capture of Baghdad, can be concluded at equally low cost.

The operations of 82nd Division were replicated by those of its brother formation, 101st Airborne Division (Air Assault). On March 30, Black Hawk and Chinook helicopters of the 101st, flying 250 sorties, airlifted two brigades of the division to positions from which Najaf and Hillah, on Highways 9 and 8, could be assaulted. The operation was sensitive, for Najaf was the site of the Golden Dome Mosque of Ali, tomb of the son-in-law of the Prophet Muhammad, a site of particular sensitivity to Shi'a Muslims. It was also protected by a mountainous escarpment which had been reinforced with fighting positions. The capture of both places was, nevertheless, essential, since they protected the routes up the Euphrates valley to the outskirts of Baghdad and had to be cleared if the rear area of 3rd Infantry Division were not to be attacked by pockets of *fedayeen* lurking in the two cities.

The 101st Airborne Division is, like the 82nd, one of the most famous fighting organizations in American military history. The 82nd, because of its nationwide recruitment during the Second World War, was known as the All-American; the 101st called itself the Screaming Eagles. With the 82nd it had jumped on

D–Day, and its infantry regiments, the 327th, 501st, 502nd and 506th, had won a reverberating roll of battle honours. In the Vietnam era it had changed role, ceasing to parachute and acquiring helicopters to make it an air assault formation. Its airborne ethos remained unchanged; like those of the 82nd, its soldiers call the rest of the infantry 'legs' and cultivate an air of superiority.

The operation to secure Highways 8 and 9 began at Najaf, where Major General David Petraeus, 101st's commanding general, deployed three battalions of his 1st Brigade, supported by a tank battalion, 1-70 Armour, to enter the city from the south. The northern approaches were covered by his 2nd Brigade. Though short of armour, Petraeus had plentiful air support, provided by his own divisional helicopters, Apaches and OH-58D Kiowa Warriors, reinforced by airforce and navy fixed wing strike aircraft. An early task was to destroy Ba'ath party headquarters, done with precision by the dropping of two JDAMs. The JDAM (Joint Direct Attack Munition) is a conventional 'dumb' bomb, to which is attached a GPS guidance unit and fins, which allows it to achieve a very high degree of terminal accuracy at a fraction of the cost of that of a cruise missile. The battle for Najaf took the form of a block-by-block clearance of the streets, under a protective umbrella of helicopters which provided close fire support and direct observation, guiding the infantry to points of resistance. Outside the city the Apaches, with their heavy armament, destroyed over 200 enemy vehicles. By 1 April, two days after the operation had begun, Najaf was secure.

The focus then shifted north to Hillah, with several objects. One was to support the marine operation at the Tigris crossing. A second was to protect the development of 3rd Infantry Division's attack on Baghdad from the direction of Karbala, farther north. Both missions would involve the 101st in combat with the Hammurabi Republican Guard Division, which had sent armour and infantry from the capital to defend its southern approaches. In one of the few episodes of organized resistance staged by the Iraqi conventional forces, 101st's infantry and supporting armour would be forced to fight step by step, relying on artillery bombardment as well as tank gunnery and air support to reduce the defences as the strongpoints were identified. The Iraqis also deployed artillery, requiring the Americans to mount counter-battery fire, directed by radar that refers incoming fire to its point of origin. Fighting persisted in Hillah and its surrounding area from 2 to 10 April; only after eight days of often intense combat could General Petraeus report that Hillah was clear of enemy and secure. The battle, though not costly in American lives, had consumed an enormous amount of ordnance, including 1,000 Hellfire anti-armour missiles, launched from helicopters, 2,000 conventional artillery rounds, 155mm and 105mm, fired by 321st Artillery Regiment, and 114 ATACMS (Army Tactical Missile System), a rocket discharged from the Multiple Launch Rocket System (MLRS), with a longer range and heavier warhead than the MLRS standard missile. Army and air force aircraft had flown 135 close support missions, against bunkers and fortified buildings, while the division's helicopters had destroyed 256 air-defence sites and vehicles, 110 guns and rocket launchers, 287 armoured vehicles, 800 other vehicles and many bunkers and other fire positions. Although the elements of the Hammurabi Division had fought better than most Iraqi troops encountered, they had lacked both the skills and the firepower to put up an effective defence.

The way to Baghdad was now open. The objectives yet to be taken – the Karbala gap, between that town and its reservoir fed from the Hadimah Dam, Baghdad International Airport, and the terminal points of the highways leading into the city – all lay within the metropolitan area. The rest of Saddam's kingdom was in the possession of the coalition forces. In the Kurdish north, never fully under Saddam's control, a coalition of Kurdish fighters, the *peshmerga*, coalition special forces and conventional American formations, notably the 173rd Airborne Brigade, had crushed the Ba'athist organization and was in control both of the countryside and the major cities. Part of the Sunni heartland, around Tikrit north of Baghdad, remained to be occupied but the behaviour of its population was not affecting the development of the campaign. In the Shi'a south the British element of the coalition force committed to Operation Iraqi Freedom had, after seizing the Fao peninsula and the port of Umm Qasr, entered and secured Basra. The liberation of Iraq from the monstrous dictatorship of Saddam Hussein was almost complete.

7

The British War

Alliances are compromises in self-interest. Some alliances are less self-interested than others. The Anglo-American alliance is one of the least. The United States and the United Kingdom have been allies since 1941 and, with understandable ups and downs, have been good friends ever since. It is a unique friendship. In 1941 Britain, battered by Hitler's and Hirohito's attacks as it was, still thought of itself as a great world power. Sixty years later, with America the only superpower, that illusion has withered. The British now realistically regard themselves as a power of the second rank. Nevertheless they take, with reason, great pride in the competence of their armed forces. The Royal Navy, the army, the Royal Air Force, greatly diminished in size though they are since they struggled to victory in the Second World War, remain military instruments of exceptional quality. They have retained the ability to motivate the young men and women they recruit to the highest level of achievement, with results that are admired by the nation and its friends and feared by its foes. Wherever they are deployed, and for whatever purpose, British forces succeed in their mission. In none of the dozens of small wars they have fought since 1945 have they been defeated. To many of the countries in which they have operated they have brought the benefits of restored peace and security.

The United States military has come to appreciate the qualities of the British forces with growing enthusiasm ever since the termination of the Cold War in 1989. Until the fall of the Berlin

Wall, which inaugurated the collapse of the Soviet Union and its client Warsaw Pact states, America was able to count on many allies in the Western world. As the Soviet threat fell away, most of its Cold War allies proved fair-weather friends. Self-interest reasserted its influence. The financial costs of sustaining forces of comparable quality to those of the United States seemed a burden better shed. It became more alluring to pursue policies that diverged from those that had assured collective security before the spectre of Communism. In 1990, when the United States called for a coalition to oppose Saddam Hussein's illegal annexation of Kuwait, most of its Cold War allies, and some newfound Middle Eastern friends, responded. When in the crisis of 2002–03, America again appealed for support against Saddam, the ranks suddenly thinned. At the roll-call before hostilities commenced, only three countries came up to the mark: Australia, Britain and Poland, though it made a token contribution. The Australians, with skeletal armed resources, could only offer special operations troops and some ships and air support. The British, however, responded as they had done in 1990. They offered, besides sizeable naval and air components, a whole division of ground troops. They had done the same in 1990 but then that British contribution was matched by France and Syria, outmatched by Egypt and dwarfed by the Americans, who provided no less than eight divisions. In 2003 Britain's division amounted to almost a third of the coalition force deployed and was appreciated by the Americans as much for the military contribution it represented as for the moral commitment its presence displayed.

The division had the same title as in 1990–91, the 1st (UK) Armoured Division, but was an unorthodox formation, the result of its having been hastily improvised from units in Britain and Germany. Its core was 7 Armoured Brigade, the 'Desert Rats', which had fought in the First Gulf War, but the rest of the division was not made up of other armoured and mechanized brigades, as would have been normal, but of two elements of Britain's rapid reaction forces, 16 Air Assault Brigade and 3 Commando Brigade. The air assault brigade consisted of 1st and 3rd Battalions the

Parachute Regiment and the 1st Battalion Royal Irish Regiment; its commanding officer, Lieutenant-Colonel Tim Collins, would become famous by making an inspiring eve-of-battle speech to his troops which President George W. Bush had displayed on a wall in the Oval Office at the White House. The air assault brigade's artillery was provided by 7 Regiment Royal Horse Artillery, and armoured reconnaissance by the Household Cavalry Regiment. The commando brigade comprised only two of its normal three units, 40 and 42 Royal Marine Commando; 45 Commando was not deployed. A Commando is equivalent in size to an infantry battalion but on lighter scales of equipment and without tracked transport. The Commando brigade had, however, brought its organic gunner unit, 29 Commando Regiment Royal Artillery.

The 1st (UK) Armoured Division also had attached to it for Operation Iraqi Freedom (Operation Telic to the British, who avoid descriptive codenames) parts of 20 Armoured Brigade and a number of individual units, allotted as required. Whilst the Desert Rats officially comprised the 1st Battalion Black Watch, the 1st Battalion Royal Regiment of Fusiliers, 2nd Royal Tank Regiment and the Royal Scots Dragoon Guards, the last two tank regiments, also at the division's disposal were the Queen's Dragoon Guards and the Queen's Royal Lancers, also armour, and four infantry battalions, 1st Light Infantry, 1st Black Watch, 1st Irish Guards and 1st Duke of Wellington's Regiment; the latter was brigaded with the Commandos for the assault on the Fao peninsula. Additional batteries of Royal Artillery provided fire support and the Royal Engineers the essential combat engineering skills. Signals, transport and maintenance were provided by the Royal Corps of Signals, Royal Logistic Corps and Royal Electrical and Mechanical Engineers.

American army regiments, formerly transient organizations, have in recent years deliberately sought to create permanent identities for themselves, the high command having recognized that tradition is an important factor in fostering regimental morale. It seems to work. The parachute regiments in the 500 series, for example, take enormous pride in their histories, which began in

Normandy, and they remain among the most effective and self-confident in the US infantry. The US Marine Corps has preserved its long-established regiments as a matter of policy, with highly beneficial effects on Corps morale. In both cases the Americans have been influenced by British example. British regiments glory in their antiquity: the oldest, the Royal Scots, dates from the early seventeenth century and is older than many of the key institutions of British public life, such as the Bank of England and, indeed, the reigning House of Windsor. By some mysterious chemistry, antiquity does not condemn regiments to senility, but seems to work as an elixir of youth. The long histories of the more senior seem to challenge fresh generations of soldiers to match the standards of courage set by their predecessors in battles long ago and challenge younger regiments to emulate them. Thus to the Royal Scots Dragoon Guards the regiment's capture of an eagle standard from the enemy at Waterloo is a triumph which demands repetition; while the Irish Guards, a comparatively young regiment founded only in 1900, is constantly in competition with the Grenadiers, the personal guard established by Charles II at his restoration to the throne in 1660.

When the British go to war, therefore, commanders do not waste nervous energy in concern over their soldiers' morale. They know that, given efficient subordinates and services of supply, they will fight with spirit and effect. The regimental system ensures that. High morale and self-confidence describe the mood of the 1st (UK) Armoured Division as it deployed for the second time in little over a decade to the head of the Gulf in 2003. The Gulf is one of the British army's historic campaigning areas. It had fought and won an eventually victorious, if difficult, campaign there in the First World War. It had put down a pro-Nazi rising in Iraq in 1941. It had fought again victoriously in 1991, beside its American comrades-in-arms, in whom it had confidence. It expected that the new campaign would have the same outcome.

General Franks allotted the British a special and separate task from that of his American formations. He correctly recognized that the American divisions, with their unmatched capacity to cover ground and to resupply themselves while doing so, were the best suited to make the long-distance strike up the central valley to Baghdad. He equally recognized that the British, with their long experience of pacification operations and their historic connections with the Gulf region, would be better suited to tackling the problem of taking and holding Basra. Iraq's second city had never fully acceded to the Ba'athist system. Its Shi'a population resented control by the Sunni of the central region. On the other hand, through its commercial association with the British, which went back as far as the days of the East India Company, it was used to their presence as traders and, indirectly, to their political and naval influence over the Gulf waters at their doorstep. General Franks's calculation that the British were the best qualified of the contingents at his disposal to deploy to the Shatt el-Arab and Basra was therefore well judged.

The attack in the south was nevertheless to begin as a joint American-British operation. The decision was taken in December 2002, while the attack on Iraq was in the planning stage, to assign a US Marine Corps formation, 15 Marine Expeditionary Unit (15 MEU), to 3 Commando Brigade. Essentially a strong infantry battalion, with attached helicopter squadrons, 15 MEU combined with the commanders to land on the Fao peninsula and seize the oil facilities, while other elements of the force, reinforced by US Navy SEAL units, landed on the oil platforms twenty-five miles offshore, the points where oil pumped from the land was transferred to tankers. At the outset 40 Commando succeeded in securing two key oil installations near the town of al Fao. When its position was judged precarious, it was reinforced by 42 Commando, flown in by USMC helicopters. The operation was supported by fire from batteries of the Royal Artillery and ships offshore, the frigates *Marlborough* and *Chatham*; another Royal Navy frigate and one from the Royal Australian Navy were also involved. After securing the wellhead facilities, 3 Commando Brigade and 15 MEU proceeded up the Fao peninsula, to take Umm Qasr and Zubayr. Coalition casualties incurred in the whole operation were light, while at least thirty Iraqis were killed and 230 made prisoner.

The American Marines commented in an after-action account on the excellence of the co-operation arranged with the British. The two corps have a long association, train together frequently and cross-post personnel to each other as a matter of course. For once it is not a cliché of alliance-speak to say that they enjoy each other's company. It is easy for them to do so, for they are similar in ethos and even in appearance; ceremonially, in dark-blue uniforms and white-topped caps, they are almost indistinguishable and in recent years the Royal Marines have adopted a semi-formal dress, greenish in hue, which closely resembles its USMC equivalent. Their rank structure, based on the primacy of long-serving senior sergeants, is similar and so is the training, with this difference: all Royal Marines have to complete the gruelling commando course, which commands high prestige in USMC eyes. The commando green beret, gained also by US Marines who successfully survive the course, is highly prized and is eagerly sought in barter for USMC kit when the two corps operate together.

The commander of the 15 MEU reported after the joint operation that co-operation had gone well from the start, when it had passed through the berm, the military sand bank on the Iraqi border, via gaps blown in it by the commando squadron of Royal Engineers, a joint task they had rehearsed together. The USMC reconnaissance unit was supported in the preliminary stage by fire called down from 29 Commando Regiment Royal Artillery. Once inside Iraq, 15 MEU was opposed by the 45th Brigade of the Iraqi 11th Infantry Division but it soon melted away as its conscript soldiers deserted the ranks. Their place was taken by fighters in civilian clothes who waved white flags but continued to deliver sniper fire without surrendering. The marines pressed on though, to seize Umm Qasr and then, after ninety-six hours of combat with the enemy, to take the Iraqi naval base of Zubayr where they were relieved by British commandos. They then departed the battle zone by helicopter to join 1st Marine Expeditionary Force fighting on the road to Baghdad.

The British marines, in their own report, paid generous tribute to the assistance received from their American comrades. The Americans provided helicopter transport, which the British lacked, as well as a great deal of electronic reconnaissance and surveillance, which the British also lacked the equipment to acquire. The information 'philosophy' of the two corps is, moreover, strikingly different. The British operate a traditional 'top-down' network, by which superiors inform subordinates of what is judged necessary. The Americans operate a 'flat' system, through a commonly available website to which all who have clearance have access. As the two corps are likely to co-operate more rather than less in the future a switch to the American system seems eventually essential. It will, however, need expensive re-equipment, a programme from which the Ministry of Defence will shrink, since it has only just completed a costly programme of radio purchase; it will also be important, as the Americans themselves recognize, to avoid increasing reliance on a system that threatens information overload. The British, in American eyes, work with too little information, the Americans, in the British view, with too much. No mastermind has yet suggested an effective compromise.

With the completion of the operation to secure the Fao peninsula, and the departure of 15 MEU to join the 1st Marine Expeditionary Force, taking with it G Battery, Royal Horse Artillery, which continued to provide it with fire support as far north as Nasiriyah, the thrust of the campaign in the south changed focus. Important results had been achieved. The Fao peninsula, the mouth of the Shatt el-Arab and the platforms and terminals at the head of the Gulf were essential to the export and distribution of oil from Iraq's southern fields. They had also been highly vulnerable to sabotage by Saddam's officials. In the event, only a handful had been set alight, while the essential pumping and separation plants had been captured undamaged. The Fao operation had been an outright success. The task following was to repeat it in Basra, which had a population of one million people.

It had not originally been intended that the British should be responsible for securing Basra. When planning began at Central Command for Operation Iraqi Freedom in the spring of 2002, the only task allotted the British, and that to 3 Commando Brigade, was the seizure of the Fao peninsula by amphibious assault, while other British forces participated in the drive north to Baghdad. While the Americans wanted the British to participate, their military participation, as opposed to their presence for political reasons, was not judged essential. It was thought, probably correctly, that the United States had sufficient available force to liberate Iraq without allied assistance. By June, however, the plan changed. The moving force seems to have been General David McKiernan, nominated as the general commander (CFLCC – Combined Force Land Component Commander), who knew the British well from his involvement with NATO's Allied Rapid Reaction Corps (ARRC) in Germany, liked them and was liked in return. He now offered the British not only a part in but control of operations in northern Iraq, through the ARRC, which has a British commander.

His proposal then encountered political objections. The northern operation, to include not only the British but also the American 4th Infantry Division, could only be mounted with the consent of the Turkish government, which would have to approve its transit from Mediterranean ports and airfields to and across the Iraqi border. Even before the Turks began to make general difficulties, they were expressing particular objection to admitting British troops to their territory. The Americans found the Turkish attitude difficult to understand. The British planners involved, through consultation with the Foreign Office, were able to offer what seemed a persuasive explanation. The Turks are deeply sensitive to British involvement in their internal affairs. In 1919, after the First World War, in which they had been enemies, the British installed an army of occupation in western Turkey, the Army of the Black Sea. It had only been removed by armed confrontation. Throughout their administration of the League of Nations mandate for Iraq, the British had managed the affairs of Iraqi Kurdistan in a manner the Turks found hostile to their national interest. Most important, in 1932, the British had argued for and successfully achieved the award of the Mosul region, with its rich oil fields, to its client kingdom of Iraq by the Treaty of Lausanne. Turkey's attitude in 2002 may have been tit-for-tat. It may have expressed some deeper-seated suspicion of British motives. Whatever the explanation, the Turks were immovable. Even before they had made it clear that they would not allow American troops to traverse their territory, they had definitively excluded any British. As a result, an alternative front of operation for the British complement had to be found. On 28 December 2002, the British told the Americans that they would deploy the bulk of their forces to Kuwait and take part in operations in the south.

That left time short. While the political crisis between Saddam and the West dragged out, with the Iraqis seeking to demonstrate that there was no justification for the taking of military measures against them, and with the Americans and British insisting the opposite, planning at Central Command went on. British planning had suddenly to accelerate. Though no deadline had yet been set, it was prudent to suppose that an invasion of Iraq would occur, without a satisfactory political settlement, by early spring. The Americans were speaking of March. That left only ten weeks for a deployment, a far shorter period than had been available before the First Gulf War of 1991. Fortunately there had been an extended exercise in Oman earlier in 2002, which had revealed certain necessary measures to be taken, including that to 'desertize' the Challenger tanks. The exercise had also left one of the units of 3 Commando Brigade in the area. Hastily the Ministry of Defence began to reinforce, sending ships and aircraft and speeding the dispatch of ground forces. Ever since the Falklands crisis of 1982, when Britain had had to assemble a long-range expeditionary force at a few days' notice, the planning organization had been honing its skills of improvisation. Now, in a hurry, another Commando was sent out to join its sister unit; 16 Air Assault Brigade, which was not encumbered by armour requiring heavy lift, was despatched, and 7 Armoured Brigade, the most experienced and readily deployable major formation on hand, was shipped from Germany. By February

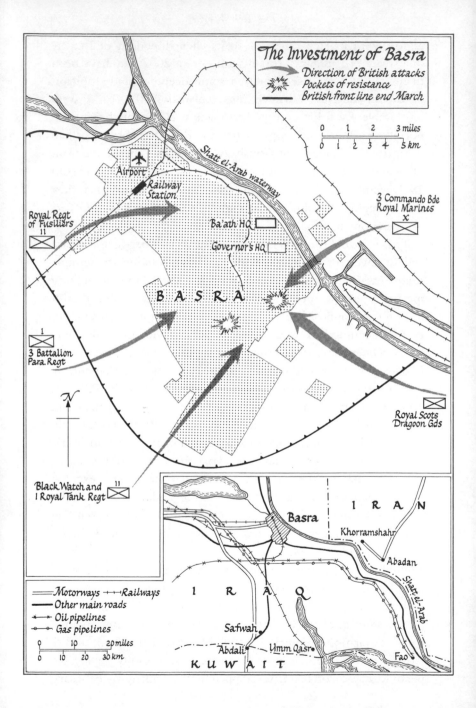

The Investment of Basra

Direction of British attacks
Pockets of resistance
British front line end March

0   1   2   3 miles
0   1   2   3   4   5 km

Airport

Railway Station

Shatt el-Arab waterway

Royal Regt of Fusiliers
11

Ba'ath HQ

Governor's HQ

3 Commando Bde
Royal Marines
X

B A S R A

3 Battalion
Para. Regt
1

N

Royal Scots
Dragoon Gds

Black Watch and
1 Royal Tank Regt
11

I R A N

Basra

Khorramshahr

Abadan

I R A Q

Shatt el-Arab

Safwah

Abdali   Umm Qasr

Fao

K U W A I T

Motorways   Railways
Other main roads
Oil pipelines
Gas pipelines

0   10   20 miles
0   10   20   30 km

Britain had the makings of a respectable intervention force in place. No other European country could have achieved the same results in the time available, not the French and certainly not the Germans. British troops, though few in number and less technically advanced than the American, had once again demonstrated their formidable readiness to respond to a challenge and competence to meet it.

Their competence was particularly suited to the problems presented by the need to isolate, enter and subdue the resistance in Basra. The British cannot match the Americans at the highest level of modern military performance. Shortage of funds deprives them of state-of-the-art equipment in the fields of target acquisition, reconnaissance, surveillance and intercommunication. In certain military tasks, however, they are without equal. Special operations is one, as American emulation of the SAS demonstrates. Counter-insurgency is another. Thirty years of engagement with the Irish Republican Army, in the grimy streets of Northern Ireland's cities, has taught the British, down to the level of the youngest soldier, the essential skills of personal survival in the environment of urban warfare and of dominance over those who wage it. Every man covering another on patrol, watching the upper window, skirting the suspicious vehicle, stopping to question the solitary male: these are the methods the British army knows backwards. Painfully acquired, they have resulted in a superb mastery of the technique of control of the streets. The army has created an artificial urban training ground where these skills can be taught. As a result they have become expert at reading the geography of an urban area − which are the likely ambush points, where bombs are likely to be planted, what observation point must be entered and occupied − and have used their mastery of urban geography to dominate. Irish Republicans hate those they call 'Crown forces' for their professionalism, since it has blocked their ambition to control the Northern Irish cities themselves. As the entry into Basra was to prove, the British army's mastery of the methods of urban warfare is transferable. What had worked in Belfast could be made to work also in Basra, against another set of urban terrorists, with a different motivation from the Irish Republican though equally as nasty.

Basra's inhabitants occupy an area about two kilometres (1.24 miles) square, with a sprawl of suburbs on the southern side. The eastern boundary of the built-up area is formed by the Shatt el-Arab, the confluence of the Tigris and Euphrates. The old city, a warren of narrow streets, is not, however, on the water. The modern city has grown up to enclose it. There are a number of tall buildings but they are few and scattered; nothing in Basra resembles the government quarter in Baghdad, with its complex of towers and ultra-modern buildings. It is a shabby, traditional Middle Eastern town, overgrown by the influx of population and bewildering to an outsider who does not know its street pattern at first hand.

Fortunately, in the years since the First Gulf War, the British intelligence services had done a great deal to set up a comprehensive network in Basra, in the expectation that, if trouble with Saddam continued, the largest concentration of Shi'a in the country could be turned against him; it would certainly yield useful information if properly exploited. It was greatly to the advantage of the British that, despite their withdrawal from empire in the 1960s and '70s, they had never fully lost touch with the region. Their long association with the Indian subcontinent and with the Gulf principalities provided a bedrock of familiarity with the political and ethnic realities; their commercial involvement in Iraq, particularly through the oil industry, sustained personal contacts; and the British services' provision of equipment and training programmes to the Gulf principalities' armed forces kept in being a body of local experts who knew the terrain and the tribes and, above all, spoke the local language. Knowledge of Arabic was a not uncommon language skill in the British army, particularly in its Special Forces and Intelligence Corps.

After the British parted company with the US Marine Corps on 23 March, their conventional ground forces were quite well prepared to undertake the isolation and capture of Basra; 7 Armoured Brigade took over the positions vacated by the 7th

Marine Regiment, 16 Air Assault Brigade those of 5th Marines. They did not, however, immediately close up to the city, but remained at a distance, forming a cordon outside the built-up area to put it under surveillance, prevent the passage of reinforcements into the city and monitor the inhabitants leaving. Each flank of the cordon rested on the river, the opposite bank of which was held by 3 Commando Brigade, while the cordon itself, about twenty miles long in circuit and crossing all the roads into the city on the west bank, was maintained at a distance of about two miles from the outskirts. The plan formed by Major General Robin Brims, the 1st (UK) Armoured Division commander, was at first to wait and watch and to gather as much information as possible from fugitives about points of resistance, whereabouts of armed bodies of fighters and the identity of leaders, military and political. Despite the efforts of the Ba'ath organization to control the population, fugitives soon began to trickle out, progressively in larger and larger groups. They sought safety, but also food and water, and were ready to talk to the British, who spread the word by mouth and printed leaflet that they had come to stay, would protect civilians and could be trusted. Meanwhile SAS and SBS teams penetrated the built-up area under cover, to reconnoitre and make touch with intelligence contacts in the city.

General Brims was resolved not to provoke a fight for the city until he was certain that it could be won quickly and easily, without causing serious damage or heavy loss of life, particularly civilian life. The policy was particularly necessary in view of the hostile attitude of much of the British media, the BBC foremost, to the war against Saddam; unlike their American counterparts, who generally supported the war and their President, home-based British journalists – not those travelling with the troops – regarded it as a neo-colonialist undertaking, doubted official justifications for its launch, particularly that Saddam possessed weapons of mass destruction, and were eager to report anything that smacked of atrocity. Ali Hassan al-Majid, 'Chemical Ali', the senior Ba'athist in the city, was for his part anxious to keep the population within the city bounds and hoped to provoke a bout of street fighting in the narrow byways that would feed Western media prejudice. He also hoped that the British forces would suffer heavy casualties, with a consequently bad effect on British public opinion at home.

'Chemical Ali's' capacity to achieve the effects he desired was, however, severely limited by the means available to him. He was personally intensely unpopular with the Shi'a population, which he had slaughtered in large numbers after the Basra uprising of 1991. His Ba'ath party organization was thinly spread in a city where it had always been regarded as an instrument of Sunni dominance. He had, finally, only the sketchiest military apparatus with which to operate. The 11th Division, the local formation of Iraq's so-called regular army, had already largely dissolved. Those soldiers who remained could be made to fight only by terror methods, which provoked farther desertions. As a result, those who would do his will were either local Ba'athists, all too aware of the fate that awaited them if the fight for the city was lost, and *fedayeen* sent from Baghdad by Qusay Hussein, Saddam's son. Many were foreigners; few had any training beyond a sketchy course in firing the Kalashnikov assault rifle and the RPG-7 grenade launcher. Of the skills at which the British infantry excelled – marksmanship, mutual support and massing firepower when attacked – they had no knowledge whatsoever.

Between 23 and 31 March the siege of Basra took the form of a stand-off, with 'Chemical Ali' trying to tempt the British inside and the British refusing to move major units downtown. They waited and watched, gathering intelligence and interrogating fugitives. Small units infiltrated the city, SAS and Royal Marine Commando SBS teams, patrols from the regular units and individual snipers, who chose fire positions and observed. The Iraqis tried to provoke a fight, by launching sorties with tanks and armoured vehicles and by mortaring the British lines. Sometimes they overreached themselves. On the night of 26–27 March a column of Iraqi tanks headed out into open country. At daylight it was intercepted by the Royal Scots Dragoon Guards, who destroyed all fifteen tanks at no loss to themselves. The Iraqi tanks involved were Soviet T-55s, when built after the Second World War excellent fighting vehicles but, by the twenty-first century, museum pieces. The British Challengers, with their 120mm guns, could destroy them at ranges too great for their own guns to reach.

By 31 March the British were becoming more aggressive. General Brims decided that his intelligence picture was sufficiently clear for him to begin infiltrating larger units into the city. One task given them was to attack Ba'ath party leaders, whom snipers were able to identify by their habit of using cell phones on the streets and visibly issuing orders to people around them. Engaging at several hundred yards, with an updated version of the bolt-action Lee-Enfield rifle, in use in the British army for over a century, they achieved a dominant psychological effect. Major Ben Farrell, a company commander in 1st Irish Guards, described the technique to *The Daily Telegraph*: 'Our snipers are working in pairs' (one man used the rifle, the other a telescope), 'infiltrating the enemy's territory to give us very good observation of what is going on inside Basra and to shoot the enemy as well when the opportunity arises. . . . They don't kill large numbers but the psychological effect and the denial of freedom of movement to the enemy is vast.' An Irish Guards sniper later described to a *Daily Telegraph* reporter how their missions worked. 'It's a bit scary going into buildings because they haven't been cleared and we don't know if they have left any booby-traps for us. But once we are here they don't know where we are and it feels OK. We can report back what is going on – to call in air strikes or direct artillery – and if they are within range of our rifles we will shoot them.'

This sort of operation – targeting armed terrorists acting singly or in small groups, without causing harm to the civilian population – is one at which British troops excel. They have learnt the skills in many terrorist-ridden environments, including Beirut and Sierra Leone as well as Northern Ireland, over the last thirty years and more.

British technique paid off in Basra, in what could be viewed as a repetition of the success of Operation Motorman against the Irish Republican Army in Londonderry in 1972. There the IRA had seized control of a large area of the city, proclaimed it to be 'Free Derry' and denied entry to the security forces. Anxious to avoid both the widening of disorder and a bad press, the army did not intervene. Over several months, however, it constructed a detailed intelligence plot and secretly rehearsed a plan to retake 'Free Derry' without provoking a costly fight in the narrow streets. When ready, it struck. Early one morning, columns of military vehicles penetrated 'Free Derry' from several directions simultaneously and within a few hours had reoccupied the whole area and reimposed civil order, without provoking armed resistance. Motorman was the indirect inspiration of the operation to take Basra.

Because Basra is much larger than Londonderry, with a far greater population, its capture could not be staged as a single coup. Having assembled an intelligence picture of where the Ba'ath power structure was located and how it worked, 1st (UK) Armoured Division began in early April to launch raids into the city, down the main roads leading into it, by columns of Warrior fighting vehicles. The Warrior is well adapted to such tasks. Relatively well-armoured and well-armed, with a 30mm cannon in its turret, and capable of speeds of 50 miles per hour or more, the Warrior has the capacity to make quick penetrations of a position and speedy withdrawals. For several days the Warriors raided in and out, destroying identified Ba'athist positions and adding to the divisional staff's stock of intelligence. Such intelligence, amplified by information gathered by the SAS, SBS and Secret Intelligence Service teams, allowed point attacks to be launched by artillery outside the city and by the coalition air forces. Among the successes achieved was the destruction of a building in which the Basra Ba'ath leadership was meeting, causing many fatalities, and another attack on what was believed to be the headquarters of 'Chemical Ali' on 5 April. It was later found to have been based on false intelligence but it was for a time believed by the population to have been successful and so helped to weaken Ba'athist control.

Finally, on 6 April, General Brims launched a full-scale assault.

The city was now ringed with British units, the 1st Royal Regiment of Fusiliers to the northwest, the 3rd Battalion Parachute Regiment to the west, the Black Watch with the 1st Royal Tank Regiment to the southwest, the Royal Scots Dragoon Guards to the south and the Royal Marines across the river, but with amphibious capability, to the east. The original plan was that, after the units had launched simultaneous but individual drives down the streets leading to the centre, they should withdraw and wait the night outside before repeating the procedure. The initial penetration, however, went better than expected: in an uninhabited factory complex, where there was no risk of causing civilian casualties, it proved possible to call in helicopter gunship strikes directed by Air-Naval-Gunfire Company (ANGLICO) liaison teams of US Marines allotted to the British armoured division. The firepower deployed inflicted heavy losses on Ba'athists and *fedayeen* defending the complex.

Such was the early success achieved by his forces that General Brims decided to persist. They were organized in 'battle groups', an improvised formation much favoured by the British and viable in a small army where everyone knows everyone else. General Brims's battle groups consisted typically of one or two companies of infantry mounted in Warrior armoured vehicles and a squadron of Challenger tanks. One battle group, which had cleared out the factory complex, was switched to attack the area of the College of Literature, a university campus occupied by 300 *fedayeen*, mostly non-Iraqi Islamic terrorists from other Arab countries, including Morocco, Algeria and Syria. Reducing the resistance of the *fedayeen*, who lacked military skills but were eager to fight to the last, took four hours, in a battle in which the British troops could not call on fire support, because of the danger of causing civilian casualties, but had to depend on their own infantry skills.

By the evening of 6 April the British were largely in control of Basra and 7 Armoured Brigade, the core of 1st (UK) Armoured Division, set up its headquarters on the university campus. The next morning, 7 April, 16 Air Assault Brigade, with two parachute battalions and the 1st Royal Irish Regiment under command, entered the narrow streets of the old city where armoured vehicles could operate only with difficulty, and set about chasing the remnants of the Ba'ath and the *fedayeen* out of the area. It proved that there was little to do. Saddam's régime recognized that it was beaten and its representatives were leaving the city.

On 8 April the British began to adopt a postwar mode. Anxious to reassure the Shi'a population that they had come to stay, they took off their helmets and flak jackets, dismounted from their armoured vehicles and began to mingle with the crowds. Soon afterwards General Brims withdrew his armoured vehicles from the city centre altogether, leaving his soldiers to patrol on foot, with orders to smile, chat and restore the appearance of normality. It was an acknowledgement that the war in the south was over. The struggle to win 'hearts and minds' – a concept familiar to British soldiers in fifty years of disengagement from distant and foreign lands – was about to begin.

The British campaign had been an undoubted success. They had secured all their objectives – the Fao peninsula, the Shatt el-Arab, the oil terminals, Iraq's second city – quickly and at minimal cost. British loss of life was slight. They had also conducted their war in a fashion that appeared to leave them, as the representatives of the coalition, on good terms with the southern population of defeated Iraq. The inhabitants of Basra made it clear, to the British soldiers who took possession of their city, that they were glad to be rid both of the representatives of Saddam's régime and of the foreign fighters who supported it. If a new Iraq were to be created from the ruins of the old, Basra seemed the most promising point at which to start.

8

The Fall of Baghdad

The pause at the end of March, which had slowed the advance of the 1st Marine Expeditionary Force and halted the 3rd Infantry Division, encouraged many media commentators, particularly in Europe, to suggest that the campaign had run out of impetus. Particularly so in France, where the public and the opinion makers were as hostile to the war as the government. *Enlisement* was a term that began to be applied, a word with special resonance for the French since it had been used to characterize the bogging-down of their army in Indo-China, in the first European war against Ho Chi Minh and General Giap fifty years earlier. *Le Monde*, organ of official opinion and of the ruling class, announced on 27 March that President Bush had been 'forced to revise his plans in the face of Iraqi resistance'. The French provincial press gloated over even gloomier predictions, forecasting a lengthening war and heavier casualties. Much was made of the forcing down of an American helicopter, allegedly by an elderly Arab with an antiquated rifle, who may merely have witnessed a case of engine failure. In Britain, too, there was a search by the media for sensationalist bad news. Antony Beevor, the author of a bestselling account of the battle of Stalingrad, was obliged to tell a newspaper executive who attempted to engage him to write about the coming battles of Saddamgrad, meanwhile swearing him to secrecy at the originality of the idea, that nine other newspapers were ahead of him and, anyhow, that he foresaw no Stalingrad in Baghdad.

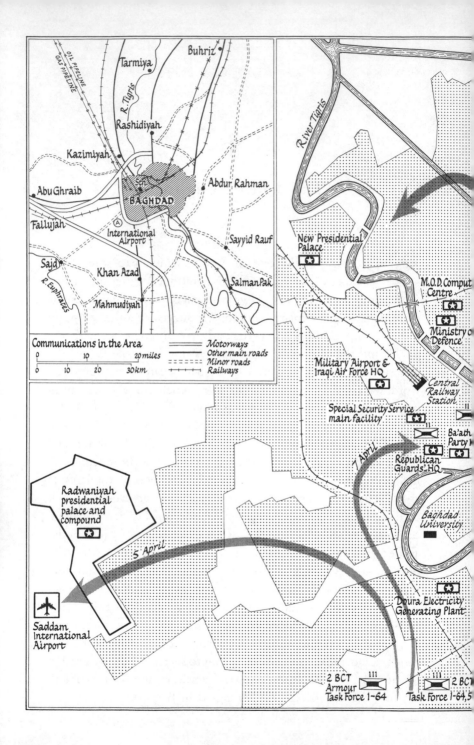

Inset map (Communications in the Area):

OIL PIPELINE
GAS PIPELINE

Tarmiya
Buhriz
R. Tigris
Rashidiyah
Kazimiyah
Abu Ghraib
Abdur Rahman
BAGHDAD
Fallujah
International Airport
Sayyid Rauf
Sajd
Khan Azad
Salman Pak
R. Euphrates
Mahmudiyah

Communications in the Area

0 10 20 miles
0 10 20 30 km

Motorways
Other main roads
Minor roads
Railways

Main map labels:

River Tigris

New Presidential Palace

M.O.D. Computer Centre

Ministry of Defence

Military Airport & Iraqi Air Force HQ

Central Railway Station

Special Security Service main facility

Ba'ath Party

Republican Guards' HQ

Baghdad University

7 April

Radwaniyah presidential palace and compound

5 April

Doura Electricity Generating Plant

Saddam International Airport

2 BCT Armour Task Force 1-64

2 BCT Task Force 1-64,5

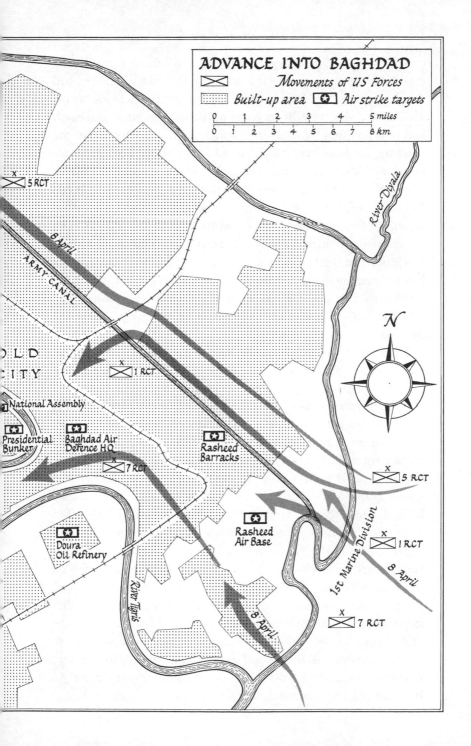

ADVANCE INTO BAGHDAD

⬒ Movements of US Forces

⬚ Built-up area ⬚ Air strike targets

0 1 2 3 4 5 miles
0 1 2 3 4 5 6 7 8 km

River Diyala

8 April

ARMY CANAL

5 RCT

OLD CITY

National Assembly

Presidential Bunker

Baghdad Air Defence HQ

Rasheed Barracks

1 RCT

7 RCT

Doura Oil Refinery

Rasheed Air Base

River Tigris

1st Marine Division

8 April

5 RCT

1 RCT

7 RCT

8 April

N

The pause had causes quite different from those identified by anti-American journalists. It had been brought about by bad weather and the need for resupply. Minor military setbacks apart, such as the difficulty of negotiating passage through Nasiriyah and of suppressing ill-organized resistance in other towns on the roads up, the Americans had achieved a pace of advance unprecedented in history, far outstripping that of the Germans towards Moscow in the summer of 1941 and even that of the British from the Seine to the liberation of Brussels in the victorious summer of 1944, following the breakout from Normandy. The Americans had suffered almost no casualties – so much for French predictions of 'heavier casualties' – and virtually no equipment losses. Their generals, moreover, were in no way discountenanced by the need to pause. Even as they accepted the necessity and organized the rush forward of resupply, they were planning the next stage of the operation.

Thus far it was the Marines who appeared to have been in the forefront, because they had been reducing resistance in the central valley, taking towns and travelling on paved roads, the modern highways which were Saddam's contribution to Iraq's communication network. The 3rd Infantry Division, by contrast, had been pushing northward on the edge of hard desert above the alluvial plain. Because the going was good, it had made excellent progress but the nature of the terrain entailed higher fuel consumption and more vehicle breakdowns. The marines had been able to re-fuel by landing C-130 aircraft, with 5,000-gallon diesel bladders, direct onto the surface of the highways. The 3rd Infantry Division, travelling on surfaces too hazardous for aircraft landings, required refuelling by wheeled tankers and also needed to set up fuel depots from which to refill. Hence, in part, the pause.

Once the pause for resupply had been completed and other stores of food, water and ammunition dumped forward, a miracle of American logistic expertise deeply impressive to attached British officers, and essential repairs and servicing completed, 3rd Infantry Division was ready by 30 March to recommence its drive on Baghdad. At the command conference on 26 March between

Generals McKiernan, Conway and Wallace, directing the operations respectively of the whole ground force, the Marines and V Corps, comprising 3rd Infantry Division and its other attached army units, it had been agreed that the Marines should continue their push up the central valley, sticking to the paved roads, while 3rd Infantry Division, with the brigades of 82nd and 101st clearing up resistance in its rear, should press on to the Karbala Gap. The V Corps operation would have five objectives. An armoured cavalry element of 3rd Infantry Division, 3/7 Cavalry, with two of the division's brigade combat teams, would lead the drive into the gap itself. The rest of 3rd Infantry Division would advance out of the desert to capture the bridges over the Euphrates south of Karbala. Then the brigades of 101st Air Assault Division would make raids in force farther south on the Euphrates and another part of 101st would mount a probing attack into the desert west of Karbala. Apart from the drive into the Karbala Gap, the subsidiary operations were intended either to capture essential objectives or to mislead the Iraqi high command as to the attackers' purposes.

The plan also had the purpose of confronting the Republican Guard, deployed outside Baghdad, with a direct military threat. The threat was double-edged. As explained to me by General Franks in the immediate aftermath of the war, the plan was to 'shape' the battlefield outside Baghdad, by using the advance of ground forces to hold the Republican Guard in place while heavily bombing its rear as a warning that, if it attempted to retreat into the city, it would suffer an even worse fate than having to engage in combat with the American armoured units. The 'shaping' plan was partly material and partly psychological in design. Its object was to deter the Republican Guard from disappearing into the built-up area, where it might indeed have created a 'Saddamgrad', by representing inactivity – staying where it was, with the chance of surrendering to the advancing Americans – as preferable to decamping, which would ensure its being carpet bombed, as during the First Gulf War.

The plan was also intended to persuade the Iraqi high command

– always supposing that it remained operational, which seemed increasingly unlikely as the war drew out – that the American attack on Baghdad would come from an unexpected direction, not out of the desert above Karbala, but indeed through the Karbala Gap. The plan also drew attention away from the approach of the Marines on the eastern flank of the city, up the Tigris.

What the Americans were preparing was a classic pincer movement, but baiting the trap so that Saddam and his sons Qusay and Uday, who had apparently supplanted in authority the senior generals as the crisis heightened, would be unable to identify from which direction the disabling blow would come. If they reacted as expected, by failing to move the Republican Guard into the capital, it would not matter what decisions they took thereafter. The fall of the city's approaches would guarantee the success of a penetrative operation to its heart.

The preliminaries to the advance into Baghdad must be the seizure of the Karbala Gap, whose shoulders were formed by Lake Razzazah and the Euphrates and up which ran Highway 8, the main road into the southwestern suburbs, and the capture of Baghdad (Saddam) International Airport, known to be of the greatest symbolic significance to the régime but which was also of high military value, its runways and facilities providing means for direct airlifted reinforcement and resupply of the forward troops. The attack on the gap was to be led by the 3rd Brigade Combat Team of 3rd Infantry Division, which had been relieved by the brigade of 82nd Airborne Division from duty on the lines of communication southward to Kuwait.

The topography of the Karbala Gap had been much studied by the US Army ever since its strategic focus had turned to the Middle East at the beginning of the 1990s. Plans to penetrate it had been practised in war games and tactical exercises without troops at all major army study centres, just as the Fulda Gap had been endlessly studied during the days of the Cold War, when US Seventh Army had stood on the defensive opposite the Group of Soviet Forces Germany in Central Europe. The Fulda Gap is the gateway to the Rhine for any invader coming westward out of what used to be the People's Republic of (East) Germany. Now the boot was on the other foot. Seventh Army – to which 3rd Infantry Division and the rest of V Corps in Iraq belonged – had to mount an offensive through a similar gap, and to traverse it at the highest speed, leaving no time for Saddam, Qusay and Uday to reposition forces to oppose it. Speed was of the highest importance because of the danger that the Iraqi engineer corps, the most competent part of Saddam's armed forces, might blow the Hadithah dam, flooding the plain of the upper Euphrates and turning it into a swamp impenetrable by armoured troops. The terrain was naturally waterlogged and had been improved as an obstacle zone by the Iraqi engineers.

The first task was to take and hold the Hadithah dam, a task assigned to army Ranger units, specialist infantry trained on commando lines. They were initially instructed only to take the dam and then pass on. On reconsideration General Franks decided that the dam had to be held against the danger of counter-attack, in the event proving a sensible precaution. The Iraqis, using troops drawn from the Republican Guard, did counter-attack and the Rangers had to endure two weeks of heavy combat, during which they were severely shelled as well as subjected to repeated attacks. Troops of the 101st Airborne Division eventually relieved them.

The next task was to secure the crossings over the Euphrates east of Karbala, near Hindiyah. There was also a dam on the Euphrates at Hindiyah which it was important to save from destruction. Manoeuvre along this stretch of the Euphrates was difficult. The river banks were high, the surrounding ground marshy, and the defending troops, drawn from the Republican Guard, proved of better than usual quality. During 1–2 April, 3rd Infantry Division was engaged in heavy combat, its helicopters providing continuous close support and the divisional artillery putting down heavy bombardment. On 1 April the division's 3rd Brigade, with two armoured battalions forward, took control of the eastern outskirts of Karbala, while the 1st Brigade man-oeuvred to attack from the other side. The culmination of the division's mission was the seizure of the Euphrates dams and bridges but swampy terrain made progress difficult.

By 2 April Iraqi resistance had been sufficiently overcome for the divisional commander, General Buford Blount, to begin planning a crossing of the Euphrates. He hoped that the intensity of his attack thus far had so knocked about the defence that it would be possible to capture a bridge on the run. The Iraqis had, as elsewhere on the great waterways, neglected to blow up the vital spans, perhaps deterred by the coalition special forces which were operating in strength in the area, perhaps because helicopter surveillance threatened demolition parties with attack. On the afternoon of 2 April, a tank unit, 3-69 Armour, reported that it had got three tanks across a bridge prepared for demolition but not yet destroyed.

The defence of river lines is notoriously difficult. Defenders are reluctant to destroy bridges which might leave friendly troops on the wrong side or be needed later for a counter-attack. It is also difficult, in the heat of action, to keep count of which bridges remain under the control of one's own side. Such failure was largely at the root in May 1940 of the French army's loss of crossings over the River Meuse, which resulted in the collapse of the Ninth Army and the beginning of the blitzkrieg. Something similar occurred on the Euphrates during March 2003. The Iraqi engineers failed to detonate the charges they had already placed in position. After the appearance of American tanks on their own side of the river, they did detonate the bridge, only for it to survive the explosions. They had miscalculated the solidity of its construction. The attacking Americans cut the wires leading to some unexploded charges and destroyed the positions in which the Iraqi engineers still sheltered. Shortly after the abortive detonations, 3-69 Armour had positioned three companies of armoured vehicles on the Baghdad bank and was ready to advance. Behind the point units, two alternative crossings were quickly thrown across the Euphrates, a medium-girder bridge to reinforce that damaged by the Iraqi engineers and a floating pontoon bridge parallel to it. The ponderous bridging trains, which had trailed behind the spearheads during the lightning advance, had begun to demonstrate their usefulness.

Once across the Euphrates, the leading tanks and armoured fighting vehicles of 3rd Infantry Division quickly reached the international airport complex. The airport is an example of how in Iraq the ultramodern and the antediluvian intermingle. Outside the airport complex the landscape has scarcely changed since the days of the Kings of Babylon – the site of whose capital lies just beyond it. The countryside presents a spectacle of sluggish irrigation canals, mud houses and palm groves. The airport itself is approached by concrete roads, interchanges and over- and under-passes. As the armoured vanguard approached the airport to take up attacking positions, fighting focused on two concrete intersections to the west, between the runways and the Euphrates. The American armoured units formed a defensive perimeter around the two intersections and awaited attack. It soon came. Saddam and his sons, or whoever was still directing the Iraqi defensive effort, correctly recognized that the appearance of the vanguard of 3rd Infantry Division at the airport presaged the downfall of the régime. Throughout the afternoon and evening of 3 April, successive waves of *fedayeen* – not the Republican Guard, which appears to have been engaged against the Marines farther to the east, certainly not the regular army, which had almost ceased to exist – launched attacks from north, east and west. They appeared in any form of transport to hand, cars, trucks, buses, or mounted on motorcycles. Their attacks were not conventional or co-ordinated military assaults. There was no support by armour or artillery. The *fedayeen* behaved like the martyrs they claimed to be, firing assault rifles and rocket-propelled grenades in unorganized rushes on the American positions, until over 400 of them lay dead on the battleground.

On 4 April *fedayeen* attacks became better organized. Tanks appeared, manned either by the *fedayeen* themselves or by the Republican Guard or remnants of the regular army. The Americans around the Abu Ghraib expressway began to take on Iraqi armour with their vehicle-mounted guns, the 120mm cannon of their Abrams tanks or the 25mm chain guns of their Bradley armoured fighting vehicles. Bradleys had not been built to engage tanks; they were up-gunned and up-armoured versions of the previous generation of armoured personnel carriers, supposed to be protected by their own tanks in manoeuvre engagements. The chain guns, however, proved remarkably effective at engaging T-72 tanks, Soviet-supplied vehicles which were supposed to be the best in the Iraqi army. The Bradleys were also supported by strike aircraft. The Bradley chain guns destroyed five T-72s. Later on 4 April Abrams tanks advanced to engage T-72s reported by the supporting aircraft to be sheltering under the concrete roadways. At ranges of a thousand metres (1,093 yards) or more, the Abrams gunners knocked out sixteen T-72s, completing the destruction of the whole Iraqi tank force that had been sent against them.

Intelligence assessments now persuaded General Blount that he had achieved both his current operational aims, the domination of the international airport and the opening of the approach into Baghdad from the west. He therefore decided to press forward from his positions encircling the airport and take it under control. By the evening of 4 April his 4th Brigade Combat Team was inside the perimeter, probing for resistance. The forward edge of reconnaissance was provided by his units of the 9th and 10th Cavalry Regiments. By early in the morning of 5 April his advanced elements were in control of the runways and the international terminal.

There had been some resistance from men on foot, perfectly pointless against the columns of American armoured vehicles. As soon, however, as the division was securely in place, Iraqi armour appeared on the airport outskirts and began an attack to retake it. It was a futile undertaking. Not only were the remnants of the Republican Guard and regular army outclassed at every organizational level from the top downward by the Americans, the obsolescence of their equipment condemned them to be massacred. During the Iraqi counter-attack on the airport, T-72s and early Cold War vintage T-55s appeared, to oppose not only Bradleys but M1A1 Abrams, the most advanced tanks in the world, armed with 120mm guns directed by laser range-finders. Twelve T-72s, two T-55s and six other armoured vehicles were knocked out in the course of the fighting, at no cost to the Americans at all.

After the defeat of the Iraqi armoured counter-attack, the American high command deemed a brief pause to consider operational options. Memories of previous bad experiences of city fighting, in Hue in Vietnam and Mogadishu in Somalia, counselled caution to some. Generals Franks and McKiernan took a different view. The campaign thus far had achieved extraordinary results, the farthest advance at speed over distance ever recorded and the disintegration of an army twice the size of the invading force. Superior equipment and organization supplied many of the reasons why such success had been won. Besides material and technical factors, however, moral and psychological dimensions had been at work. Daring and boldness had played parts in the campaign as significant as dominance in the air, greater firepower or higher mobility on the ground. Franks and McKiernan were now convinced that the opposition had lost, if it had ever possessed, the means to organize an effective defence of Baghdad. Permission was given to launch deep reconnaissance probes – 'thunder runs' – into the centre of the city.

The two American generals may have been influenced by the example of the British operation which had successfully secured Basra, in turn itself modelled on earlier operations in Northern Ireland. They may independently have come to the conclusion that raids into the city would not be effectively opposed by what remained of Saddam's forces. Whatever the inspiration, in the early morning of 5 April 3rd Infantry Division's armoured spearhead, 1st Battalion 64th Armoured Regiment (1-64), moved out of its overnight positions to attack up Highway 8 directly into the southern suburbs, with the 'régime district' of ministries and residential palaces as its objective.

Central Baghdad was still full of fighters of various denominations, Saddam *Fedayeen*, Republican Guard, regular army and foreign fanatics; the intelligence staff's assessment was that only two Republican Guard brigades and 15,000 *fedayeen* remained available to Saddam, who had apparently transferred control of the defence to his two sons, Uday and Qusay, neither qualified to direct fast-moving military operations. Few of the defenders on the morning of 5 April, moreover, were prepared for the appearance of the Americans. Iraqi disinformation had done them a disservice. Though denials by the Minister of Information, Muhammad Saeed al-Sahhaf, soon to be celebrated about the world as 'Comical Ali', that the invaders had reached the capital, mixed with assertions that they were being thrown back with heavy losses, brought heart to supporters of the régime, they did nothing to present the fighters on the ground with the facts. The advancing Americans of 1-64, moving at high speed down boulevards leading to the city centre, found fighters eating breakfast, evidently oblivious of imminent danger. Farther down the street other fighters, alerted by the sound of approaching gunfire, hastily manned defensive positions. They drenched the American armoured columns with fire from their Kalashnikov assault rifles and RPG-7 grenade launchers, all of it ineffective against the armoured skins of Abrams tanks and Bradley fighting vehicles. The deeper the Americans penetrated, the more intense became the martyr impulse. Fighters appeared in hundreds along the sides of the streets into the city, mounting suicidal assaults with weapons instantly overpowered by those of the invaders.

The Americans on the ground were supported by Americans in the air, flying A-10 Warthog anti-tank aircraft. American gunship helicopters also added to the carnage, attacking Iraqi military positions and vehicles identified in the city streets. The fighting was not altogether one-sided. An Abrams tank was set on fire by a hit from an RPG-7 launcher but the crew were able to evacuate the vehicle without loss. Many of the armoured vehicles of 1-64 had been hit by anti-armour weapons, mostly RPG-7s, but none had been disabled. After repair and re-supply, 1-64 was ready for the next phase of operations. It had suffered no human casualties at all. By contrast hundreds of Iraqi fighters had been killed in the street combat.

There had also been heavy fighting during 5 April, persisting into 6 April, on Route 1, the highway leading out of Baghdad to Tikrit, Saddam's seat of family and tribal power. It ran due north out of the city through a series of concrete intersections and, as the American pincers closed round Baghdad from west and east, it became the only remaining escape route out of the city to what might still be a place of refuge. The 3rd Brigade Combat Team of 3rd Infantry Division was ordered to take and hold it, against at first small parties of escapees but later a flood of motorized fugitives protected by tanks of the Republican Guard. The fight to prevent their leaving lasted for ten hours and was heavily contested, eventually resolving into an armoured battle between Republican Guard tanks and the 7th Cavalry for control of the last bridge the road crossed out of the city. Eight tanks were destroyed before the Americans closed off the exit.

General Blount's soldiers now controlled the western perimeter of the capital, as the Marines did the eastern. The Iraqis lacked the means to break the cordon from the outside and, though there were still considerable numbers of soldiers and fighters within the city, Blount had concluded that they lacked the spirit or organization to conduct an effective defence. He decided on a second 'thunder run', to be mounted by his 2nd Brigade Combat Team, led by Colonel David Perkins. If it made a successful penetration the raid would become a permanent occupation of the city centre. Perkins, who proposed the raid, was convinced that occupation was now possible, since he sensed from the tempo of the fighting that the defenders were on the point of collapse. Generals McKiernan and Franks, conferring with the divisions and brigade commanders via their sophisticated communications system – which allowed the high command to call up images of the battleground on their television screens in 'real time' – concurred.

Soon after 2nd Brigade Combat Team left its line of departure, however, the fighting took an unpleasant turn. The key points on the way towards the centre, particularly the 'régime district' of ministries and palaces the Marines were attacking from the other direction, proved to be three concrete overpasses on the network of internal city streets, codenamed by the Americans Curly, Larry and Moe. On the advance towards them, an Iraqi surface-to-surface missile, one of the few fired during the campaign since the fighting on the Fao peninsula at the outset, impacted near Perkins's headquarters, killing five soldiers and damaging several vehicles. The missile strike caused disorganization and brief delay. Soon after it, however, 2nd BCT had resumed the advance, led by 1st Battalion 64th Armored Regiment, with seventy Abrams tanks and sixty Bradley armoured fighting vehicles. The enemy they encountered were mainly *fedayeen*, now somewhat better organized since the first 'thunder run' of 5 April. Obstacles had been improvised by overturning buses, trucks and construction vehicles, and strongpoints and barricades had been constructed along and across the streets. The obstacles were pushed aside by the tanks, acting as bulldozers. Colonel Perkins then judged the way into central Baghdad to be open and ordered 1-64 and its sister unit, 4-64, to press ahead. The régime district of ministries and palaces was an hour away. The district in between, formed of parks and wide avenues, offered good fields of fire and could easily be defended against *fedayeen* human-wave attacks. Blount approved Perkins's plan on condition that his lead elements could be re-supplied with fuel and ammunition.

The fight for central Baghdad, launched up Highway 8 towards the Moe, Curly and Larry overpasses, became during 7 April essentially one of passing the resupply columns forward to the fighting troops. Responsibility for the operation moved to another battalion of 3rd Infantry Division, 3rd Battalion 15th Infantry Regiment (3-15), commanded by Lieutenant Colonel Steven Twitty. Twitty's rapid assessment was that to guarantee the arrival of resupply at the engaged units he would have to secure and hold the three overpasses, Moe, Larry and Curly, the first a mile apart, Curly two miles farther on. Twitty committed his conventional infantry, mounted in Bradleys and protected by Abrams tanks, to Moe and Larry. Curly he had to consign to the battalion's support units, which had some Bradleys but were largely equipped with obsolete M-113 armoured personnel carriers or with armoured engineer vehicles. The men of these units, trained for but not normally assigned to the infantry role, were suddenly to find themselves in the front line. Fortunately their commander, Captain Zan Hornbuckle, was much respected in the battalion as a leader and under his command 3-15 was successfully to defend all its strongpoints. Hornbuckle deployed his vehicles in cordons around Moe, Curly and Larry, which were encircled by entrenched Iraqi positions. As soon as the soldiers of 3-15 appeared, the Iraqi defenders began to attack, charging in successive waves on foot and in vehicles they had appropriated, taxis, cars and pickup trucks mounting machineguns, the ubiquitous 'technicals' of Muslim fighters all over the Middle East and Africa. In the aftermath of the battle for the overpasses, it became apparent that many of the enemy were not Iraqi but Syrians, who had crossed the border to fight the Americans in prosecution of the war against the Great Satan. They used mortars, could call on artillery but preferred, as almost all fighters in Iraq did throughout the campaign, to rely on RPG-7 rocket launchers, firing their projectiles in salvoes at close range. In response every unwounded American, and even some of the wounded, turned their weapons against the enemy.

The fighting was hottest at strongpoint Curly where Hornbuckle's Sergeant-Major, Robert Gallagher, who had been wounded in the debacle in Mogadishu in 1993, convinced his senior officer that it was essential to demand reinforcements. B Company of 3-15 was alerted at short order and raced northwards to the relief, armoured vehicles intermixed with resupply trucks, with all soldiers, combat specialists or not, firing their weapons as they advanced. When B Company, 3-15, arrived at strongpoint Curly, five of the resupply vehicles, loaded with ammunition and fuel, were sent up in flames by *fedayeen* fire but the other fifteen survived and the American garrison of the position sustained the defence.

At strongpoints Moe and Larry the fight had meanwhile been going on for six hours. The American defenders were attacked by a car bomb driven by a suicide bomber at Larry but obstacles improvised by combat engineers arrested its impetus before it reached its target point. Car and bomber were destroyed by the detonation. At Moe combat engineers improvised other obstacles to block suicide bombers, while the commander on the spot organized counter-attacks to engage columns of Iraqi fighters set on attacking the position. Sixty Iraqi vehicles were destroyed and hundreds of *fedayeen* killed. All American forces in the city centre, despite 3-15's delivery of fuel and ammunition, were now short of supplies. A reorganization of supply with the vehicles that had reached the focus of the fighting was hastily arranged and reinforcements from another battalion of the 3rd Infantry Division, 2nd Battalion 7th Infantry Regiment (2-7) were hurried forward to support 3-15. Strongpoint Moe was swiftly resupplied. Then 3-15 proceeded at high speed into central Baghdad. During the night of 7–8 April the centre and the régime district, already partly under the control of the 1st Marine Expeditionary Force, was completely secured.

The Marines had meanwhile closed up to the Tigris and its tributary, the Diyala river, on the south-east corner of the capital. In the right angle formed by the confluence of the Tigris and the Diyala stood a sprawl of poor housing, known as Saddam City, and a prison, military offices and the Rashid military air base. On the other side of Saddam City the roads led to the régime district, contained within one of the wide meanders of the Tigris. The three marine regimental combat teams, with their attached tank and armoured reconnaissance battalions and supporting artillery, were now deployed very close to the heart of the capital, in line with RCT 7 on the left, RCT 1 in the centre and RCT 5 on the right, across a front of about six miles. Between them and their objectives, however, lay the Diyala, which had steep banks offering few crossing points. There were two bridges in RCT 7's area but for once the Iraqi engineers had done their work. A narrow pedestrian bridge had a ten-foot gap in the centre, the four-lane concrete Baghdad Bridge had lost fifty feet of its centre span. The marine engineers reckoned that the gap in the pedestrian bridge could be repaired by pushing planks across, making it usable by infantry, but the concrete bridge would require major work. The bridging train would have to bring up and emplace metal spans to make it possible for tanks to be passed across.

Once over, the plan was for the Marines to push ahead in strength into the city and hold the ground taken. Unlike the army units of 3rd Infantry Division they did not intend to mount probing raids but to fight and take territory. The different plans reflected different organizations. Despite its title, 3rd Infantry Division had a heavy complement of armour of several types but relatively few foot soldiers. The marine regimental combat teams, by contrast, were largely infantry units. Traditionally the US Marine Corps has been and remains an infantry force and its battalions are trained and expect to fight on foot. Once across the river, they would fight their way down the city streets to secure the centre. The problem was to get over the Diyala, which was defended on the far bank by Iraqi entrenchments.

The initial crossing was made over the pedestrian bridge. Ferreting about in the debris that littered the area, the Marines of K Company, 3rd Battalion 7th Marines had found the necessary planks and also a metal gate. Shouldering the bridging material and formed in single file, they charged onto the broken bridge towards the far bank, thirty yards away. Iraqi artillery was firing – the artillery commander was heard on radio intercept attempting to correct his battery's fire – and one shell killed or wounded four Marines just behind the point of assault. The assault team, however, reached the gap in the bridge, dropped the metal gate across it, threw the planks on top and charged on to gain the far bank. There was a little firing but it was ineffective. Almost all the defenders had fled and their entrenchments, when overrun, were revealed to be wrongly sited. Instead of having been dug behind the lip of the river bank, they were on the forward, exposed side and so useless.

The Marines who had crossed the pedestrian bridge at once fanned out to search the houses on the city side, breaking down doors, surveying the interior and shouting 'clear' as they raced from one to another. (Elsewhere in the city the Americans took paint canisters with them, to spray 'C' on buildings which had been found empty of enemy or obvious booby traps.) Journalists and photographers jogged along with the fire teams; this was a media war and the crossing of the Diyala one of its reportorial high points. Beyond the houses on the river bank stood a grove of palm trees, which threatened danger. It proved to be full of abandoned military equipment but the enemy had fled. Five hundred yards beyond the bridge the Marines paused to form a perimeter. A defensible bridgehead had been secured and the follow-up units could cross in safety. Still, however, danger threatened. First one and then another vehicle approached the marine positions down roads leading to the river and were engaged with machine-gun fire. Both were stopped, neither proved to be a military vehicle, several civilians were killed. The marine officers cursed. Such incidents had proliferated throughout the campaign. Civilian vehicles had time and again driven at high speed into firefights, as if their occupants were oblivious to the dangers of war all about them. It was pointless to order young Marines to hold their fire. Too many apparently disoriented civilian drivers had proved to be armed *fedayeen* or suicide bombers, bent on destruction. Yet some who were shot up as they careered into American roadblocks clearly were disoriented or in denial. One of the most bewildering characteristics of this strange war was the apparent refusal of civilians to accept that a war was indeed going on. They drove about, in vehicles easily mistaken for the 'technicals' used by fighters, as if the Americans should understand that they were on a family outing or their way to market, as they often were. The result was the spectacle of dead fathers or slaughtered children in bullet-riddled cars skewed across the roadway; incensed American soldiers, stricken with guilt at what they had done, took refuge in feigned indifference: 'Why didn't they stop? How can we tell? I've got a family too.'

The seizure of the pedestrian bridgehead simplified the crossing problem. While marine engineers worked to mend the break in the concrete Baghdad Bridge into Saddam City, another battalion had regained the bridge farther north and pontoon bridges were being laid in other places. The three marine brigades were now jostling for position to lead the charge into central Baghdad. An argument was also in process between commanders about whether to raid or to mount push-and-hold penetration operations. As intelligence accumulated, it was becoming clear that eastern Baghdad was a 'target rich' objective. Beside the Rasheed military airport, there was also the Saddam *Fedayeen* training centre, the Atomic Energy Commission, Baghdad University campus, the Directorate of General Security Headquarters, the Ministry of Defence, *Fedayeen* headquarters and one of Saddam's palaces, the Al Azamiya. Eastern Baghdad was divided by marine staff officers into three regimental zones, while the regiments subdivided zones into battalion sectors, nine altogether. The battalion sectors were farther subdivided into six. Once one sector was secured, the troops were to move on to the next.

The advance of 1st Marine Expeditionary Force into eastern Baghdad during 7–8 April was not heavily opposed. Such resistance as the Marines encountered was disorganized. The abandoned Atomic Energy Commission was secured without meeting resistance. The advance into the university area on 9 April was more strongly opposed; stay-behind *fedayeen* made a stand in the middle of the campus, firing RPG-7s or Kalashnikovs at the advancing marines. There was, however, no real defence. Of the regular army and the Republican Guard there was no sign. The night of 8–9 April was disturbed by sporadic, ineffective firing. On 9 April, with the university campus taken, the Marines pressed on and soon reached Firdos (Paradise) Square, dominated by one of the many statues of Saddam Hussein found by the invaders throughout Iraqi cities. Iraqi opponents of the régime had already attempted to pull the statue down by throwing a loop around its neck and using muscle power. A marine armoured engineer vehicle now amplified their efforts. Its cable loop broke the statue's supports and Saddam's image collapsed face-forward revealing a shoddy framework of metal struts that had held it upright.

The fall of the Saddam statue on 9 April, televised across the world, was taken by its media to mark the fall of the Saddam régime. Yet despite the cinematic sensation of the event, many in the media resisted the impulse to exult. As representatives of the *bien pensants* in Europe and even parts of North America, many television and print journalists declined to celebrate the fall of the dictator the toppling of his statue symbolized. Monster though he clearly was, his humiliation at the hands of the capitalist system – the United States, the world's largest economy, Britain, the fourth – rankled. In Saddam's own world, many followed the media lead. Iraqis who had suffered under his selfish autocracy rejoiced. The beneficiaries were downcast, as was 'the Arab street' in general. A Jordanian refugee from Palestine told a BBC correspondent in Amman, 'It's just too painful. We Arabs were once a great nation. We were in Spain for 700 years. And where are we now? We're beaten in our own homes.'

To most Europeans and Americans for whom the Arab kingdom of Spain and the Muslim domination of the Balkans, if remembered at all, are footnotes of history, Muslim fellow-feeling for Saddam is inexplicable. They genuinely regard him as a would-be accomplice of Hitler and Stalin who, like them, terrorized his own people and wished to mount a campaign of conquest and revenge against the liberal democracies of the West. Confident in the benevolence of their own societies, to which the Third World apparently wishes to migrate *en masse*, Europeans and Americans fail altogether to understand the hatred felt by the world's outsiders, particularly fundamentalist Muslims, for their way of life. It is possible for Westerners intellectually to grasp the essentials of Muslim belief, that religious teaching should predominate in public affairs, that women should be modest in manner and dress and outwardly subordinate to men, that the premodern texts of the Koran and *Sharia* law should be accorded the respect due to literal truth; but they do not regard such beliefs as applying outside what they regard as the closed borders of the Muslim world. They are particularly resistant to the view that Muslim secularists, such as Saddam, should enjoy the liberty to organize a Muslim society as they choose while simultaneously invoking an Islamic right – the basis of the Ba'athist idea – to a special place in regional and ultimately world affairs. Saddam, as dictator of Iraq, was that most dangerous of individuals, a Muslim who could dodge between religious and secularist appeals to authority, personally loyal to neither creed, adept at exploiting the power of both over the minds of his followers.

The fall of Saddam's statue on 9 April was swiftly followed by the occupation of the premises from which he and his intimates had exercised their dictatorial regime. The 'palace' so-called of Tariq Aziz, Saddam's Deputy Prime Minister, was quickly taken. The occupation of the five 'palaces' – large, vulgar, recently built villas – allotted to Saddam's inner family swiftly followed. Not without loss; though a hundred *fedayeen* were killed in the fight for the palaces, twenty-two Marines were wounded, in exchanges of fire with assault rifles and rocket launchers. The capture of Baghdad had been in many respects a model of a modern military operation, cunningly planned with every electronic aid, skilfully executed by highly trained troops. Even the best battles, however, have their price for the victors. The cost had been paid by the soldiers of the 3rd Infantry Division and the 1st Marine Expeditionary Force.

9

The War's Aftermath

The toll of coalition fatalities was nevertheless surprisingly light, 122 American, 33 British. Of the British dead, six had been killed in action, the others in accidents or by 'friendly fire'. A higher proportion of Americans were killed in combat but, again, most were victims of accident and some of attack by their own aircraft. Almost all were young, under thirty, some very young. War is a young man's – now also a young woman's – business; one American who died was Army PFC Lori Ann Piestewa, aged twenty-three. Almost all the British dead bore identifiably traditional British names, Stratford, Allbut, McCue, Evans, Ballard, Tweedie. One, however, was a citizen of the Irish Republic, Ian Malone, serving in the Irish Guards, another a black Zimbabwean, Christopher Muzvuru, an Irish Guards piper. A high proportion were senior NCOs or junior officers, evidence of the dangers always attaching to leadership in combat.

Among the American dead, too, many were NCOs or junior officers, marine gunnery sergeants, army warrant officers, captains, second lieutenants. The names testify to the kaleidoscopic origins of the American nation. Many were Hispanic or Slav, from recent immigrations, others Teutonic or Scandinavian from the great North European influx of the nineteenth century. A considerable number were as British as those of the 1st (UK) Armoured Division's dead, Tristan Aitken, Nicolas Hodson, George Mitchell, Wilfred Bellard, names that might have been found among the emigrants on the *Mayflower*. The American armed forces are truly representative of the American people, who so devotedly support their soldiers, sailors and airmen.

The number of Iraqi dead has not yet been counted. Since there were no great battles in the war, it is unlikely that casualties in the Iraqi armed forces were high. Most of the conscripts of the regular army drifted away before the fighting began. Casualties may have been higher among the Republican Guard but it, too, avoided heavy combat. Such serious fighting as was done was by 'fighters' – not uniformed soldiers but Saddam's political militiamen, devotees of the Ba'ath party and foreigners, Islamicist volunteers from Syria, Algeria and other Muslim countries seeking the opportunity to give their lives for the faith. The total of their dead will probably never be known but must have amounted to several thousand. The number of civilian dead was much lower, thanks to the careful precision of coalition air attack on populated areas.

Prisoners there were none. In the heat of combat such small groups as offered their surrender were made captive but they were not long detained. One of the first acts of the occupiers was to decree the disbandment of the Iraqi army and the battlefield detainees were released to their homes, whither most of their comrades-in-arms had already made their own way. The only Iraqis the victors sought to apprehend were leaders of the régime and identifiable violators of human rights.

In retrospect the disbandment of the army was a serious mistake, one of several made by the American interim administration in the immediate aftermath of the Saddam régime's collapse. It released several hundred thousand young men onto the unemployment market, leaving them unpaid and discontented, at precisely the moment when the need became apparent to rebuild Iraq's security forces. The mistake was repeated when the national police force was not kept in being. The occupiers had defensible grounds for both acts, since they feared that retention of the army might perpetuate the power of a major Ba'athist institution, while the police force was tainted by violations of human rights. The occupiers argued, persuasively, that the police force would have to be recreated, from freshly recruited entrants trained by Westerners.

The disappearance of the police – which could probably not have been averted in the immediate aftermath – had regrettable effects in the days following Saddam's downfall. Looters appeared in thousands and began to pillage. At first their targets were the office buildings of the régime in the government quarter of Baghdad; seventeen out of twenty-three ministries were ransacked. American troops managed to protect the Ministry for Oil, the resumption of oil production being judged essential to the country's reconstruction, but there were too few troops to save the others. Then the looters turned to nongovernmental facilities, including hospitals and schools. The looters, some ex-prisoners released from the city gaols, others simply the poor of the back streets, stole anything portable. Computers were a favourite piece of booty, and air-conditioning units, but eventually completely worthless items were carried or wheeled away. In the process enormous quantities of documents, essential to reorganization and reconstruction, were destroyed or irretrievably dispersed. Looting spread wider. The looters began systematically to strip copper wire out of the telephone networks and electrical distribution systems, making communication and power, interrupted by the war and the damage war had caused, impossible to restore without elaborate and expensive repair. There was also cultural damage. Iraq, home to the world's oldest civilizations, was a treasure trove of antiquities, originally collected by European scholars, later piously preserved by dedicated Iraqi scholars and conservationists. For some weeks it was believed that the Iraqi National Museum had been emptied of its treasures, a story that led to wild denunciation of the invasion in the Western press. Later, fortunately, it was discovered that the museum staffs had been able to hide almost all the exhibits in the vaults.

Looting was destructive but merely anarchic. After a few chaotic weeks there was little left to steal, householders in the richer quarters were defending their properties and the American troops had established rough-and-ready order in the streets. Looting, however, merged into and was succeeded by organized attacks by intransigents on the occupying forces. Anarchy, in the Sunni central region, gave way to insurgency, organized and vicious. The attackers were the same people as the 'fighters' who had raised most of the resistance to the invasion in March and April. They were ex–Saddam militiamen, *fedayeen*, Ba'ath party members and foreign fighters, whose numbers were reinforced by an influx of Islamic extremists from other Arab countries, filtering across the unguarded borders. Their methods, familiar to the Israeli troops fighting the *Intifada* but also to the British with experience in Northern Ireland, were those of terrorism – attacks on patrols by gunmen who disappeared into side streets, roadside car bombs – intensified by the self-sacrifice of suicide bombers. The British in the Shi'a south were spared the worst; an appalling incident, when six military policemen training Iraqi police recruits were massacred, proved to be an isolated event, apparently provoked by a local dispute over possession of weapons. It was the Americans in and around Baghdad, in the 'Sunni triangle', who were consistently attacked, leading to a steady drip of deaths. In August the 'fighters' extended their reach. On 14 August a car bomb exploded outside the Jordanian embassy, killing seventeen. On 19 August a suicide truck bomber drove into the United Nations headquarters in Baghdad, killing the Special Representative, Sergio Viera de Mello, and twenty others. On 28 August a leading Shi'a cleric, who advocated co-operation with the Americans, was killed by a car bomb in Najaf, one of Shi'ite Islam's holiest cities. A few days later Akila al-Hashemi, one of the women members of the American-sponsored Iraqi Governing Council, was assassinated outside her house. American military deaths continued almost day by day, to reach 500 by the end of the year.

The fighters persisted despite the evident approval most Iraqis showed for the overthrow of Saddam. Polls demonstrated that 80 per cent of Iraqis welcomed the dictator's fall. Support was absolute in the Kurdish north, which had effectively reverted to self-rule, and almost universal in the Shi'a south where, after a brief period of instability, the British had succeeded in restoring order and winning the co-operation of the inhabitants, much assisted by the early restoration of essential services. The Sunni recalcitrants were either Saddam loyalists, whom defeat had deprived of privileges and employment, or foreigners who had entered Iraq to carry on the war against the Great Satan of America. A leading terrorist group was Ansar al-Islam, allied to al-Qaeda, which had briefly occupied a 'liberated zone' in the Kurdish north, during the period when Kurdistan had escaped from Saddam's control. Its members fled after the American occupation to Iran, then infiltrated back again. The spiritual leader of Ansar al-Islam, the mullah Mustapha Kriekar, in exile in Norway, compared the activities of Ansar al-Islam in Iraq to al-Qaeda and the Taleban in Afghanistan. 'The resistance', he told an Arabic language television channel, 'is not only a reaction to the American invasion, it is part of the continuous Islamic struggle since the collapse of the Caliphate. All Islamic struggles since then are part of one organized effort to bring back the Caliphate.'

It was anomalous that Saddam's apparent avengers should have invoked the Caliphate, since his secularist régime was anathema to Islamic fundamentalists. Their appeal to the Caliphate also partook of myth rather than reality. The last Caliphate, which had its seat in the Ottoman capital at Istanbul, had no connection, either by endorsement of the *Umma*, the Muslim community, or by blood, with the family of the prophet, to justify its status. Endorsement by the *Umma* was the Sunni orthodoxy, blood descent the Shi'a orthodoxy. The Ottoman Turks had simply assumed the Caliphate, by right of conquest, at the beginning of the sixteenth century. The Ottoman Caliphate, moreover, had been abolished by a secular Muslim, Mustapha Kemal, in 1925; no Westerner had been involved. Not even by the most tortuous theological logic could the infidel West be held responsible for the Caliphate's termination.

It was most unlikely, in any case, that a dominant constituency for the re-establishment of the Caliphate could have been assembled in post-Saddam Iraq. The surviving Ba'athists were secularist, so were many of the Sunni population. The Shi'a, though a majority in Iraq, were a minority in the Muslim world. Whatever views they advanced about the Caliphate would have been rejected by most of their co-religionists in the wider Muslim lands. Indeed, even among the Shi'a, the beliefs and the methods of the terrorists were an abhorrence. The Western conquerors, uninvolved as they were on one religious side or the other, were therefore pursuing an objectively uncontroversial policy in their efforts to establish an efficient, modernizing post-Saddam regime.

Unfortunately, the American efforts got off to a bad start. The British in the south, with their long imperial experience, took the pragmatic view that the priority was to establish law and order, working with whoever appeared co-operative, and to restore essential services. By September electricity supplies in Basra had been returned to normal and most other facilities, such as schools and hospitals, were operating efficiently. Crime was under control, the streets were safe and terrorism had been quashed. The Americans adopted an ideological approach. They sought an immediate transformation of Iraq from a tyranny to a functioning democracy, believing that liberation from Saddam would motivate a sufficient number of pro-democratic Iraqis to assume effective governmental functions within a few months. To oversee the democratization of Iraq, the US Department of Defense, the Pentagon, which had assumed the lead function, appointed a retired general, Jay Garner, to lead a team of Pentagon-vetted officials with authority to institute governmental functions. General Garner's organization, the Office of Reconstruction and Humanitarian Assistance (ORHA), was answerable to the expeditionary commander, General Tommy Franks. The State Department had, before the war, drawn up an elaborate collection of policy documents, the 'Future of Iraq Project', suggesting guidelines for reconstruction and transitional governmental procedures. On the Pentagon's assumption of responsibility for Iraqi postwar affairs, however, they were set aside. The future of Iraq was to be decided, paradoxically, by the dictates of a military organization committed to idealistic democratic goals. Its brief was to hand over the administration of the country to a group of unpolitical Iraqi leaders within ninety days.

It became quickly apparent that the Garner transitional régime was inadequate to its task. Its personnel were naïve and undertrained, it lacked a rational plan of procedure. On 12 May Garner was replaced as presidential envoy by Paul Bremer, a former counter-terrorism expert at the State Department. He also had close Pentagon connections. Bremer established better relations with Central Command, which had fallen into quarrels with Garner's team. He also made it a priority to tackle the problem of terrorism. ORHA became the Coalition Provisional Authority (CPA), with largely new personnel.

Bremer began at once to create a new Iraqi police force, with an initial strength of 40,000. Training academies were set up and Western police leaders brought to Iraq to instruct the trainers in Western policing methods. The trainers proved both enthusiastic and brave; bravery was needed, since the terrorists instantly targeted the men in new uniform. Recruitment remained a difficulty. The CPA had set its face against enlisting former servants of the Saddam régime but ex-policemen provided the most obvious enlistees. It was Bremer who also decided ill-advisedly on the complete disbandment of the army. A future Iraq would need a properly trained army and there was no better time to establish one than when large numbers of Western troops, models of what post-Saddam soldiers should be, were present on the territory. Bremer, however, was determined to make a clean sweep. As a result, several hundred thousand ex-soldiers were demobilized and turned onto the employment market which could not absorb them. Discontented and unpaid, they easily yielded recruits to the terrorist campaign.

Bremer also decided to exclude members of the Ba'ath party from new government employment. He thereby deprived the CPA of the services of most of the country's most experienced experts and officials. His dilemma repeated that of the Allied Military Government of Germany in 1945. It had originally adopted, for moral and ideological reasons, a policy of de-Nazification, treating all former members of the Nazi party as disqualified to resume the positions they had held under Hitler.

Since almost everyone in a position of responsibility had been obliged to join the party, or had found it difficult not to do so, post-1945 Germany was deprived in the crisis of surrender and occupation of the services of those people most urgently needed for the country's reconstruction. As a result there was a compromise: de-Nazification was accelerated, sometimes dispensed with altogether. Principal beneficiaries of the policy of turning a blind eye were the German secret weapons scientists, such as Wernher von Braun, who was transformed from a Nazi favourite to an American citizen at headlong speed. Ironically it was his principal invention, the V-2 rocket, which, in its Iraqi version, formed a principal target of UNSCOM's and UNMOVIC's inspections.

The CPA was eventually obliged to adopt the attitude of the postwar occupiers of Germany, interviewing Ba'ath party members on a pragmatic, person-by-person basis and exempting from penalty almost all those judged necessary to the reconstruction programme.

De-Ba'athification did not apply in the selection of members of the Iraqi Governing Council (IGC), established in July 2003. Its twenty-five members represented all Iraq's ethnic and religious groups, Sunni, Shi'a, Kurds, Christians, Assyrians, Turkoman and others; three were women, an unprecedented departure from normalities even in Saddam's secularist society, where women's nominal equality had not accorded them political representation. None had been Ba'athists. Their consequent unfamiliarity with the exercise of power at first hampered their ability to launch and direct reconstruction programmes. Shortage of funds, however, was not one of their problems. On 10 June 2003, Paul Bremer announced that $100 million was to be made available for reconstruction, all the money to be spent through Iraqi companies, so as to provide employment and credit to domestic businesses. In the longer term, finance for reconstruction would be supplied by Iraqi oil revenues. The initial funds were a transfer from the American treasury.

The status of the Coalition Provisional Authority, and of the Iraqi Governing Council, was regularized on 22 May 2003 by the adoption at the UN of Resolution 1483, which declared an end to the régime of sanctions against Iraq, in force since 1990, and gave legal authority to the occupation of Iraq by the coalition forces. The export of oil, destined to pay for the reconstruction, was authorized, the proceeds to be vested in the CPA. On 16 October the Security Council extended its approval of postwar arrangements in Iraq by adopting Resolution 1551, which recognized the legitimacy of the Coalition Provisional Authority and urged the establishment of a constitutional conference to assist the Iraqi Governing Council in settling the future government of Iraq.

The governments which had most stridently opposed the war, France and Germany foremost, continued to express their hostility to the coalition's actions. Russia, at first an opponent, relented; in October it decided to back the Americans. The French and Germans remained intransigent. Though they both demanded 'rights' in the determination of Iraq's future form of government, basing their claims on ill-defined appeals to 'international democracy', they declined to offer money to Iraq's reconstruction programme. Both declined to provide troops to the international force, which by 2004 included contingents from thirty-five countries, such as Japan, Italy, the Netherlands, Denmark, Romania, the Czech Republic, Norway, Portugal and South Korea.

Despite the enlargement of the international occupation force, and the creation of a new inspection team, the Iraq Survey Group (ISG), in succession to UNSCOM and UNMOVIC, the one front in which the coalition failed to make progress was in the location and identification of Iraqi weapons of mass destruction. The ISG, which was led by David Kay, the American former UN weapons inspector, published its interim report in October 2003. Its content, and his subsequent testimony to the Senate Armed Services Committee in the last week of January 2004, lent comfort to the opponents of President Bush in the United States and to the many critics of the war in Britain. Both were taken to substantiate the view that there was no reliable intelligence support for Anglo-American allegations of Saddam's continuing possession and development of weapons of mass destruction and their means of delivery. Dr Kay in fact said no such thing. While admitting that he doubted if large stocks of WMD would be found, an embarrassment to both the American and British governments which had advertised before the invasion their certainty of such discoveries, he qualified his doubts about the WMD threat by stating his belief in the existence of smaller stocks of WMD still hidden on Iraqi territory, Saddam's sponsorship 'right up to the end' of such programmes as the refinement of the deadly poison ricin, his maintenance of a ballistic missile development programme, assisted by the import of foreign technology, and the resumption of nuclear weapons development. He also revealed to *The Sunday Telegraph* that he had evidence of the transfer by Saddam of WMD to Syrian territory.

It was, however, the headline elements in Dr Kay's testimony, rather than his careful qualifications in detail, that were seized upon by the anti-war constituency. Its spokesmen were compromised in the United States because of their association with the campaigns of Democratic candidates running against George W. Bush in the current presidential election campaign; their message was also offset by the expert evidence of a few stalwarts in the media, such as Judith Miller of *The New York Times*, a veteran of weapons inspection on the ground, who continued to demand that attention be paid to the evidence for WMD. On the whole, the anti-war party, though strident, failed to capture control of opinion among the American people who remained in the majority supportive of their President and armed forces. That was not the case in Europe, where the French and Germans, governments and peoples alike, remained hostile. It was equally not the case in Britain. There the moderate majority continued to support Prime Minister Blair's Iraqi policy, but many professional politicians and much of the media took a different view. Their suspicions, essentially that Britain had gone to war for unsubstantiated reasons, found endorsement in a broadcast by Andrew Gilligan, a BBC reporter specializing in defence affairs, on 29 May 2003. At 6.07 a.m., on the *Today* programme, the BBC's flagship morning radio news channel, Gilligan revealed that 'a British official who was involved in the preparation of the dossier' – the dossier being an intelligence assessment of the threat presented by Iraq's WMD, prepared by the Joint Intelligence Committee and submitted in September 2002 to the Prime Minister – had claimed it was 'transformed in the week before it was published to make it sexier'. As an example he cited the statement that 'weapons of mass destruction were ready for use in forty-five minutes'. The 'official' said, according to Gilligan, that the 'forty-five minute' statement was not in the original draft of the dossier, was included 'against the wishes' of some involved in the dossier's preparation and came only from one source, instead of the usual two or more.

The broadcast attracted widespread interest, which grew. Its truth was denied by the Prime Minister's official spokesman, Alastair Campbell, after he and Gilligan had both given evidence to the House of Commons Foreign Affairs Committee (FAC) on 19 June and 25 June respectively. During late June the interest of the media, that of the BBC in particular, and of the government focused on identifying Gilligan's 'official'. The mystery was partially dissolved on 1 July when a letter, written the previous day, was received at the Ministry of Defence. It came from Dr David Kelly, a scientific civil servant with great experience in the arms control field in general and Iraqi WMD in particular, and revealed that he was the 'official' Gilligan had cited. He carefully defined what had been discussed in the Charing Cross Hotel, over a glass of apple juice. He emphasized that he had in no way said anything to undermine government policy, revealed that he supported the war, because he regarded Saddam as a threat to regional peace, and admitted only that he had conceded that the 'forty-five minute' claim might have been added to the dossier 'for impact'. There were no witnesses to their conversation and no evidence of its content, except for Gilligan's skimpy and barely decipherable notes.

Two consequences followed from the receipt of Dr Kelly's letter at the Ministry of Defence. One was that he was required to give evidence before the Commons Foreign Affairs Committee, in public and on television, on 15 July, and before the Intelligence and Security Committee (ISC) on 16 July; the other was that, over the course of the next days, Dr Kelly was revealed by the government, in a convoluted and less than frank way, to be Andrew Gilligan's 'official' (it was a complication of the story, wholly unfair to Dr Kelly, that he had somehow been characterized, and would so be described by much of the media, as an 'intelligence officer', which he was not). Dr Kelly was roughly handled by several members of the FAC, particularly a Labour member, Andrew Mackinlay, a backbencher who went out of his way to scorn Dr Kelly, a highly distinguished scientist and devoted government servant, as 'chaff' and 'a fall guy'. Many viewers were stunned by Mackinlay's performance, which many felt was unworthy of a Member of Parliament.

By the time of Dr Kelly's appearance before the FAC, confirmation of his name as Gilligan's 'official' had been made public, through a curious guessing game devised by the Ministry of Defence, which declined to publish his name but agreed to confirm it if it was put to the Ministry by a newspaper or broadcasting agency. *The Financial Times* was the first organization to make the correct guess.

As soon as publicly identified, Dr Kelly left his house in Oxfordshire with his wife for the west of England, to take refuge from press attention. He later returned to his daughter's house in Oxford and it was from her home that he travelled to London on 15 and 16 July to attend the meetings of the Foreign Affairs and Intelligence and Security Committees. He then returned to his own house where he joined his wife. They spent the morning of 17 July together though for most of the time he was working in his study. Colleagues at the Ministry of Defence sent him a number of e-mails about the progress of the inquiry and he sent e-mails himself and made and received telephone calls. He and his wife then had lunch together. She found his state distressed. He was sunk in silence. After lunch he said he would go for a walk and, after returning briefly to his study, he set out. He did not return. As the evening drew out his family became concerned and his daughters searched for him. After midnight they called the police. Early next morning, after the organization of a police search, his body was found in remote woodland. Its state suggested he had committed suicide, by cutting his wrist and taking an overdose of painkillers. The official inquiry later conducted by Lord Hutton into the circumstances of his death confirmed that to be the case.

The death of Dr Kelly provoked a full-blooded political crisis in the United Kingdom. The Prime Minister immediately announced, the day following Dr Kelly's death, that an inquiry would be held into the circumstances, to be conducted by Lord Hutton, a senior Law Lord. It first met on 11 August and concluded its work on 25 September. It exercised wide powers. Among the witnesses called were the Prime Minister himself, the Secretary of State for Defence, the Chairman of the Governors of the BBC and its Director-General.

Lord Hutton's report, published on 28 January 2004, caused consternation. Opponents of the war had expected that the judge would find, in his analysis of the documents brought in evidence, grounds for criticizing the government's decision to go to war; the report included, among much other material, the 'September dossier' which Andrew Gilligan, in his broadcast of 29 May, alleged had been 'sexed up' to improve the government's case. Against the expectations of much of the media, the Conservative opposition in Parliament and many members of the Parliamentary Labour Party, Lord Hutton decided, by contrast, to reserve almost all his criticism for the BBC. He found that Gilligan's allegation, that the government's warning of Iraq's ability to deploy weapons of mass destruction within 'forty-five minutes' of receiving the order to do so was based on information it knew to be false, was 'unfounded', and that it was inserted at a late stage into the dossier not because its veracity was doubted by intelligence officers but because of its late reception. He also dismissed the allegation that the Chairman of the Joint Intelligence Committee had yielded to pressure applied by Alastair Campbell, the Prime Minister's

Director of Communications, to insert material that supported the government's case for war which was not supported by intelligence evidence. He recognized that the JIC Chairman, John Scarlett, had been willing to assist the government but only in so far as the facts did so as well.

Turning to the BBC, he was almost unsparing in his strictures. He found Gilligan's allegations about the 'forty-five minute' claim and the circumstances of its insertion to be unfounded. He found the BBC's system of exercising editorial control to be 'defective', as was its procedure for investigating complaints. He criticized the Governors of the BBC for failing properly to investigate the complaint against the Gilligan broadcast and so for persisting in a failure to apologize for which a proper investigation would have shown the necessity.

The government did not altogether escape Lord Hutton's criticisms. Those focused on the pathetic circumstances of Dr David Kelly's death. David Kelly was a distinguished scientist who had spent a life of duty in the scientific civil service. Scientific civil servants occupy an ill-defined and anomalous position, superior to that of middle-rank penpushers but inferior, and made to feel inferior, to the Whitehall grandees who mingle on terms of equality with ministers, despite the fact that they can be of an intellectual eminence not found elsewhere in government service. Like all government servants they are forbidden to speak in any undirected way to the media. Some, however, and David Kelly was one, are given a loose and undefined permission to brief the media on matters of public interest. They are thus put in an indefensible position, apparently allowed to speak to journalists but liable to disciplinary action if what they say causes embarrassment. Poor David Kelly fell headfirst into that trap.

Lord Hutton conceded that Dr Kelly, when the trouble broke, was given support by a few of his immediate civil service superiors. The hierarchy effectively disowned him. Sir Kevin Tebbits, the most senior civil servant in the Ministry of Defence, described Dr Kelly in a letter to the Secretary of State as 'a relatively junior official' and 'not the Government's principal adviser on the subject [of Iraqi weapons of mass destruction], nor even a senior one'. Yet Dr Kelly knew more about Iraqi weapons of mass destruction than anyone in Britain. It is testimony to how little real experts are valued within the government hierarchy that he could be discussed so dismissively. Lord Hutton was moved by compassion. At the end of his report he adopted as his conclusion on the circumstances of Dr Kelly's death the opinion of the Professor of Psychiatry at Oxford University who had examined the evidence. He judged that Dr Kelly had killed himself out of a 'profound sense of hopelessness', of his life's work having been 'not wasted but . . . totally undermined'; these feelings were compounded by fear that the civil service intended to take disciplinary action against him, perhaps end his work in Iraq or even dismiss him from government employment.

David Kelly was not the only victim of the 'September dossier' affair. The Chairman of the Governors of the BBC, Gavyn Davies, resigned on the day of the Hutton report's publication. Greg Dyke, the Director-General, resigned a day later. No such indignities had ever before been visited upon an institution which continued to regard itself, with some justification, as 'the greatest news-gathering institution in the world'. A little later, in the first week of February 2004, the British government announced that it would undertake an inquiry into the workings of the intelligence services over the Iraq crisis. Its announcement followed one similar by the United States government.

Thus the certainties that had inaugurated the brief and brilliant campaign to overthrow the tyranny of Saddam Hussein petered out in recrimination. Objectively the world was undoubtedly a safer place as the result of his downfall, besides being morally purged of one of the most wicked dictators of modern times. Subjectively it was even more divided than it had been when the 'war on terror' was undertaken after the atrocity of 11 September 2001. The Muslim world in general, the Arab world in particular was confirmed in its grievances, particularly that the West was prepared to use its overwhelming military superiority to keep Muslims subordinate. 'Europe', the Europe of the Franco-German plan to create a federal union strong enough to stand on terms of equality with the United States as a world power, had been humiliated by the failure of its efforts to avert the war. Liberal opinion, dominant throughout the European media and academia, strong also in their American equivalents, was outraged by the spectacle of raw military force supplanting reason and legality as the means by which relations between states are ordered.

Reality is an uncomfortable companion, particularly to people of good will. George H. W. Bush's proclamation of a new world order had persuaded too many in the West that the world's future could be managed within a legal framework, by discussion and conciliation. The warnings uttered by his son that the United States was determined to bring other enemies of nuclear and regional stability to book – Iran, North Korea – was found by his political opponents profoundly unsettling. The reality of the Iraq campaign of March–April 2003 is, however, a better guide to what needs to be done to secure the safety of our world than any amount of law-making or treaty-writing can offer.

Postscript to the Vintage Edition (2005)

The end of the campaign to defeat Saddam's forces in April 2003 was succeeded, as described in Chapter 9, by a period of lawlessness and looting. The lawless elements came from the city poor and the former inmates of Saddam's prisons, unwisely released by the coalition forces in the moment of victory. By August, however, disorder was becoming purposeful and was designed to contest control of Iraq's cities in the central region with the American occupiers and to destabilise the postwar governmental Iraqi regime. There were attacks on the Jordanian embassy and on United Nations headquarters in Baghdad, on a Shi'a religious site in Najaf and on a leading member of the Iraqi Governing Council, all with fatal consequences.

Such attacks persisted during the winter of 2003–04 and by March 2004 had swelled into a full-scale insurgency. While the Kurdish north settled into peace and a form of self-government, and the Shi'a south, centered on Basra, also accepted the regime sponsored by the British occupiers, Baghdad and the 'Sunni triangle' to its west, north and south of Fallujah, relapsed into disorder. There were daily attacks on American forces, on supply columns along the main roads, on the new American-sponsored security forces, army, and police, and on Iraqis who co-operated with the American occupiers.

Outline arrangements for the future government of Iraq had been signed between the Coalition Provisional Authority (CPA), in effect the American military government, and the Iraqi Governing Council (IGC), an appointed interim administration, on 15 November 2003. Negotiations between the IGC, the

Americans and leaders of the Shi'a community, the Grand Ayatollah of Najaf foremost, resulted in the promulgation on 8 March 2004 of the Transitional Administrative Law (TAL), which laid down that governmental power in Iraq would be transferred to an Iraqi Interim Government (IIG), by 30 June 2004. The IIG was entrusted with the functions of government until the holding of elections to establish a Transitional National Assembly of Iraq (TNA) not later than 31 January 2005. The TNA is intended to select an Iraqi Transitional Government, which will in turn draw up a constitution, to be ratified by referendum in October 2005, under which a definitive national government will be elected by democratic procedure in December 2005.

These constitutional procedures threaten the interests of many groups in Iraq and of their supporters in neighbouring countries. The new constitution will be accepted by the Kurds of the north as long as it recognises the rights they have acquired, perhaps to be institutionalised by the establishment of a federal structure, since Saddam's fall. The two leading Kurdish parties, the Kurdistan Democratic Party (KDP) and the Patriotic Union of Kurdistan (PUK), are prepared to co-operate if the eventual constitutional government concedes Kurdish semi-independence. Among the rights they seek are those of control over the rich oilfields around Kirkuk. The constitutional government will, however, also have to accommodate the aspirations of the sizeable Turkmen community, ethnically Turkish, which is supported by Turkey. Turkey's interest is complicated by its opposition to any enlargement of Kurdish power, given the sizeable overlap of Iraq's Kurdish population into Turkey proper. Semi-independence for Iraq's Kurdish population, inside a federal structure, would palliate Kurdish nationalist aspirations. Turkey fears that it might strengthen Kurdish pressure to create an autonomous Kurdish state, embracing the Kurds of Iran and Syria as well.

The Shi'a of Iraq, like Iraq's Kurds, have also greatly benefited from Saddam's downfall. Though governing as an Iraqi nationalist, he was a figurehead of Sunni hegemony within Iraq and so a representative of the minority community's traditional dominance over other Arab Muslims. The Sunni, a minority in Iraq proper but a majority in the Baghdad region, have long been the better educated of Iraq's Arab communities, richer and better adapted to sharing in and exercising governmental power. Saddam repressed the Shi'a, even though Iraq is the homeland of their sect's holiest sites, at Najaf particularly. He refused them the right to celebrate their rituals and he excluded them from government. The fall of Saddam and the dissolution of the Ba'ath party in Iraq (it remains the ruling party in Syria) have revived Shi'a political aspirations. They have been allotted a proportion of places in the Interim Government and, with the holding of elections and the referendum in 2005, can expect to be fairly represented in a future sovereign administration. Their claims have been skilfully negotiated by their spiritual leader, Grand Ayatollah Ali Sistani. Sistani belongs to the moderate, quietest wing of Shi'a religiosity, which deprecates involvement in day-to-day politics. Unfortunately his leadership is encroached upon, if not directly challenged by, that of Moqtada al-Sadr of Najaf, a young cleric with a fervent following among the poor and powerless. Sadr has links with fundamentalists; he also belongs to a political tradition with a troubled and troublesome history. His ancestors fought the British in the 1920s; his father, Ayatollah Sadiq al-Sadr, was killed on Saddam's orders in 1999. Since 2003 he has made Najaf, where he controls the mosque associated by pious Shi'a with the deaths of their holy men, Ali and Hussein, into a stronghold of resistance to the American occupiers. During 2004 Najaf has been the scene of constant fighting between Sadr's followers and American forces; a showdown has been postponed, largely because of American reluctance to conduct military operations in the vicinity of the Shi'a holy places, but it may be expected that, unless Sadr moderates his intransigence, there will be a definitive offensive against him before the elections of 2005.

Meanwhile the Sunni, who have enjoyed dominance within Iraq ever since the days of Ottoman rule, are coming to terms with the demise of their privileged position. Their main props as a minority, the Sunni-controlled Ba'ath Party, the army and the police, were dissolved immediately after Saddam's fall. Some Sunni leaders have attempted to secure their community's future position by co-operating with and taking places within the Interim Government; others have not. The troubles within the 'Sunni triangle', around Fallujah and Ramadi west of Baghdad, have been mounted and directed by Sunni extremists, discontented by their loss of power but also motivated by their connections with al-Qaeda and other fundamentalist bodies. The most important of these Sunni movements is al-Jam'iya al-Salifya al-Mujahida. As its title implies, it adheres to the Islamic belief that religion demands a return to the values and system of the first Muslim centuries (Salafism) and that it regards attack on non-Muslim forces as a religious duty. It has been responsible for many of the attacks on American troops, roadside bombings, ambushes, shootings and kidnappings, though some kidnappings have been carried out directly by al-Qaeda cells present in Iraq, notably those led by Abu Musab al-Zarqawi. Zarqawi, a fugitive from justice, has specialised in beheading his kidnapped victims, the murders recorded on video and broadcast by unofficial Arab television services. Other Islamist groups, such as Kataeb al-Faruk and the al-Dawa party, a military wing of the Muslim Brotherhood, underpin Sunni nationalism but do not espouse violence.

Indigenous violence has been reinforced by the incursion of aggressive Islamist groups from neighbouring countries, particularly Syria. Generally allied to al-Qaeda, and often experienced in fighting in Afghanistan, the foreign insurgents, of whom Zarqawi is representative, are not seeking to establish political positions for the future but to undermine the American occupation and to kill Americans and those Iraqis who co-operate with them. Their interest is in an unstable, not a stable, Iraq, since instability in Iraq may also heighten instability in neighbouring Muslim countries, particularly Saudi Arabia, in which the leaders of al-Qaeda originate, and Jordan, whose monarchist regime fundamentalists particularly dislike. Al-Qaeda refuses to recognise the permanence of existing frontiers and seeks the overthrow of all moderate Muslim governments, which it wishes to replace with a Salafist regime as a preliminary to the restoration of the universal Caliphate.

The insurgency has resulted in a steep rise in deaths among the coalition forces; by the end of February 2005 they totalled 1,500 American and nearly 100 British deaths. Iraqi civilian deaths from all causes are estimated at between 10,000 and 33,000. The focus of the fighting has been in the 'Sunni triangle' and at Najaf, where Sadr's Mahdi army operates. Most Western soldiers have been killed by terrorist methods such as drive-by shootings, roadside booby traps, and suicide bombings. As the insurgency developed, however, between March and June, the American forces did suffer conventional casualties when they mounted operations to overcome the opposition in Najaf, Karbala, and neighbouring areas. Their poorly equipped opponents suffered far worse and also lost ground; they retained, nevertheless, their centres of resistance because of American reluctance to press attacks to a conclusion during the sensitive period before the presidential elections at home. The Americans were also deterred from exerting maximum force by the revelation of mistreatment of Iraqi prisoners in the Abu Ghraib prison. Small though the number of American soldiers accused of misbehaviour was, the news story compromised the claims of the American forces to have come as liberators and undermined the resolution of American commanders to exert their authority in regions of disorder. The final pacification of central Iraq had to await the reelection of President George W. Bush in November 2004 and the election of an Iraqi Transitional National Assembly (TNA).

The creation of the TNA will, it may be hoped, be assisted by the development of the new Iraqi national police force and national army. In retrospect it will probably be seen that the gravest mistake made by the Coalition Provisional Authority (CPA) was to dissolve the existing army and police force in the aftermath of the coalition's victory. The decision to do so, though explicable in terms of America's anti-imperialist past, might not have been taken by a European power, such as Britain, with a less idealistic approach to pacification problems. Britain, during its conquest of India in the nineteenth century, in military circumstances not dissimilar from those facing the Americans in Iraq, suspended moral judgement and expended considerable care and effort to keep in being but win over the forces of its defeated enemies, as during the conquest of the Sikh kingdom of the Punjab in the 1840s. The Sikhs, like Iraq's Sunni, were a dominant regional minority. Having beaten them in battle, the British incorporated their regiments into their governing system, with great success. The Sikh regiments became a mainstay of Britain's Indian Army and in 1947 transferred their loyalty to the new Republic of India.

A similar incorporation would have been possible in April 2003; instead several hundred thousand policeman and soldiers found their employment and their pay stopped, and were turned loose onto the employment market. Finding no work, they were readily recruited into resistance and wrongdoing. Many of them seek reemployment in their former occupations. Those who report to recruiting stations have been the victims of terror attacks by supporters of the old regime and Islamist fundamentalists. Such attacks, however, do not appear to be a deterrent. The recruitment, training, and organisation of the successor security forces continues, at a rate which promises that the Iraqi Transitional Government will command sufficient force to ensure law and order, the condition of life which is at the forefront of Iraq's hopes for the future. Until the new army and police force have reached effective size and capability, nevertheless, Western troops will have to remain.

The presence of a large American army in Iraq, together with the threats levelled by its internal instability, makes the future of the country a matter of keen concern to its neighbours, Iran, Saudi Arabia, Syria, Jordan, Turkey and Israel.

Iran, as the largest Shi'a country in the Muslim world, is a traditional protector of Shi'a minorities elsewhere and has a particular interest in Iraq because of the presence there of the

Shi'as' holiest places. The religious powerholders in Tehran have undoubtedly sponsored the infiltration of Shi'a militants into Iraq during the disorders of 2004. On the other hand, Tehran's principal national interest at present is the development of its military nuclear capability, which is being closely watched by the International Atomic Energy Authority. The United States makes it clear that it disapproves strongly of Iran's nuclear programme, to which Israel is even more sensitive. The United States has recently begun to supply Israel with 'bunker-busting' missiles, which might be used *in extremis* to repeat the preemptive attack mounted against Iraq's Osirak reactor in 1981. Were Iran to proceed to producing weapon-grade nuclear material, which it has the capability to do, or is close to acquiring, the United States might well feel impelled to use its Iraqi-based army to take preemptive action, possibly even by ground invasion. Militarily the ayatollahs' Iran is no more of a match for US power than was Saddam's Iraq. The likelihood is, therefore, that Iran will desist from exacerbating the troubles in Iraq, since its leaders are aware that after the Republican victory in the 2004 presidential elections there will be strong pressure from the Washington neoconservatives to take preemptive action against them, both to punish them for meddling in Iraq and to eliminate Iran's nuclear potential.

Iran has an additional interest in the outcome of Iraq's postwar settlement, which is the future of its oil production. Iraqi territory contains the second largest oil reserves in the world, whose output has been limited since 1991 by international sanctions against sales. Limitation of Iraqi oil supply to the world market benefits Iran, itself a major oil producer, and so gives it an interest in fostering the disorder that inhibits a return to full production. Iran cannot, however, risk being identified as a sponsor of disorder for its own sake and will probably, as a result, desist from malevolence.

The interest of Saudi Arabia in Iraq's future takes a different form. The country is the heartland of Islam; its ruler, indeed, now prefers to identify himself as 'the Guardian of the Two Holy Places' (Mecca and Medina) rather than as King. Its status as an oil producer is not threatened by Iraq's return to the international oil markets, since its reserves exceed in volume those of any other country. Its internal stability is, however, closely linked to that of Iraq, because the population of its Eastern Province, where most of its oil is located, is Shi'a. The Saudi royal family, which rules as an autocracy, is therefore threatened by the rise of Shi'a power in Iraq. It is also threatened, paradoxically, from the opposite direction by the infiltration into the Kingdom of Iraq of al-Qaeda operatives whose principal ambition is to bring down Saudi royal power. The leaders of al-Qaeda are Saudi nationals. Although they are almost indistinguishable in belief from the Wahabi sect which has been dominant in Arabia since the eighteenth century, they seek its overthrow, and that of the royal family, so that the oil power of the kingdom can be harnessed to the reestablishment of the universal Caliphate. The Saudi royal family therefore finds itself in a difficult position. It is linked, currently inextricably, by its alliance to Washington. Washington values the connection, as long as the Saudi government will alter oil output to regulate market prices in favour of Western consumers. The Americans, however, because of the Saudi link to al-Qaeda, have come to regard Saudi Arabia as a suspect quantity in the Global War on Terrorism (GWOT). The American neoconservatives have convinced themselves that a principal means towards the defeat of al-Qaeda is the reform of the Saudi political system, favouring the development of representative institutions and the exclusion of Wahabi clerics from access to power. The Saudi royal family thus finds itself in a quandary. Theologically and therefore socially, since religion informs Saudi society at every level, it has no means of detaching itself from the Wahabi clerisy. Politically, practically, and commercially, it is tied to an American government which has no truck with theology and wants the world's largest oil producer to become a modern state. That outcome the Saudis are bound to resist, for reasons that penetrate the heart of their society, but which will be increasingly difficult to sustain against the emergence of a truly modern society in an American-sponsored Iraqi democracy. While the postwar situation in Iraq

develops, the Saudi Arabian government will be forced to persist
with its policy of domestic repression of Islamic terrorism which,
in 2003–04, claimed the lives of 85 victims, most of them
Westerners. Terrorism is a threat to the authority of the Saudi
royal government which cannot be ignored, since the emigration
of Western experts to a revived Iraqi oil industry would be a
serious blow to Saudi prosperity.

Saudi Arabia is in an unenviable position. Though a rich country,
with the ability to increase its income at will by amplifying oil
production, its young population is discontented. Saudi youth know
that a vast proportion of oil wealth goes to support the extravagant lives of the bloated royal family (7,000 strong) while their own
prospects of gainful employment are limited. Although the government finances free education up to university level, too many Saudi
students choose courses in Muslim theology, and so find employment elusive. Per capita income is actually falling. The royal government, at a realistic level, would wish to see the country's youth
trained in modern science and technology, so that its principal assets
could be managed by the native-born. Ideologically, however, it
prefers an educational system of which the clergy approves, since
that defers trouble. In the long run, however, trouble between the
royal house and its subjects is inevitable; it is, indeed, already breaking
out. At present, many of the troublemakers slip into Iraq to wage
jihad against the Western troops. Some are, moreover, already
choosing the Westerners working in Saudi Arabia as their targets.
If a successful home-based terror organization can be established
in Saudi Arabia proper, it will probably be too late for the royal
government to institute reforms that would secure its position.

Jordan, another monarchical state, is also threatened by disorder
in Iraq. Early in Saddam's regime, the then-king, Hussein, made
the mistake of supporting the annexation of Kuwait. It was a
serious foreign policy error, subsequently retrieved by ostentatious obeisance to the United States. Obeisance continues, under
a new king. Meanwhile Jordan exerts careful control over its
border, so that, unlike Syria, its territory is not useful to terror-

ists seeking to infiltrate Iraq from the north. Its main connection with post-Saddam Iraq is as an *entrepôt,* from which supply convoys deliver essential goods to the Iraqi economy. Attacks on the supply convoys, which kill or injure many nationalities working as transport drivers but a consistent number of Jordanians also, do not endear the dissidents to Jordanian opinion. The Jordanian government will support any strong, non-Islamist administration that emerges in Baghdad. It is an embarrassment to the Jordanian government that the most ferocious of the Islamist fighters operating in Iraq, Abu Musab al-Zarqawi, is a Jordanian national.

At the outset of the 2003 war, Jordan's mistake of 1991 was repeated by Syria. Not expecting the American intervention, or its power, the Damascus government was foolish enough publicly to express its desire that the Western invasion would be defeated. Washington, which has long regarded the Syrian Ba'athist regime with hostility, responded, in the aftermath of Saddam's fall, by accusing Damascus of permitting Islamic fighters to cross into Iraq from Syrian territory, and of hiding numbers of the Saddam regime and even Iraqi weapons of mass destruction. Alarmed at the strength of the American reaction, Syria attempted to reingratiate itself with Washington, to little effect. In November 2003 the US Congress passed a law (the Syria Accountability and Lebanese Sovereignty Restoration Act) that imposed a regime of severe sanctions against Syria. During the Iraqi internal disorders of 2003–04 Syria has been lying low, attempting to distance itself from the troublemakers, but failing to restore good relations with the United States. The restoration of law and order in Iraq and the creation of a democratic government will, as Damascus realizes, serve further to isolate it in an Arab world remade in the image the United States seeks to foster. If a tier of pro-American Arab states including Saudi Arabia, Jordan, Iraq, and a Lebanon detached from Syrian control is brought into existence, Syria will find itself isolated, particularly because its closest relations are with non-Arab Iran, which stands high on America's blacklist. The neoconservative lobby in Washington will pursue 'regime change' in Syria if it sees the opportunity to achieve it.

Turkey's main anxiety vis-à-vis Iraq arises from the nature of the eventual settlement of the country's Kurdish north. Turkey has its own Kurdish problem, as the homeland of the largest of the Kurdish minorities. It fears the emergence of a sovereign Kurdish state, particularly if such a state, as is highly probable, would seek to incorporate irredentist Kurdish territories elsewhere. Turkey got off to a bad start with the United States at the outset of the Western effort to replace the Saddam regime, by refusing to allow the US 4th Infantry Division to operate against the Iraqi army from its territory. Since Saddam's fall, Turkey has repaired relations and certainly gives no help to the Iraqi dissidents. The Ankara government welcomes the creation of a democratic regime in Baghdad and will support it.

The last Middle Eastern state on which Iraq has impinged historically is Israel. Under Saddam's predecessors, Iraq participated actively in the Arab-Israeli war of 1948, while Saddam himself had directly attacked Israel with Scud missiles during the Gulf War of 1991. Saddam, however, was among the least threatening of Israel's Arab neighbours during the periods 1980–90 and 1991–2003, because his military operations against Iran (1980–88) and then with the Western powers (1990 and years following) left him little energy to engage in operations against Israel or even to support other Arab states, such as Syria, which did sustain hostilities. Saddam was not therefore high on Israel's list of enemies once it had destroyed the Osirak nuclear plant in 1981 during his years in power. Nevertheless the Israeli government is glad at his downfall and will seek to establish mutually tolerant relations with the new Baghdad government, which the United States, as Israel's protector, will certainly seek to foster.

The nature of future Iraqi–Israeli relations, supposing that democracy in Iraq takes root, will nevertheless be dominated, as other Israeli–Arab relationships are also, by the Palestinian question. Israel's best hope is that a future Iraqi government will adopt an Egyptian attitude, sympathetic theoretically to Palestinian nationalism but committed pragmatically to co-operation with Tel Aviv. Iraq's democrats cannot favour the militants of the intifada, since such fanatics resemble all too closely the Iraqi terrorists who are seeking to prevent the emergence of representative government in their homeland.

Beyond Iraq, in the autumn of 2004, the repercussions of the Western military operations to liberate the country from Saddam's dictatorship and the Ba'ath Party's institutional tyranny persisted. The Iraq war dominated the American presidential election campaign, with the Democratic Party candidate, Senator John Kerry, promising to extricate American troops from Iraq as quickly as possible if he were elected, and President George W. Bush insisting that he would keep them there until the job – manning the establishment of a pro-Western, democratically oriented regime is – were achieved.

In America the debate over Iraq, though intense and at times passionate, remains essentially bipartisan. It is a debate over detail, not principle. In Britain, which in October 2004 still deployed nearly 10,000 troops in the country, there was, by contrast, widespread and organized protest against involvement in the war itself. Although the antiwar movement, which was led by such familiar left-wing bodies as the Campaign for Nuclear Disarmament, was unable to achieve such turn-outs as marched in the months before the beginning of the war in March 2003, it succeeded in assembling a crowd of 15,000 to demonstrate in Central London in October 2004. More worrying for the Prime Minister were the positions taken by the Liberal Democrat Party, which continued to insist that the war was illegal and to demand the immediate withdrawal of British troops from Iraq, and by groups of his own backbenchers who expressed similar views. The Prime Minister had been obliged, by media but also by parliamentary pressure, to appoint the Hutton Committee of inquiry into the intelligence reports underpinning resort to war in 2003. In 2004, in order to quell persisting dissatisfaction over legal justification for the war, he appointed a second committee, under the chairmanship of Lord Butler, Master of University College, Oxford, a former Cabinet Secretary, to reexamine the matter. Butler, though less emollient than Hutton, concluded by endorsing the government's decisions also. Nevertheless discontent persisted, threatening to undermine the Prime Minister's appeal to the country in the forthcoming general election of 2005.

Meanwhile, within Iraq, disorder persisted. Though American operations around Najaf had, by October, largely quelled the insurrection of the Mullah Sadr's Mahdi Army, a Shi'ite organisation, resistance by Sunni forces at Fallujah persisted. In mid-October the American high command in Iraq was preparing an offensive against the city, designed to destroy resistance and, with the co-operation of the new Iraqi national army, to impose law and order within the 'Sunni triangle'. Operations against and within Fallujah by the US 1st Marine Division, in which British troops, notably the Black Watch, played a supporting role, were mounted throughout September, October, and November 2004. Heavy casualties were inflicted but, even by mid-November, no definitive result had been achieved. However, the internal situation was calm enough in January for the promised elections to be held. Despite intimidation, over eight million Iraqis, mainly Shi'a, voted in what observers described as fair and well-conducted polls. The Kurdish parties secured an overwhelming majority in the north. The Shi'a parties were elected in the south and center. Few Sunni candidates secured sizable votes. A Shi'a coalition controlled the Transitional National Assembly, though as late as mid-March it had failed to agree on the appointment of ministers.

Appendix 1

Coalition Order of Battle

UK
ROYAL NAVY AND ROYAL MARINES

HMS *Ark Royal* (aircraft carrier)

HMS *Ocean* (helicopter carrier)

HMS *Liverpool* (Type 42 destroyer)

HMS *Edinburgh* (Type 42 destroyer)

HMS *York* (Type 42 destroyer)

HMS *Marlborough* (Type 23 frigate)

HMS *Richmond* (Type 23 frigate)

HMS *Grimsby* (minehunter)

HMS *Ledbury* (minehunter)

HMS *Brocklesby* (minehunter)

HMS *Blyth* (minehunter)

HMS *Chatham* (Type 22 frigate)

HMS *Splendid* (Swiftsure class submarine)

HMS *Turbulent* (Trafalgar class submarine)

RFA *Argus*

RFA (Royal Fleet Auxiliary) *Sir Tristram*

RFA *Sir Galahad*

RFA *Sir Percivale*

RFA *Fort Victoria*

RFA *Fort Rosalie*

RFA *Fort Austin*

RFA *Orangeleaf*

The amphibious force
Numbered some 4,000 and included:

HQ 3 Commando Brigade
40 Commando Royal Marines
42 Commando Royal Marines
29 Regt, Royal Artillery (105mm Light Gun)
539 Assault Sqn, RM
59 Commando Sqn, RE

Helicopter air groups aboard *Ark Royal* and *Ocean* included:
845, 846, 847, 849 Sqns

ARMY
1 (UK) Armoured Division:
Headquarters and 1 Armoured Division Signal Regt
30 Signal Regt (strategic communications)
The Queen's Dragoon Guards (reconnaissance)
1st Bn The Duke of Wellington's Regt (additional infantry capability)
28 Engineer Regt
1 General Support Regt, Royal Logistic Corps
2 Close Support Regt, Royal Logistic Corps
2nd Bn, Royal Electrical & Mechanical Engineers
1 Close Support Medical Regt
5 General Support Medical Regt
1 Regt, Royal Military Police
plus elements from various units including:
33 Explosive Ordnance Disposal Regt
30 Signal Regt
32 Regt Royal Artillery
(Phoenix UAVs)

7th Armoured Brigade
Headquarters and Signal Sqn
Royal Scots Dragoon Guards (Challenger 2 tanks)

2nd Royal Tank Regt (Challenger 2 tanks)
1st Bn The Black Watch (Warrior infantry fighting vehicles)
1st Bn Royal Regt of Fusiliers (Warrior infantry fighting vehicles)
3rd Regt Royal Horse Artillery (AS90 self-propelled guns)
32 Armoured Engineer Regt
plus elements from various units including:
Queens Royal Lancers (Challenger 2 tanks)
1st Bn Irish Guards (Warrior infantry fighting vehicles)
1st Bn The Light Infantry (Warrior infantry fighting vehicles)
26 Regt Royal Artillery
38 Engineer Regt

16 Air Assault Brigade
Headquarters and Signal Sqn
1st Bn The Royal Irish Regt
1st Bn The Parachute Regt
3rd Bn The Parachute Regt
7 (Para) Regt Royal Horse Artillery (105mm Light Guns)
23 Engineer Regt
D Sqn, Household Cavalry Regt
3 Regt Army Air Corps (Lynx & Gazelle helicopters)
7 Air Assault Bn, Royal Electrical & Mechanical Engineers
13 Air Assault Support Regt, Royal Logistic Corps
16 Close Support Medical Regt
156 Provost Company RMP

102 Logistics Brigade
Headquarters 2 Signal Regt
36 Engineer Regt
33 and 34 Field Hospitals
202 Field Hospital (Volunteer)
4 General Support Medical Regt
3 Bn, Royal Electrical & Mechanical Engineers
6 Supply Regt, Royal Logistic Corps
7 Transport Regt, Royal Logistic Corps

17 Port & Maritime Regt, Royal Logistic Corps
23 Pioneer Regt, Royal Logistic Corps
24 Regt, Royal Logistic Corps
5 Regt, Royal Military Police
Specialist Royal Engineer teams
Airfield engineer support units from 12 Engineer Brigade
Elements from 11 Explosive Ordnance Disposal Regt
Elements from additional Royal Logistic Corps Regts

ROYAL AIR FORCE
Composite sqns formed including elements from:

9, 13, 31, 39 (1 PRU) Sqns, RAF Marham
12, 14, 617 Sqns, RAF Lossiemouth
11, 25 Sqns, RAF Leeming
43, 111 Sqns, RAF Leuchars
6, 41, 54 Sqns, RAF Coltishall
1, 3, IV Sqns, RAF Cottesmore
8, 23, 51 Sqns, RAF Waddington
33 Sqn, RAF Benson
10, 99, 101, 216 Sqns, RAF Brize Norton
24, 30, 47, 70 Sqns, RAF Lyneham
120, 201, 206 Sqns, RAF Kinloss
7, 18, 27 Sqns, RAF Odiham
RAF Regt

AUSTRALIA

NAVY
HMAS *Kanimbla*
HMAS *Anzac*
HMAS *Darwin*

AIR FORCE
One RAAF sqn F/A-18
Three RAAF C-130
Two P-3C Orion

ARMY
Special forces task group including SAS, and 4 Royal Australian
 Regt

POLAND

200 special forces

USA

Elements included

US ARMY
Special Operations Command
5th Special Forces Group
75th Ranger Regt
160th Special Ops Aviation Regt

3rd Infantry Division
1st Bn, 39th Fd Artillery Regt
11th Aviation Regt
1st Brigade
 2nd, 3rd Bns, 7th Infantry Regt

3rd Bn, 69th Armor Regt
1st Bn, 41st Fd Artillery Regt
2nd Brigade
  3rd Bn, 15th Infantry Regt
  1st, 4th Bns, 64th Armor Regt
  E Troop, 9th Cavalry Regt
  1st Bn, 9th Fd Artillery Regt
3rd Brigade
  1st Bn, 30th Infantry Regt
  1st Bn, 15th Infantry Regt
  2nd Bn, 69th Armor Regt
  D Troop, 10th Cavalry Regt
  1st Bn, 10th Fd Artillery Regt
Aviation Brigade
  1st Bn, 3rd Aviation Regt
  2nd Bn, 3rd Aviation Regt
  3rd Sqn, 7th Cavalry Regt

82nd Airborne Division

2nd Brigade Combat Team
  1st, 2nd, 3rd Bns, 325th Airborne Infantry
1st Bn, 82nd Aviation Regt

101st Airborne (Air Assault) Division

1st Brigade, 101st Airborne Division
  1st, 2nd, 3rd Bns, 327th Infantry Regt
2nd Brigade, 101st Airborne Division
  1st, 2nd, 3rd Bns, 502nd Infantry Regt
3rd Brigade, 101st Airborne Division
  1st, 2nd, 3rd Bns, 187th Infantry Regt
101st Aviation Brigade
  2nd Bn, 17th Cavalry Regt
  1st, 2nd, 3rd, 6th Bns, 101st Aviation Regt
159th Aviation Brigade
  4th, 5th, 7th, 9th Bns, 101st Aviation Regt

Divarty [Divisional Artillery]
  1st, 2nd, 3rd Bns, 320th Fd Artillery Regt

173rd Airborne Brigade
  1st, 2nd Bns, 508th Infantry
  173rd Engineer Detachment
  173rd Brigade Recon. Company
  Battery D, 3rd Bn, 319th Airborne Fd Artillery

US MARINE CORPS
1 Marine Expeditionary Force
1st Marine Division
1st Marine Regt
  3rd Bn, 1st Marines
  1st Bn, 4th Marines
  1st, 3rd Bns, Light Armored Recon.
5th Marine Regt
  1st Bn, 5th Marines
  2nd, 3rd Bns, 5th Marines
7th Marine Regt
  1st, 3rd Bns, 7th Marines
  3rd Bn, 4th Marines
  1st Tank Bn
  1st, 2nd, 3rd Bns, 11th Marines (artillery)

2nd Marine Expeditionary Brigade
2nd Marine Division
  1st, 3rd Bns, 2nd Marines
  2nd Bn, 8th Marines
  1st Bn, 10th Marines
  2nd Amphibious Assault Bn
  2nd Recon. Bn
  2nd Light Armored Recon. Bn
  2nd, 8th Tank Bns

15th Marine Expeditionary Unit

24th Marine Expeditionary Unit

26th Marine Expeditionary Unit

US AIR FORCE
Special Ops
16th Special Ops Wing (AC-130)
20th Special Ops Sqn (MH-53M)
193rd Special Ops Wing (EC-130E)

Ali Al Salem AB, Kuwait
386th Air Exped. Group
118th Fighter Sqn (A-10)
41st Electronic Combat Sqn (EC-130)

Al Jaber AB, Kuwait
332nd Air Exped. Group
52nd Fighter Wing
22nd, 23rd Fighter Sqns (F-16)
172nd Fighter Sqn (A-10)
332nd Exped. Air Support Ops Sqn
332nd Exped. Intelligence Flight
332nd Exped. Rescue Sqn (HH-60G)
552nd Air Control Wing (E-3 AWACS)

Masirah AB, Oman
355th Air Exped. Group
4th Special Ops Sqn (AC-130U)
8th Special Ops Sqn (MC-130E)

Thumrait AB, Oman
405th Air Exped. Wing
405th Exped. Bomb Sqn (B-1B)

28th, 34th, 37th Bomb Wings (B-1B)
55th Wing (RC-135)

Al Udeid AB, Qatar
379th Air Exped. Wing
49th Fighter Wing (F-117)
4th Ops Group (F-15)
336th Fighter Sqn (F-15)
93rd Air Control Wing (E-8 JSTARS)

Al Dhafra AB, UAE
380th Air Exped. Wing
9th, 57th Recon. Wings (U-2)
11th, 12th, 15th Recon. Sqn (RQ-1A)

Prince Sultan AB, Saudi Arabia
363rd Air Exped. Wing
14th, 22nd Fighter Sqns (F-16)
67th, 390th Fighter Sqns (F-15)
457th, 524th Fighter Sqns (F-16)
363 Exped. Airborne Air Control Sqn (E-3 AWACS)
38th Recon. Sqn (RC-135)
99th Recon. Sqn (U-2)

Diego Garcia
40th Air Exped. Wing
509th Bomb Wing
20th, 40th Bomb Sqns (B-2)

RAF Fairford, United Kingdom
457th Air Exped. Group
23rd Bomb Sqn (B-52)
509th Bomb Wing
9th Recon. Wing

US NAVY

Theodore Roosevelt Carrier Battle Group

USS *Theodore Roosevelt* (CVN 71)
   Carrier Air Wing 8
USS *Anzio* (CG 68)
USS *Cape St George* (CG 71)
USS *Arleigh Burke* (DDG 51)
USS *Porter* (DDG 78)
USS *Winston Churchill* (DDG 81)
USS *Stump* (DD 978)
USS *Carr* (FFG 52)
USS *Arctic* (AOE 8)

Harry S Truman Carrier Battle Group

USS *Harry S Truman* (CVN 75)
   Carrier Air Wing 3
USS *San Jacinto* (CG 56)
USS *Oscar Austin* (DDG 79)
USS *Mitscher* (DDG 57)
USS *Donald Cook* (DDG 75)
USS *Briscoe* (DD 977)
USS *Dey* (DD 989)
USS *Hawes* (FFG 53)
USNS *Kanawha* (T-AO 196)
USNS *Mount Baker* (T-AE 34)
USS *Pittsburgh* (SSN 720)
USS *Montpelier* (SSN 765)

Kitty Hawk Carrier Battle Group

USS *Kitty Hawk* (CV 63)
   Carrier Air Wing 5
USS *Chancellorsville* (CG 62)
USS *Cowpens* (CG 63)
USS *John S. McCain* (DDG 56)
USS *O'Brien* (DD 975)
USS *Cushing* (DD 985)

USS *Vandergrift* (FFG 48)
USS *Gary* (FFG 51)
USS *Bremerton* (SSN 698)

Abraham Lincoln Carrier Battle Group
USS *Abraham Lincoln* (CVN 72)
   Carrier Air Wing 14
USS *Mobile Bay* (CG 53)
USS *Shiloh* (CG 67)
USS *Paul Hamilton* (DDG 60)
USS *Fletcher* (DD 992)
USS *Crommlein* (FFG 37)
USS *Reuben James* (FFG 57)
USS *Camden* (AOE 2)
USS *Honolulu* (SSN 718)
USS *Cheyenne* (SSN 773)

Constellation Carrier Battle Group
USS *Constellation* (CV 64)
   Carrier Air Wing 2
USS *Valley Forge* (CG 50)
USS *Bunker Hill* (CG 52)
USS *Higgins* (DDG 76)
USS *Thach* (FFG 43)
USS *Ranier* (AOE 7)
USS *Columbia* (SSN 771)
USS *Milius* (DDG 69)

Nimitz Carrier Battle Group
USS *Nimitz* (CVN 68)
   Carrier Air Wing 11
USS *Princeton* (CG 59)
USS *Chosin* (CG 65)
USS *Fitzgerald* (DDG 2)
USS *Benfold* (DDG 65)
USS *Oldendorf* (DD 972)

USS *Rodney M. Davis* (FFG 60)
USS *Pasadena* (SSN 752)
USS *Bridge* (AOE 10)

Amphibious Task Force East
USS *Saipan* (LHA 2)
USS *Gunston Hall* (LSD 44)
USS *Ponce* (LPD 15)
USS *Bataan* (LHD 5)
USS *Kearsarge* (LHD 3)
USS *Ashland* (LSD 48)
USS *Portland* (LSD 37)
Marine Aircraft Group 29

Amphibious Task Force West
USS *Boxer* (LHD 4)
USS *Bonhomme Richard* (LHD 6)
USS *Cleveland* (LPD 7)
USS *Dubuque* (LPD 8)
USS *Anchorage* (LSD 36)
USS *Comstock* (LSD 45)
USS *Pearl Harbor* (LSD 52)

***Tarawa* Amphibious Ready Group**
USS *Tarawa* (LHA 1)
USS *Duluth* (LPD 6)
USS *Rushmore* (LSD 47)

***Nassau* Amphibious Ready Group**
USS *Nassau* (LHA 4)
USS *Austin* (LPD 4)
USS *Tortuga* (LSD 46)

***Iwo Jima* Amphibious Ready Group**
USS *Iwo Jima* (LHD 7)
USS *Nashville* (LPD 13)
USS *Carter Hall* (LSD 50)

Mine Countermeasures Div. 31

USS *Ardent* (MCM 12)
USS *Dextrous* (MCM 13)
USS *Cardinal* (MHC 60)
USS *Raven* (MHC 61)

Appendix 2

What follows is my record of a long conversation I held with General Tommy Franks, CENTCOM and campaign commander, during a visit he paid to London shortly after the war. I saw General Franks alone, apart from the presence of two of his staff officers. I subsequently sent the record to General Franks for his approval of its accuracy.

REVIEWING THE IRAQ WAR WITH GENERAL FRANKS, 1 JULY 2003 AT THE GROSVENOR HOUSE HOTEL, LONDON by JOHN KEEGAN

1. During the course of a long presentation, General Franks outlined for me, with remarkable frankness and great clarity, the course of the Iraq crisis and the ensuing war, from the point of view of Central Command and himself as commander. He described the campaign from the inception of the planning until the present moment. He also answered a number of questions I put, though I put few because I did not wish to break the flow of his highly fluent discourse. Moreover, General Franks organized his presentation so effectively that few questions were necessary. As I remarked afterwards to his Executive Officer, his briefing was the most impressive I have ever received from a military officer.
2. General Franks began by dating the inception of planning,

which he put in the month of December 2001. He was then requested by the President to visit him at Crawford, Texas, to outline Central Command's existing plan for an operation against the Saddam régime in Iraq. The plan existed simply as a planning requirement, in accordance with its policy of preparing plans for foreseeable eventualities, and was *not* predicated on a *casus belli*.

3. General Franks told the President that the plan, when he examined it, struck him as too 'heavy' in conception, making little allowance for the use of surprise or for responding to the unfolding of events. It envisaged the deployment of up to 500,000 ground troops with a full range of heavy equipment. General Franks called this plan 'the heavy bookend'. He asked his staff to plan a 'light bookend', for an operation that would be mounted largely with special forces, the total numbers to be deployed amounting to about 50,000 at most.

4. The 'bookends' were planning devices. By examining likely outcomes at either end, and at points in between, by discussion, paper exercises and computer modelling, he expected to arrive at an eventual plan that would achieve the desired outcome, the defeat of the Saddam military structure; the staff procedures would also determine the necessary force size, points of entry, axes of advance, objectives and subordinate tasks, including those of airpower. As planning proceeded, the operational concept moved away both from the 'heavy' and 'light' bookends to settle somewhere between the two. The eventual choice of force was two divisions for the initial phase, the 3rd Infantry Division and the 1st Marine Expeditionary Force, with the British 1st Armoured Division to be committed in the south against Basra; the 82nd Airborne and the 101st Air Assault Divisions were earmarked for intervention later.

5. At a later point, General Franks also touched on the role of the 4th Infantry Division which, before 19 March, had been brought to the eastern Mediterranean embarked. At the outset it was expected that permission would be given by the Turkish government for the division to land, to deploy in southern

Turkey and to intervene in northern Iraq. In the event the Turkish government withheld permission. It nevertheless proved possible, General Franks explained, to make use of the 4th Infantry Division, in the following way: using covert deceptive means, information was passed to the Saddam régime suggesting that, after an interval, the Turkish army would exert its political authority to extract permission for the division to land and intervene in the coming operation. This deception was believed, with the result that two Republican Guard and several Iraqi regular army divisions were retained north of Baghdad and so took no part in the defence of the country against the coalition offensive.

6. General Franks also disclosed that, before the operation opened, his staff had established contact with the commanders of several of the Iraqi regular army divisions in the south. He was hopeful that the divisions could be brought over before the fighting began. In the event, Saddam installed Ba'athist teams at these divisional headquarters and frustrated the attempt at subversion – though, in practice, the divisions did not resist very strenuously. He emphasized the importance of the Ba'athist forces, and others loyal personally to Saddam, including *fedayeen*, throughout the campaign. It was they, he agreed, who did much of the fighting. He deprecated, however, their effectiveness. All too often, he said, once operations began, they simply set up their base in the local Ba'athist headquarters of a town and operated from there. As the locations of such headquarters were either known to Central Command or readily identifiable, it was not difficult to destroy them, thus often neutralizing the Ba'athists associated with them.

7. As preparations were being finalized, the ultimate phases of the plan came to be denoted, General Franks said, as 'Five, eleven, sixteen, one-two-five.' The formula stood for five days for the President and Prime Minister to make last-minute adjustments to the plan, eleven days of 'final flow', the concluding military adjustments, then sixteen days of special

operations, followed by 125 days of decisive fighting. As he pointed out, the end of the 125 days had not, on 1 July, yet been reached; he was not, therefore, seriously concerned that sporadic attacks on coalition forces were continuing, as that eventuality had been foreseen.

8. The general then turned to the war itself, taking it front by front. There had, he said, been five fronts, the southern, the western, the northern, the Baghdad front and the intelligence front. The northern front has already been dealt with above, in his references to the deception over 4th Infantry Division. The management of the intelligence front he narrated by describing the way in which his personal command centre was arranged in his headquarters at Qatar. In front of his desk, he said, he had four screens which he viewed continuously. One displayed, at five-second intervals, the different outputs of the main television news channels, CNN, Fox, BBC; he needed to know what each was broadcasting because public coverage of the war so closely affected strategy. A second screen displayed the location of friendly ground units at the front of contact, a third the location of air units, the fourth the current intelligence estimate, including the location of enemy units. It was possible to superimpose the images if desired and it was also possible to call up an 'eyeball vision' picture of critical encounters in progress. General Franks was emphatic, however, that despite the theoretical ability thus provided for him to intervene in the conduct of small-unit operations, he declined to do so, regarding such interference by high command in the responsibilities of the local commander as undesirable, indeed deplorable. He had learned in Vietnam, he recalled, as a cavalry unit leader, how little 'Snowball Six' (the superior commander), overflying the battle-field in a helicopter at several thousand feet, could grasp of what was transpiring in a firefight.

9. In describing what occurred on the southern front he addressed two main topics: the employment of special forces and the use of armour in built-up areas. He had, he said,

forty-eight special forces teams available, drawn from American Special Forces and British and Australian SAS. Many were deployed into the operational area before the main ground force crossed the Iraq–Kuwait border on 19 March. They had both reconnaissance and strike roles. One of their most important operational roles was to identify 'Scud pans' – points from which Scud missiles could be launched – in the western Iraqi desert. The Scud needs an area of hard-standing from which to launch. The special forces teams surveyed the desert to identify 'soft' areas, which form the majority of the desert surface, and 'hard' areas, the minority, which could then be targeted by airpower. In the two nights either side of 19 March, special forces also destroyed all Iraqi watch posts on Iraq's borders with Saudi Arabia, Kuwait and Jordan, so as to assure the governments of those countries that the Saddam régime was deprived of the opportunity to launch Scud attacks into their territories.

10. Special forces also targeted bridges and crossing points across the Euphrates and Tigris, to forestall attempts by Saddam's forces to demolish them before the arrival of coalition ground troops. The ability of the coalition to cross the large water obstacles (which I found so mysterious when I was commenting daily on the war in my newspaper) was thus explained: the defences of the bridges had already been overcome. Nevertheless, the general said, it was necessary to bridge, with engineering bridge columns of the National Guard, at some points, where demolitions had succeeded; the bridging columns also used ferries and pontoons as necessary.

11. About the use of armour in built-up areas, such as Basra and Nasiriyah: the general emphasized that it was a deliberate policy not to block city highways by using airpower to demolish buildings, so that tanks could manoeuvre freely and target points of resistance with their main armaments. The policy, he said, proved highly successful. Tanks operated with great success, against conventional thinking, in built-up areas.

Some Iraqi units were able to immobilize tanks, by using RPGs against their road wheels, but the number of successful attacks was few. The Iraqis suffered heavy casualties in attempting to 'swarm' tanks with foot soldiers.

12. Turning to the western front, the general responded at length to my question about using the 'hard' desert to bypass the area of paved roads west of the Euphrates and press the advance on Baghdad. He said that it was a misunderstanding to think that the advance from Basra to Baghdad had been achieved across the gravel desert. In fact, most of the advance had been made along the highways and it was only just short of Baghdad that the 3rd Infantry Division's armoured columns had left the paved roads to make use of a 'spit' of naturally hard surface between Karbala and the adjacent lake to press forward.

13. He turned finally to discuss the Baghdad front. Baghdad, he said, had always been seen as the critical focus of the offensive, and the place where the 'tipping point' of the campaign would occur. The exact focus was Baghdad International Airport. It was a location of vital prestige to the régime. Its capture intact would also – as the Ba'athists would recognize – permit the reinforcement of the ground offensive with troops and supplies virtually at the point of final assault – at the place of victory or defeat. General Franks reflected here on what he called the 'inside-out' nature of the air attack on Iraqi formations defending Baghdad. He stressed very strongly that he sought to avoid 'collapsing' the Republican Guard into the city, thus filling its buildings and streets with the better-trained Iraqi soldiers. He wanted them to remain outside. With that object in view, airpower was used to attack the divisions' rear areas and lines of retreat, so as to persuade the enemy that they were safer where they were. The procedure was successful. Few of the Republican Guard left their positions and the divisions were engaged and neutralized by advancing American units well outside the city limits. They were unable to manoeuvre so as to defend Baghdad airport

so that, as it began to fall into American hands, the 'tipping point' was reached.

14. Because the built-up areas of Baghdad had deliberately not been devastated by air attack, he was able to use armour in a novel way inside the city. In an aside, the general revealed that he had never cared for the use of the term 'shock and awe' and, though no doubt the initial bombing of the government quarter did cause shock and awe, he had not seen that effect as the point of the air offensive. He saw the point as the dislocation of the command and administrative structure. The forecasts of Baghdad becoming 'another Stalingrad' were proved wrong; armoured units were able to fight with almost the same freedom of action inside as outside the urban area, and to achieve rapid and decisive results. Main armament was fired effectively, down boulevards, at ranges of as much as 1,000 metres (1,093 yards).

15. In answer to a question, General Franks said it was his impression that, once large-scale operations began, the Iraqi command and control system was not effective. He did not think that anyone was in charge, 'anyone' including Saddam, Uday or Qusay. He believed that the Iraqi defence system 'went onto automatic', simply reacting as it had been trained to do in peacetime, not responding to American attacks by calculated counter-thrusts.

16. After taking over an hour and a half of General Franks's time, I felt I had trespassed long enough on his patience and goodwill. I also felt, correctly, that I had acquired a comprehensive overview of the sequence of the war's main events, and of the interaction of offence and defence. The General's presentation was a *tour de force*. No military analyst could have expected more in the time available.

17. In retrospect, I nevertheless recognize grey areas and blank spots in my understanding. For example, were there critical engagements in the ground fighting and, if so, when, where and between which formations? How important was the role of the air forces – in ground attack, in heliborne operations,

in interdiction? How important was intervention by 82nd Airborne and 101st Air Assault? Was there at any stage, as the media alleged, a shortage of force on the ground? Was it true, as alleged, that there was a lack of 'force protection' on the march up to Baghdad? Was there a 'wobble week'? On that subject, did the embedded media assist or detract from the evolution of the operation? Could the British have taken control of Basra earlier than they did?

Bibliography

Armstrong, K. *Islam*, New York, 2000

BBC News, *The Battle for Iraq*, London, 2003

Coughlin, C. *Saddam: King of Terror*, London, 2002

Dodge, T. *Inventing Iraq*, London, 2003

Hertoghe, A. *La guerre à outrances*, Paris, 2003

Hiro, D. *Desert Shield to Desert Storm*, London, 1992

Kampfner, J. *Blair's Wars*, London, 2003

Murray W. and Scales, R. *The Iraq War*, Cambridge, Mass., 2003

Shawcross, W. *Allies: The United States, Britain, Europe and the War on Iraq*, London, 2003

Stothard, P. *30 Days: A Month at the Heart of Blair's War*, London, 2003

Tripp, C. *A History of Iraq*, Cambridge, 2002

Watson, B. et al., *Military Lessons of the Gulf War*, London, 1993

West, B. and Smith, R. L. *The March Up: Taking Baghdad with the 1st Marine Division*, New York, 2003

Zinsmeister, K. *Boots on the Ground: A Month with the 82nd Airborne Division in the Battle for Iraq*, New York, 2003

Index

ALSO BY JOHN KEEGAN

INTELLIGENCE IN WAR
The Value—and Limitations—of What
the Military Can Learn About the Enemy

Intelligence gathering is an immensely complicated and vulnerable endeavor. And it often fails. Until the invention of the telegraph and radio, information often traveled no faster than a horse and rider. In the twentieth century, photo analysts didn't recognize Germany's V-2 rockets for what they were; on the other hand, intelligence helped lead to victory over the Japanese at Midway. In *Intelligence in War*, John Keegan illustrates that only when paired with force has military intelligence been an effective tool, as it may one day be in besting al-Qaeda.

Military History/0-375-70046-3

THE FIRST WORLD WAR

In this magisterial narrative, Keegan has produced the definitive account of the Great War, a cataclysm that left ten million dead. He sheds fascinating light on weaponry and technology, shows us the doomed negotiations between the monarchs and ministers of 1914, and takes us into the verminous trenches of the Western front. His panoramic account of this vast and terrible conflict is destined to take its place among the classics of world history.

History/0-375-70045-5

FIELDS OF BATTLE
The Wars for North America

Spanning more than two centuries and the expanse of a continent, Keegan demonstrates how the immense spaces of North America shaped the battles and wars that were fought on its soil. He revisits fields of combat from Quebec to Little Bighorn and retraces Washington's triumph and McClellan's defeat on battlefields only a few miles apart. Once again, Keegan's scholarship gives Americans a brilliant reassessment of their military heritage.

History/0-679-74664-1

THE BATTLE FOR HISTORY
Re-fighting World War II

In this engaging and concise volume, Keegan evaluates books on World War II that range from general histories to biographies of the war's principal figures, from accounts of individual campaigns to studies of espionage and resistance. What emerges is an essential guide for any serious student of World War II and the riveting story of how the war has been refought by two generations of its chroniclers, as told by one of the greatest of them all.

History/War/0-679-76743-6

A HISTORY OF WARFARE

In this encyclopedically learned and immensely gripping book, one of our foremost military historians demolishes the famous dictum that war is the continuation of policy by other means. Analyzing centuries of conflict—in societies from those of the Amazon to the Balkans—Keegan unveils the deepest motives behind humanity's penchant for mass bloodshed. *A History of Warfare* is a masterpiece of military scholarship, irresistible in its style and terrifying in its implications.

History/0-679-73082-6

WAR AND OUR WORLD

Is war a natural condition of humankind? What are the origins of war? Is the modern state dependent on warfare? How does war affect the individual, combatant or noncombatant? Can there be an end to war? In a series of brilliantly concise essays, Keegan addresses these questions with a breathtaking knowledge of history and the many other disciplines that have attempted to explain the phenomenon. The themes of *War and Our World* are essential to understanding why war remains the single greatest affliction of the twenty-first century.

Military History/0-375-70520-1